GOOD HEALTH!

Stories from the Lives of Pioneers in the Health Services

In memory of my wife Susie Nelson

Also recorded by Jack Gillespie:

Our Cornwall: the Stories of Cornish Men and Women
Our Cumbria: the Stories of Cumbrian Men and Women

GOOD HEALTH!

Stories from the Lives of Pioneers in the Health Services

Recorded by

Jack Gillespie

TABB HOUSE

First published 1993
Tabb House, 7 Church Street, Padstow, Cornwall, PL28 8BG

Copyright © Jack Gillespie 1993
and the contributors

ISBN 1 873951 00 0
Cased edition 1 873951 15 9

'Psychiatric Hospital Attendant: Robert Rowe' was first published in
Our Cornwall and 'District Nurse in Cumbria: Constance Gate' first
published in *Our Cumbria*.

Typeset by Exe Valley Dataset, Exeter
and printed by Short Run Press, Exeter

CONTENTS

PREFACE

MY AIM was to record in informal conversations the personal stories and professional experiences of men and women now retired who through their efforts and skills helped to develop Britain's health services from the earlier years of the twentieth century.

Amid the proposed changes and problems of the National Health Service, it is good to remind ourselves of, and appreciate, the contribution of the people who in past years devotedly committed their professional lives to the care of their fellow-citizens.

The book contains transcribed recordings by a cross-section of people such as a former Director of the Institute for Cancer Research, GPs, nurses, the Principal Medical Officer on board the Royal Yacht *Britannia*, the President of a Royal College, a hospital porter, professors in different areas of health services, a psychiatric hospital attendant, the founder of a hospice, a catering manager, a hospital chaplain and many others, illustrating a wealth of character, skills and dedication.

There is a point I should like to emphasise. The contributions in the book are, with one or two exceptions, sound-recorded responses to questions in informal conversation. They make no pretensions to literary style which the contributors, some of whom are distinguished authors in their own disciplines, would use in considered writing. I hope such off-the-cuff responses may give a fresh simplicity to tales of men and women worthy of our respect and gratitude.

The book, apart from intrinsic and historical interest, aims to benefit the Cancer Research Campaign and all royalties will be donated to that cause.

Jack Gillespie

ACKNOWLEDGEMENTS

THANKS are due to the following who have allowed me to use photographs: Professor Sir Thomas Symington, Captain Surgeon David Dalgliesh, Peggy Fulton, Roger and Margaret Woods, Dr Peter McKenzie, Dr John Wilkinson, Joseph Tyrer, Eileen Lennon, Dr L. Hockey, Professor R. Girdwood, The Rev. Murdoch Mackay, Major-General Frank Richardson, Ann Weatherill, Clarice King, *Westmorland Gazette*, Dr Helen R. Buck, Jessie Barron, Tom Chambers, Dr L. Dummer, Kelvin Rees, Eileen Daws, Dr Sheila Cochrane, Andrew Shaw, Beryl Skidmore, the Edinburgh Royal Infirmary, and Constance Gate. I am also grateful to Joyce Griffiths for her help with proof-reading.

List of Illustrations

Cancer Research

PROFESSOR SIR THOMAS SYMINGTON
KT, MD, DSc (Hon.), FRSC, FRCP (Glasgow), FRS (Ed.)

Formerly Professor of Pathology, University of Glasgow, Professor (Emeritus) University of London, formerly Director of the Institute for Cancer Research (London)

MY STORY starts in Muirkirk in Ayrshire on April 1st, 1915. My father was a miner in the Kames colliery there and he died in the influenza epidemic of 1918 when he was twenty-nine years old. What I remember of him was told me by my mother, a typical good Scottish housewife who believed profoundly in the value of education. My father's death was a tragedy for her as I was only three and my sister was born six months after his death.

We moved to Grandfather Steven's home to live with my mother's brother Bob Steven, a very fine man who had a great influence on my early life. He had taken the diploma of the Royal Technical College (ARTC) in Glasgow, and when war broke out in 1914 he refused to go into the pits and joined the Army. When he came back from the war he became the chief mining lecturer for Ayrshire. I really had a new father in Uncle Bob, who used to say to me later "Although I never married, I brought up two children."

Uncle Bob was a great socialist, an ILP (Independent Labour Party) man of the old Jimmy Maxton, Keir Hardie tradition. He talked often to me about Hardie and what happened when Hardie was lecturing to a group at Glenbuck near Muirkirk. After the lecture, when he went to the home of his host a knock came at the door and he was asked, "Is Keir Hardie staying the night with you?" and before he could answer was told, "If he is, don't come to your work tomorrow." Keir Hardie, thinking of his host, said, "No, no, I can't allow this." And he walked the thirteen or fourteen miles back to Cumnock from Glenbuck.

Uncle Bob was a great reader and my collection of Dickens and Hardy were inherited from him. He liked those books and when I was young he would read me passages from them. These old socialists were tremendously interested in the need to educate the working man. I think the first thing I really remember was the 1921 strike when I went with other children to the miners' soup kitchens which Uncle Bob helped to finance. During the strike he promoted sports days for the miners and their children and held gala days for them. He was very interested in football, and from the time I was five would take me to the Scotland-England international matches at Hampden Park in Glasgow.

I also went to ILP meetings with him and would fall asleep at the back of the hall. Indeed I went everywhere with him and was happy to do so. He was, as I said, a good man who believed in socialism and the need to educate the worker and improve his lot. Sadly, in later years he became rather disillusioned with politics.

I speak about my uncle because of the influence he had on others. He had a wonderful relationship with the young miners and did a great deal to ensure they had a chance to further their education. On a Monday night after the lads finished their work in the pit, they would go to his mining class in the local school from about five o'clock till about twenty past seven and study maths, science, geology and technical drawing. After school he would take them to the cinema where I joined them to see *The Lost World*, which we followed each week. On a Saturday his students from different parts of Ayrshire would meet in Kilmarnock and I would go with them in the afternoon to see a football match. Nowadays it would be unheard of, but on the Saturday night after the football match those boys went to his class at the Technical School in Kilmarnock for more mathematics, science and technical drawing. Uncle Bob certainly put his beliefs into practice. As I was now about eight years of age, all this affected me and I became conscious of the value and importance of education.

To keep the young men together during the summer, Uncle

Bob would organise rambles into the hills around Muirkirk. To maintain their interest he arranged for someone to lead the ramble and give a talk to the students when we reached our destination. The leader was often an old miner with a know-ledge of botany. On the way, as we sat around a hastily-built fire and enjoyed a sandwich lunch, he would describe to us a variety of wild flowers.

Another old miner with an interest in industrial archaeology would gather us around the cairn, which was erected to the memory of John Macadam, and show us the remains of the first macadamised roads which Macadam built on the outskirts of Muirkirk.

With evening continuation classes in winter and rambles in summer, Uncle Bob kept those boys together. Some of them became mines inspectors, others mine managers in this country and abroad. Many of his students went to the Royal Technical College in Glasgow and became mining lecturers. One of them, Professor George Hibberd, became Professor of Mining at Glasgow University. When Uncle Bob retired he went to work for a short time with Professor Hibberd. Later that year in 1951 he developed pneumonia and died.

In later years when my wife and I were pioneering Friends of the Hospice in Ayrshire, a member of the audience told us that my talk reminded him of the lectures he attended as a young miner by Bob Steven, the finest teacher he ever met. It was wonderful that he was remembered with such affection by one of the young miners he trained.

From Muirkirk public school I went on to the secondary school, Cumnock Academy. I could do mathematics and science quite well but I was really interested in sport, which I think is a normal adolescent pursuit. Mr Bridges our English teacher had an influence on me. He used to come in with his *Glasgow Herald* and announce to the class the poem from Keats or Wordsworth we had to learn. We knew when he started reading we had to learn as much as we could by heart until he had finished the *Herald*. I remember some of those poems to this day. When I went into general practice later in Coatbridge and saw patients dying from tuberculosis, I used to think of that English class and imagine the poet Keats sitting with a friend who was dying of tuberculosis and writing the 'Ode to a Nightingale':

> . . . The weariness, the fever and the fret
> Here, where men sit and hear each other groan;
> Where palsy shakes a few, sad, last grey hairs,
> Where youth grows pale, and spectre-thin, and dies;
> Where but to think is to be full of sorrow
> And leaden-eyed despairs,
> Where Beauty cannot keep her lustrous eyes,
> Or new love pine at them beyond tomorrow.

I found I could remember many of the poems I had learned at Cumnock Academy and being able to recall them in later years made me appreciate and enjoy them.

I remember the headmaster of Cumnock Academy, Mr Martin, saying to me "You will do mathematics and physics", and one day his secretary came into the class and asked if there was any pupil interested in medicine. When she asked me, I said "No." In 1932 I went to Glasgow University. In the first year I studied physics, chemistry and mathematics. Then, in the summer of 1933, Uncle Bob introduced, as one of the speakers for his students, a young man who had taken an Honours degree in biochemistry at Glasgow University. I was so impressed with him and his lecture that I decided to change my course and take my degree in biochemistry. It's interesting how someone you meet can impress you and change your whole life. Later that summer when I went back to see the headmaster at Cumnock, he said to me "You are doing mathematics and science, aren't you?" "No," I said, "I'm doing biochemistry." He asked what it was and I replied, "I don't know but it's something to do with milk!"

When I returned to the university, I enrolled for the Honours degree in chemistry with biochemistry as my special final year subject. When I graduated in biochemistry in 1936 I had the choice of going to Germany to the University of Freiburg to take a Ph.D. degree or going back to the university and doing medicine. The professor said to me "If you really want to make the best of your training in chemistry, I suggest you do a medical degree.' This meant another five years study but I managed to win one or two bursaries which helped. As it turned out, that was how I met my wife Margaret who was in the same class as I in medicine. Nine years was a long time to spend at university and I was getting tired by the end of it.

When I graduated in medicine I felt I couldn't afford to go into hospital as a resident and be paid only 19s.2d. a week, so I went into a busy general practice in the Lanarkshire town of Coatbridge, where I saw life as it was in a bustling industrial town. I worked with Dr Jim Sweeny and thought very highly of him. I learned how to run maternity and other clinics and if during the night I got into difficulty with a patient, he was always very willing to come out and help. I saw many children with severe gastro-enteritis, and I also saw many skin and infectious diseases I had not met as a student, but the one thing that really worried me was tuberculosis. I had seen many of my young school friends dying of tuberculosis and encountered it frequently in this practice. It was a very confusing illness which presented itself in many different ways, so I took a post in East Fortune Sanatorium. I worked under Dr Charles Cameron, who later became Professor of Tuberculosis in Edinburgh, and I learned from him that tuberculosis was a general not a local disease, one that affected the whole body. The outcome for patients with tuberculosis in those days depended upon their resistance and whether or not they were able to deal with the tubercle bacillus. The discovery of chemotherapy virtually put an end to tuberculosis as a dreaded illness.

I left the sanatorium to go into the Army and while waiting for my call up took a temporary post in general practice in the small village of Cleland in Lancashire. Margaret was working as an assistant medical officer in the hospital there and in March 1943 we were married. One day she met Dr McCallum Lang, the Medical Officer for Health for Lanarkshire, who suggested that I, having a degree in biochemistry, should be doing pathology. For some reason my army call-up papers were lost and this is why I landed in pathology and my army service was delayed until 1947.

So I came to the Royal Infirmary in Glasgow to work in pathology with Professor Blacklock. Margaret had done her undergraduate course with Blacklock. She thought highly of him and he liked her but he didn't know me, so I'm sure it was because of my wife that he agreed to take me. I now learned a lot more about tuberculosis, since Blacklock was an authority on the subject. In addition, it was the beginning of my research career.

One day I was called into the professor's office. He handed me two tumours and asked if I could identify them. They were, he said, chromaffin tumours, and in life they secrete large amounts of noradrenalin and adrenalin directly into the patient's blood. This causes a tremendous rise in the patient's blood pressure and causes severe headache. I remember going into the history of the first of the two patients from whom the tumours had been removed surgically. The consulting physician who had been called to see the patient by a general practitioner found her blood pressure extremely high. He sent her into his wards at the Royal Infirmary. When he went to the hospital to see the patient, he asked his resident"What did you make of the blood pressure?" And when he was told it was normal he realised that he was dealing with a tumour of the medulla or central part of the adrenal gland. These two tumours started me on work on the human adrenal gland that lasted more than twenty-five years, ending in 1969 when I published my book on *The Functional Pathology of the Human Adrenal Gland.*

In November 1947 I was called up to the Army as a pathologist and was immediately posted as a major to Malaya in charge of the laboratories in Kuala Lumpur, where I wrote a thesis on my adrenal gland research for the Doctor of Medicine degree which I was awarded.

I was in Malaya only a few weeks when the emergency, due to communist terrorism, started. I had to prepare all the transfusion fluids and set up a blood transfusion service. I arranged to blood-group every soldier who came into Malaya. Whenever there was an ambush I would be told the blood group of the casualties and then phone the commanding officers of the units stationed around Kuala Lumpur and tell them I'd need so many group As, so many group Bs, group Os or group ABs. Plenty of soldiers would volunteer since they knew they could be on the next casualty list. I would recheck them and ask if they had had any contact with any local women in the last few weeks. If they had, I'd say, "Just disappear and I'll say no more about it. But go to the special treatment centre." I rechecked the blood group of the volunteers and passed them to my assistant in the room adjacent to the operating theatre. He took their blood and in turn passed it to the surgeon in the theatre who would transfuse the patient.

One thing Malaya showed me was that dollar earnings from the export of tin and rubber were greater than the dollar earnings of the United Kingdom. This was the kind of colonial exploitation people talked about but I began to appreciate the many contributions Britain had made to the country by the provision of education, the legal system, public health and many other things. Unfortunately, I felt we trained local people to be second but never first in command of activities in their own country.

When I was in Malaya I became familiar with the fine work the scrub typhus research group was doing under Dr Raymond Lewthwaite, who was Director of the Institute for Medical Research in Kuala Lumpur. He had left Malaya at the time of the Japanese invasion and gone to Burma where he made contact with an American typhus research group. After the war he induced them to come to Malaya and test out the effect of their new antibiotic drug chloromycetin in patients with scrub typhus. I saw about a hundred patients there with scrub typhus and they all recovered after treatment with the new drug. Dr Lewthwaite told me that when he came to Malaya in the 1920s, if four of his colleagues went into the jungle on a survey, three would come back with scrub and one would die. Lewthwaite found that the illness was caused by the rickettsia, a type of organism slightly larger than a virus and he showed that the rickettsia was carried by the trombiculate mite that lives in the ears of rats. When soldiers went through the scrub land of a deserted native village which had been invaded by rats, the trombiculate mite would get onto their skin and bite them, leaving a black mark or an eschar. The patient would develop an illness like pneumonia and often there was myocardial or heart involvement. Chloromycetin cleared all this up.

One day the old family doctor in our unit was waiting in my laboratory when I arrived. He had taken blood for a blood culture from a patient who was the wife of the Assistant Provost Marshal in Malaya. She was very ill and when I examined the culture media I found she was suffering from typhoid fever. We contacted the Americans who were working with Dr Lewthwaite. "What about trying chloromycetin on our patient with typhoid fever?" we asked. They did, and in twenty-four hours the blood had cleared and the patient survived. This was the first case of typhoid fever treated with chloromycetin.

My next job was to find the typhus carrier and we finally traced it to her house-boy so we brought him in for treatment. Some time afterwards the lady came back for a check-up. She looked worried. Then she told me the house-boy had run away from hospital before his treatment was finished and he was now working as house-boy with the NAAFI Manager. So panic stations! I immediately phoned the manager and explained the position. "Oh," he said, "he's the best house-boy I've ever had." I told him he had to get rid of him straight away, and he did.

Before I went to Malaya I had been an assistant in the Department of Pathology at the Royal Infirmary in Glasgow and before I was called up had received a salary only as a lecturer. When I had been in Malaya about six months, I got a letter from Professor Blacklock to say that the lecturer was leaving the department and he himself had accepted the Chair of Pathology at Barts hospital in London. I therefore applied for the post of Senior Lecturer at the Royal Infirmary in Glasgow and was appointed when I was still in Malaya.

Soon after I returned from army service I became very involved in research on the human adrenal gland and in the ensuing three years published a number of papers and gave lectures on the work. Eventually I was given the vacant Chair of Pathology at Glasgow Royal Infirmary.

I had a very good relationship with the Principal, Sir Hector Hetherington, a tremendous person. I told him I thought it was important to send my young assistants abroad for a year to learn new techniques and bring them back to the Royal. He was very much in favour of that and to this effect I went away for three months to America where I made contact with scientists interested in the adrenal gland. I attended the Laurentian Hormone Conference in Colorado and met all the people I wanted to see. I went to research departments in Chicago, Minneapolis, the Mayo Clinic in Rochester Minnesota; to Montreal, Boston, New York, and set up links with the people there, who became life-long friends. I selected excellent young doctors from my department and arranged for them to spend a year in America and when they came back to my department they brought new ideas and new techniques with them.

When medicine was nationalised I had about £50 a year for my research but after nationalisation a quarter of a million pounds of endowments from each of the big Scottish hospitals was put into a Scottish Hospital Endowments Trust which was advised by an advisory committee. This was a boost for medical research in Scotland and in about 1953 my grant went up from £50 a year to £5,000. I remember lecturing on my work at the Mayo Clinic and saying what a difference nationalisation of medicine had made.

Dr Wright, who had been Margaret's boss, told me that Robert Macfarlane, the biscuit manufacturer, would like to endow something in the name of his father, Sir James. Sir James had helped to raise money to set up Canniesburn Hospital so that the Royal Infirmary technicians would have private facilities that would compete with the nursing homes in the west end of the city. Dr Wright told me John Macfarlane's brother Robert and his sister both had rheumatism and they wanted to set up a Chair in Rheumatology. Dr Wright persuaded them to think again, and they agreed to endow the first Macfarlane Chair in Cancer Medicine. With that money we were able to bring senior professors in medicine from this country and abroad to work with us at the Royal Infirmary.

I went to see Lord Erskine, who was the Chairman of the Scottish Hospital Endowment Research Trust and told him we had a visiting professorship and I wanted to set aside a lab. for it. The Royal Infirmary had agreed the visitor should have the McGhee Cancer Fellow to work with them but I needed technical help and finance for equipment. He arranged for the Endowment Research Trust to provide it.

This was a fine collaborative effort between the new grant-giving body, the Royal Infirmary and the University and it was a great success. The first man who came to Glasgow was Rupert Willis, a very distinguished Australian pathologist. When I was trying to attract the scientists, I would approach their wives first. I found if the wives were happy to come, the professors would be likewise, but of course we had to have a house for them. The Royal Infirmary sold some old property, and bought a very nice flat in Great Western Road and furnished it.

A distinguished professor came every two years and worked with a young assistant and technician in a well-equipped laboratory in my department of pathology. Rupert Willis was followed by Professor Ivanovitch from Szeged University in Hungary, where I had lectured. A number of Hungarian scientists worked with me in Glasgow.

Professor Engel was our next visitor. He was Professor of Biochemistry. One of my assistants had worked with him at Harvard. Then we had Professor David Glick from Stanforth University. These were all distinguished men whom I had visited during my three months tour of America or my lecturing abroad.

During part of the '60s and early '70s I was involved with developments in medicine in East Africa. In 1960 there were only five medical schools in an area of Africa south of the Sahara and north of the Limpopo, and one of the medical schools was at Makerare, in Kampala, Uganda. In 1962 Sir Arthur Porritt's report on medical aid to developing countries invited British universities to explore the possibility of creating links with overseas universities. In response to Porritt the University of Glasgow decided to send a delegation to East Africa under the Dean of the Faculty of Medicine, Professor Charles Fleming. I was a member of that delegation. In the East Africa Federation it had been agreed that the medical school should be at Makerare in Uganda, the science faculty in Nairobi in Kenya, and the law faculty with President Nyerere in Dar-es-Salaam in Tanzania.

Our delegation went first to Makerare in Uganda, where we found a first-class medical school run mainly by senior expatriot British doctors. The standard of teaching and training was as good as that in any British medical school, but the number of doctors who graduated there was insufficient for the needs of the three countries. After visiting Nairobi and Dar-es-Salaam the delegation decided there was a need to establish another medical school, and on our return to Glasgow we recommended to the faculty that Nairobi should be chosen as the site for it. This was accepted, and Glasgow sent out a strong team of senior physicians, surgeons and obstreticians to initiate the teaching programme. A good relationship had been established with Makerare, and they allowed half of their final year students to complete clinical training in Nairobi, with good results. One of my senior pathologists, Dr Stuart Kennedy, became clinical sub-dean and in 1967 the medical faculty in the University College of Nairobi was inaugurated. Thus in two and a half years there was an active development of undergraduate teaching in Kenya and an upgrading of the ancillary hospital services. Our work was paying off.

When the delegation went to Kenya, Professor Ian McIntyre, of the Veterinary School in Glasgow, had already established a veterinary training school in Nairobi and he and his colleagues helped with much of the early training of medical students in anatomy and physiology. I had the responsibility for developing and running the laboratories and with this in mind induced my senior colleague Dr Hector Cameron to go with his family to Nairobi. Hector played an important part in planning the new Kenyatta National Teaching Hospital which was funded by the British Government. He was responsible for undergraduate teaching of pathology and ran the diagnostic services in pathology, bacteriology and haematology. He, like his senior colleagues in medicine, surgery and obstetrics were made professors, and together they created a fine medical school where they trained African staff who would eventually take over their own school. Indeed, East Africa owes them a debt of gratitude, since each sacrificed his own position in Glasgow to help create the medical school in Nairobi.

When our delegation visited Dar-es-Salaam in Tanzania, I met Dr Rankine, a young Australian physician who had already started his own medical school there, and he took me to see the twenty young students who were in the class. He taught physiology and the surgeon took anatomy but they had no one to teach pathology the following year. He asked for my help. I was very impressed with his enthusiasm and although my department was actively committed in Nairobi I agreed to help. Dr Slaven, now Professor of Pathology in St Bartholomews Hospital in London, and his wife Brenda, a biochemist, went to Dar-es-Salaam for two years, ran the laboratories and taught the course. I saw President Nyerere, who was interested in the developments, and with his help arranged for two young African doctors to come to Glasgow and be trained. Those young men played an important part in establishing the Medical School in Dar-es-Salaam and training African staff to take over from them. Each year for eight years I visited Nairobi and Dar-es-Salaam, took part in the professional examinations and watched the progress of our venture. Sadly, I do not know what is happening now in either school.

Most of the medical staff who worked with me in Glasgow had been my students. They were now experienced consultants with many scientific publications, ready to move on to senior academic appointments in this country and abroad. The African venture had reduced the number of young local doctors I was now training, and by 1969 my adrenal research was completed. Maybe this was the time to move on and take on a new challenge.

I was a member of the Medical Research Council (MRC) and in 1969 was one of the group who carried out an external review of the Institute for Cancer Research in London. The Institute was in receipt of a block grant of two million pounds from the MRC and Cancer Research Campaign (CRC) and following the report of the external review group it was decided to cut the block grant to one million pounds, to provide the Institute's basic facilities; the other one million would require to be won on the basis of a five-year programme and a three-year project application by the staff. At that time the Institute had directors of clinical research, radiotherapy, physics and of biophysics, and also a director of the Chester-Beatty Laboratories. A committee under Sir Edward Hale recommended that there should be only one overall director. I got a letter from Lord Halsbury, Chairman of the Committee of Management, inviting me to become the director. It was a difficult decision to make. My family was settled in Glasgow, but in the end I decided it was a challenge which I must accept. I spent the next seven and a half years there as Director of the Institute for Cancer Research.

My first task was to create a proper divisional structure with a senior person in charge, who had the responsibility of preparing a submission document on the work of the division, and a justification for existing staff and equipment. The submissions were assessed by a scientific committee of representatives from the MRC and CRC, which in the end decided to approve only £400,000 of the one million requested. However, they agreed to give me the whole sum for a period of seven years, but it was my responsibility by the end of this time to have justified the whole sum.

Since over forty scientists were involved, I had to introduce a retraining programme. It proved successful, and at the end of five years all divisions in the Institute were on a sound scientific and financial footing. I learned from experience at the Institute that when scientists lose their creativity they can provide a valuable service working in a team with younger scientists, and can play an important role working with doctors on problems they encounter in patient care. My experience at the Institute showed how scientific and financial accountability could be achieved by programme submissions and then assessment by an experienced external site-visits group; something, as I describe later, which could be used to improve patient care, and justify medical and financial accountability in the Health Service today.

My time at the Institute was stressful but I feel worthwhile. I was able to establish a close link between clinicians in the Royal Marsden Hospital, from which the Institute had sprung, and scientists in the Institute. In the autumn of 1975, my elder son Robin developed cancer and although he was treated in the Marsden, he died in February 1977. I stayed on for a further six months, but I felt my interest and enthusiasm had gone. I had completed the job, the work of the Institute was going well and I decided to retire and return home to Scotland.

Two years later Margaret and I thought there was a need for a hospice in Ayrshire and we began to work towards that end. A committee was set up and it met in our house. Margaret wrote the philosophy of the hospice and along with a friend and the local paper, *Ayrshire Post*, gave some money to provide prizes for a competition among the schools of Ayrshire to produce a logo for the hospice. It was won by a young male student from Mauchline.

Margaret and I visited different villages in Ayrshire to set up 'Friends of the Hospice' in each one. A very good group in Troon was established and the lady running it, Mrs Margaret Toner, asked me to come and talk to the school children about the hospice. This was not a very easy thing to do. How do you get over to children that this is not just a place where people go to die? That it is a place where they go to live, be well cared for and after a short period go back home? Nevertheless, children are quick to realise that in the end the day will come when they will lose the grandfather or grandmother to whom they are very attached, and that this could occur in a hospice.

I decided to explain this by relating the conversation I had with my grandson Andrew when he was seven. I found him in bed looking at a caterpillar in a jar and when I asked what he was looking at, he said this was Charlie. Teacher had given it to him and said he was to watch it carefully at home when Charlie would turn into a beautiful butterfly. He wondered how this could be, and I explained to him that the developing butterfly was being carried like a child inside the mother and when the time came the caterpillar would die and the butterfly would be born. He thought what I said was interesting and went on to say "Maybe I'll become a doctor." He added "Grandpa, I don't think you'll ever see me as a doctor." – "How is that?" – "Because," pointing upwards, "you'll be up there." Seeming to sense I would be disappointed, he said quickly "But you'll always be in my heart, and when I want to see you I'll call you down and we can have a talk and then you can go back up again." I thought this was a good philosophy when teaching a child what a hospice is: 'the grandfather and grandmother, the father and mother; all must die, but they'll always be in your heart.' I've talked to children in many schools about the hospice and this approach has gone over without any difficulty.

I remember Professor Lewis Engel used to say to me "When you create a bandwagon, make sure it's got wheels, otherwise it won't run." After a lot of pioneering work the hospice had got wheels and was beginning to go. But I had been having trouble with my eyes and I thought the time had come for us to jump off, and this is what my wife and I did. Fortunately the Ayrshire hospice is now well established and a great success.

Publication of the Government White Paper 'Caring for Patients' stimulated my interest. It might make the Health Service financially accountable, but would it improve patient care at a time when doctors appear to have less and less influence on medical accountability? It made me consider the role consultants had played in the service and how that role has changed and what I felt should be done.

In my early days each hospital had a medical superintendent and also in each medical and surgical unit a chief of wards. If he was a good chief, the unit was a happy one, but if he ran a poor unit, there was a disgruntled group of consultants.

The medical superintendent was able to alter the waiting lists of each unit if he thought it necessary. In those days medical accountability was in the hands of the medical superintendent and the chiefs of wards. After the war and creation of the Health Service things changed and every consultant had control of beds allocated to him and in addition controlled his own waiting list. But now there was no one who could change the consultants' clinical care of patients. It is true that divisions of surgery, medicine, laboratory medicine and other specialities were created and democratically elected chairmen appointed to the divisions. However, the chairman had no power over the clinical care of patients by the consultant nor of their training of junior medical staff. The post of General Manager was created in the 1980s and the General Manager has taken over the role of the Medical Superintendent but without his medical knowledge. He may say "I can deal with the chairmen of each of the divisions" but the chairman has no power over the consultants, their treatment or actions.

I believe my own experience at the Institute of Cancer Research may give some clue as to what could be done. At the age of fifty-five I gave up my own research to direct the medical and scientific activities of the Institute. What, I feel, is needed for hospitals, whether they are National Health Trust or National Health Service hospitals is to appoint to each one a full-time medical director of fifty-five to sixty years of age. The director would be a well-respected clinician who would give up all clinical work and co-operate with the general manager. Between them they would be responsible for financial and medical accountability in the hospital. The medical director would be chairman of the chairman's group and along with the general manager of the hospital would prepare a submission document of the work done by each division in the hospital, what they would like to do in the next five years and what staff and financial help would be required in that period. There would be, as I had in the London Institute, a quinquennial visit to each division in the hospital; in other words, a medical and financial audit. The Department of Health would be required to make up a list of consultant doctors who would serve on the visiting team to visit the hospital, assess the patient care, the justification for present staff and requests for new staff. For example, a division of surgery with three general and three special units would require three days for a site visit.

If we are to have medical and financial accountability, the general manager and medical director need to organise a site visit to all departments in the hospital and, so that the work of the hospital was not interrupted, site visits could be spread over a period of five years. Thus the division of surgery and nursing administration could be done in the first year, medicine and all aspects of hospital management in the second year, laboratory medicine, pharmacy and catering in the third, and radiology, radiotherapy and ancillary services in the fourth. This would allow one year free and give time to start the next quinquennial.

It is proposed by the Government that each hospital should have an internal audit committee and while I agree with this, the work of the committee would be enhanced if they had an external assessment of all divisions in the hospital.

How much money, you may ask, would it take to appoint a full-time medical director in each hospital in the country with more than two hundred and fifty beds, which is the number required before the hospital can be considered for a Hospital Trust status? I calculate it would take twenty million pounds to cover the whole of British hospitals, and two million for Scotland alone. This would allow the appointment of a director on a top-grade salary with merit award. Since the Government has allocated thirty-one million pounds for 1990–91 for the creation of audit committees, part of this sum could be used to create the medical director appointments. Since the British Health Service is the biggest employer of labour in this country, the measures I have proposed would go a long way to promote the two objectives, better medical care, and also medical and financial accountability in the Health Service. This I believe is a positive approach to the future.

These convictions are based on years of experience at different levels of the Health Service in Britain, years for me rich in satisfaction and fulfilment.

A Consultant's Memories

DR PETER MCKENZIE
OBE, D.Univ., FRCP, FFCM

Formerly Consultant Physician in Charge, Belvidere Hospital, Glasgow

I WAS born in the Vale of Leven, a mile from the south end of Loch Lomond. The Vale people just took the beauties of the valley and Ben Lomond and the Loch for granted, always referring to them as the 'Loch' and the 'Ben'. Indeed, from my bedroom window, I had a panoramic view of the Ben which each day had its varying display of colour and was probably at its best in winter when it was capped with snow. The folk in the Vale were essentially a kirk-going people but without any sanctimoniousness. The majority of the men had a trade, mainly engineering, and worked in the local dyeworks and in the shipbuilding yards on the Clyde. There was a collective spirit of wishing to excel – and excel they did in soccer, shinty and rowing. There was also a great musical tradition in the Vale with choirs that always seemed to be at Festivals – and the area even boasted its own Opera House.

In *Tom Brown's Schooldays* there is a sentence which says that there is something special about being brought up in a valley. I would subscribe to that, but of course I might be biased.

I have always been fascinated by trains and I love train journeys. In my boyhood we knew the time of day by the trains; their times did not change in the twenty years between the wars. In the summer there were boat trains for Loch Lomond and there were five steamers on the loch at that time. And there was, to us, the very funny story of the American tourist who asked a porter at Renton station, "Does this train stop at Balloch Pier?" and received the reply, "Well, if it doesn't there'll be a helluva splash!"

In May 1932 my father was returning home on the Balloch train and was in conversation with one of the regulars who was a teacher and who enquired what I was going to do. I was then in my sixth year at the Vale of Leven Academy but at that time there was no advice whatsoever about careers. As I had done rather well in maths and science, I had decided to go to Glasgow University to take an MA, BSC (which was not an unusual combination then) with a view to teaching. My father vouchsafed this information to his teacher friend on the train and his immediate reply was "He must be off his head! Teachers are walking the streets. Has he never thought of doing medicine?"

This was the time of the Depression and it was very real in the Vale of Leven where 76% of the insured population (almost entirely male, of course) were idle. This was equalled only by the constituency in Wales of George Thomas, who was Speaker of the House of Commons and is now Lord Tonypandy. All work had ceased on the Cunarder 534 (later the *Queen Mary*) in John Brown's shipyard in Clydebank and one of the main dyeworks had closed down. Many people were on short commons, but they kept up their legendary aggressive cheerfulness and I certainly do not remember the belligerent resentfulness which the media always portrays in the people at that time. They certainly did not blame everyone in sight.

Had I thought of medicine? No, I had not, but my Highers seemed all right for entry. The very next morning I made for Glasgow University to see about entry into medicine. I landed in Dumbarton Road and soon found three adjacent gates, all with no marking. From left to right facing, these gates were, and are, the entrances to the Western Infirmary, the University and Kelvingrove Park. The University tower was far to the right and so I entered the Elysian fields of Kelvingrove Park. The further I went along the roadway the further I seemed to get from the University, so I made a frontal attack and found quite a high spiked fence barring my way to the high Olympus. With youthful agility I climbed this obstacle and then scrambled up the steep grass slope to the front of the University below the tower. And so I literally scrambled over the breast of what was to be my Alma Mater!

I was confronted by a uniformed man who had obviously observed my rather unusual route of entry. He asked me what I was up to and I explained that I wished to enquire how to get into medicine. He directed me to the Adviser of Studies, a Dr John Thompson, whose room was at the top of a turreted staircase. Following a rather brusque "Come in", I found myself in the presence of a formidable-looking man who asked me what I wanted. I told him I would like to study medicine. "What Highers have you got?" I told him. "That's all right. Get a Certificate of Fitness and come up in October." And that was it; I had been advised! I was to learn that John Thompson's brusqueness was legendary and later I was to know him well and to find that behind this gruffness was a most likeable and kindly man. He was a life-long supporter of the University Athletic Club and was greatly liked.

That is how I entered medicine. I have often shuddered to think that I might have missed the opportunity to be in what in many ways is the most wonderful profession of all. And for me it all resulted because of my father's conversation in the train to the Vale of Leven in 1932.

So I entered the Medical Faculty in 1932 and the following episode took place at the end of my third year as a medical student. One Sunday evening early in July 1935 my friend, Duncan McIntyre, who was training to be a music teacher at the Athenaeum in Glasgow, appeared at our house in Bonhill. He had formed a band to play on the new paddle steamer the *Marchioness of Lorne*; he was the pianist, a fellow student Peter Jenkins was the violinist and old professional Sam played the trumpet. Duncan had been called back for a special course at the Athenaeum and, presenting me with a white-topped sailor's hat with a harp on the front, asked if I would replace him on the *Lorne*. We had frequently performed as four hands on the piano at local concerts; indeed had been referred to as young 'Rawitz and Landauer'; so he considered I was capable. Not without a lot of hesitation, I agreed; then I asked what did they play? He said it was easy; Scottish selections and the song of that year, 'When I grow too old to dream'. He added – "Don't worry. You'll manage!"

With considerable trepidation, and arrayed in my cap, I duly joined the steamer at Dunoon. We began with a Scottish selection and very shortly my trepidation was justified when Sam exploded "That's nae use. You couldnae hear you behin' a bliddy caur ticket! Thump it oot!" So I duly thumped it 'oot' while Sam went aft to collect the 'thank offerings' from the passengers. (I was to learn that the bag was known in the trade as the 'bottle'). So I played on the *Marchioness of Lorne* for the rest of the season and it was a most interesting and pleasurable experience. It was the *Lorne*'s first year in service. She was a lovely wee paddle steamer, almost as broad as she was long. She had triple expansion engines with working crank shafts wholly visible to the passengers, as in all the Clyde paddle steamers. Of course, it was the standing joke that 'faither', going below for a dram, always said he was 'just going to have a look at the engines.'

The main commitment of the *Lorne* was the piers of the Holy Loch, beginning at Gourock, then Kilcreggan, Cove, Blairmore, Strone, Hunter's Quay, Ardnadam and Kilmun. The Holy Loch was the afternoon cruise and there was a morning and evening run to Kirn and Dunoon. In those days there was also a considerable number of what would now be called 'summer communities', for there were many villas adjacent to each of the piers. Overnight the *Lorne* lay at Kilmun and on the early morning sailing she collected the business people who were *en route* to their offices in Glasgow.

My memories of playing in the band are very vivid. Every Clyde steamer had a band. It was an amenity expected and enjoyed by the passengers. Peter Jenkins was an excellent violinist. When I arrived on the *Lorne* Sam had criticised my pianissimo but I thought he was dreadfully poor. His main (and important) duty was collecting from the captive audiences but his performance was to improve dramatically – of that later. During the two-hour trip round the Holy Loch we gave two performances – one at the piano and then one at a small organ at the forecastle.

We lived in digs on the front at Gourock at a cost of £1 a week for dinner, bed and breakfast, Monday to Friday. In 'pennies', we collected enough to give us each £5 clear per week, and that was a considerable sum in 1935. There was always a last run to

Dunoon on a Saturday evening and there was time for us to divide the 'takings' in a pub there. I remember so well that Sam kept the money in a large sock – and the publican changed the coppers into silver or notes. Also, the last run was always a lucrative one as so many of the passengers had had a good dram and were very open handed. On quite a number of Friday nights we played at dances at Kilmun.

I have said I would recount the incident which improved Sam's trumpet playing out of all recognition. When I joined the *Marchioness of Lorne*, Peter Jenkins said he did not know what had happened to Sam – his playing was so poor compared with the previous year. He seemed to be short of breath or something. Well, one day when we were sitting in the 'lounge' between performances Sam, for some reason or other, was poking down his trumpet with a piece of wire. It stuck and when he pulled it, out came a large plug of tar within which were embedded Glasgow tram tickets. He realised that someone had plugged his trumpet in a pub in Glasgow! Anyway from then on he 'blew a gale'. Indeed, I had to request him to change his direction away from my left ear lest I sustain a ruptured tympanic membrane.

There was a kind of unwritten rule among the bands on steamers that you did not play requests from 'drunks', which in effect was to be an accompaniment to their vocal efforts. One Saturday a request came from a man who had been enjoying himself: "Hey, gie us the 'Rose o' Tralee' ". We indicated that we did not know that song – and he certainly indicated what he thought of us! It was very common for us with our white caps to be mistaken for the purser, and later, when he encountered me, he fumbled for his ticket and said "See that bliddy baun' up there. They should be thrown over the side. They don't even ken the 'Rose o' Tralee' ".

We always had our lunch on board and a right good lunch it was – I think costing one shilling. The sailing for the afternoon was at two o'clock and there was always time to go for a walk in Gourock after lunch. One day I cut it too fine and I ran onto the pier to find the gangway had been withdrawn and the *Lorne* had started to move. However, the tide was such that the *Lorne*'s railings were level with the pier. I made a run and a jump and landed nicely on the deck. There was a great jingling of the bridge bells – the *Lorne* reversed and the gangway was replaced.

The Captain, whom I had got to know very well – probably because I was a medical student – came off the bridge, took me by the arm and I was ignominiously marched down the gangway with the admonition – "Let that be a lesson to you!" I was only off for one trip and, fortunately for me, we remained good friends.

A final note about my happy days on the *Lorne*. Each Saturday we did the last run to Dunoon and thereafter I took a bus from Gourock to Glasgow and boarded the last bus from Glasgow to Balloch. When I arrived home at midnight there was the welcome from father, mother and brother eager to hear the happenings of the week on the *Lorne* and there was always the enjoyment of a great supper of ham and eggs.

The other day I was at the top of the Lyle Hill in Greenock, which has such a grand panoramic view of the Clyde Estuary, and it was almost totally empty of shipping. What a contrast to the 1930s! In addition to sea-going ships passing to and fro to the extensive Glasgow docklands, the Firth then was alive with pleasure steamers, all with their distinctive coloured funnels, criss-crossing their way over the estuary. That is all gone, but having had the opportunity of world wide travel I have no doubt at all that there is no finer scenic estuary than the Firth of Clyde.

I have always taken pride in the fact that I did surgical and medical residences in Glasgow Royal Infirmary. When I qualified in the late thirties it was not obligatory, as now, to spend the first year working in hospital. The number of posts available in the teaching hospitals was quite limited, usually two per unit, and these posts were eagerly sought after; indeed, there was a common belief that to get one you had either to be first in the clinic or your father had to know the 'chief'. It certainly was not for financial gain: an honorarium of £25 for the six months, which in effect was £4.3s.4d. per month less 3s.6d. for the papers in the mess. Well, in my third year I did quite well in the junior clinical classes in surgery and medicine and was accepted as house surgeon to Mr Milne McIntyre and house physician to Dr J.C. Middleton, when I would eventually qualify.

In the middle of my six months in surgery Jock Middleton asked me to come over to the medical side to see him. In his characteristic almost whiny voice he told me that he had made a terrible mistake insomuch as he had promised three people for two places for the next six months' residency. My other two colleagues arrived and it was agreed that we should draw two names out of a hat and that the unsuccessful one would be assured of a residence the following six months. I drew the blank – and I was quite upset. I was out of a job for the next six months!

That very evening I went by train to the Vale to let my folks know of my setback. I was joined in the compartment by David Stewart, who had recently completed an Arts degree and was now in the divinity faculty. He was *en route* to his parents' home on Loch Lomondside. Their home was a most unusual one; it was part of the southern gatehouse of the Colquhoun Rossdhu Estate. On either side of the large gates, which are surmounted by the Clan Colquhoun Crest, are two cube-like buildings which have large arched windows. The Stewarts lived in the one near the Luss Road and it was divided into an upper and lower room, with the floor visible through the large windows. At one time the gatekeeper's house consisted of the two buildings – the second being the bedroom and separated from the living quarters by at least forty yards. One can imagine the inconvenience on a winter night! However this part of the gatehouse has long been bricked up.

I told David Stewart my sad tale and he asked if I had ever thought of going as a ship's surgeon. That would fill in the six months pleasurably. He told me that Lord MacMillan, who was chairman of the Shaw, Saville and Albion shipping line, was rather keen on people who had a connection with Argyllshire. That very night on returning to the Royal I wrote to Lord MacMillan requesting a job as a ship's surgeon, preferably going to Australia, where I could visit my uncle and aunt in Melbourne. I had corresponded with them since childhood. My connections with Argyllshire were somewhat tenuous but I indicated that for several years I had gone to the Isle of Jura on holiday. Within forty-eight hours I received a letter offering me the post of Assistant Surgeon on the ss *Jervis Bay*, sailing for Australia via Malta, Port Said, Suez, Colombo and then round the Australian coast, leaving in mid-November 1938 and returning mid-March 1939 – all within my six available months. It was to prove a wonderful experience!

I had never been to London and arranged to spend a few days there before joining the *Jervis Bay*. On Sunday evenings I had heard on the wireless outstanding preaching by Pat McCormack and Dick Shepherd from St Martin's-in-the-Fields and I determined to visit this famous church. About half-past six on the Saturday on my London visit, as I began to ascend the steps of St Martin's, I was confronted by a gentleman with a microphone. He said "I am Michael Standing of *In Town Tonight* – we are just going on the air. I would like to interview you." There were two girls with him who in answer to his questions just giggled and he quickly came to me. Before going on the air he had heard me speaking to my friends and he (not surprisingly of course!) said "There is no need to ask where you come from."

In Town Tonight was a programme which had an immense listening public. It began with the Knightsbridge March by Eric Coates; then there was a background of London traffic which was brought to a halt with the screeching of brakes. Thereafter there were, among other items, interviews with people who were visiting London. Michael Standing began by asking my name. It may seem very precious now but in 1938 medicals were very conscious of advertising, so I said that I was a doctor and that medical etiquette precluded me from giving my name. However, I did reveal that I was on my way to being Assistant Surgeon on the *Jervis Bay* which was sailing to Australia. He asked me about my hobbies and I told him I was very keen on music and that we had a considerable collection of recordings on classical music at home in Bonhill, Dunbartonshire. He then asked me what I thought of modern jazz music and I said (with, I suppose, a kind of musical pomposity) "I would rather not comment on that!"

Later I phoned home to hear my folks' reaction to my achieving the fame of being on *In Town Tonight*, because like most people they usually listened to that programme. However, my father asked "Were you on the wireless tonight?" Unfortunately on that night he had switched off prior to going down to the village to procure his Saturday evening football paper. Crossing Bonhill Bridge over the River Leven someone enquired of him "Is your Peter in London tonight?" My voice had been recognised by one of my former classmates.

But on the Monday morning there was a paragraph about the

interview in the now defunct, but then very popular daily paper *The Bulletin*. On the 'Pertinent and Otherwise' page, it read *Bonhill for Doctors* 'These street interviews in *In Town Tonight* have a pleasant air of unexpectedness. I liked the doctor from Bonhill, Dunbartonshire on Saturday night who withheld his name in the sacred cause of etiquette but gave his hobby as music. Bonhill seems to be strong in artistic doctors. There is Dr Cronin for instance.'

I may add with all my early prejudice and rivalry that Dr Cronin came from Dumbarton *not* Bonhill. (Apart from his undoubted literary attributes I would not like to claim that he came from the Vale of Leven).

The Captain of the *Jervis Bay* was very friendly towards me and often referred to me as *In Town Tonight*. My senior colleague was a Welshman with whom I got on very well. Both of us were fond of poetry and could repeat great parts of Palgrave's *Golden Treasury* by heart. I specially remember, in the Mediterranean sun, reciting together the whole of Keats' 'Ode to the Nightingale'. The arrangement my senior made with me was that I did most of the work, he collected the fees and I went ashore at all the ports of call. This suited me admirably – I was keen to do the work. Although essentially a new graduate, in the Royal I had had quite an experience of minor surgery, for example, dealing with fractures. In preparation for my trip as ship's surgeon I had been allowed to do six appendicectomies (under supervision, of course) and also I had given many ether and chloroform anaesthetics.

The Captain offered me leave at Melbourne (while the ship went to Sydney and Brisbane) to visit my uncle and aunt and later he presented me with his complimentary ticket to visit Cairo and the Pyramids, allowing me to leave the ship at Suez and rejoin at Port Said. I kept a diary of the trip and I wrote it up assiduously. It is a record of another era. Sulphonamides had just become available but I do not remember having any on the *Jervis Bay*. The contents of the diary make a story in itself but I will desist from that. In addition to the diary I have a collection of good photographs, and one of them was to be of historic interest.

I was fortunate enough to be taught about photography by my father's cousin who had taken it up after the Great War. As a boy, I had a plate camera and did all my own developing and printing in a darkroom in the basement of our house. However, in preparation for my trip I acquired a Zeiss-Ikon camera and all my films were contained in special foil for tropical use. In Malta I took a picture of the *Jervis Bay* and HMS *Hood* lying in the Grand Harbour at Valetta. They were to become the most famous North Atlantic casualties of the Second World War.

In Winston Churchill's *The Second World War* he vividly describes the sinking of the *Jervis Bay* and to read of the *Jervis Bay* described as an 'armed merchant-cruiser' makes me realise just how stretched our resources were for protection of our convoys. At most, the *Jervis Bay* was capable of achieving 14–15 knots and on the first deck there were openings in place of cabins which were reputed to be for gun emplacements. During my voyage we used one of these openings for the burial at sea of one of the passengers.

The *Jervis Bay* arrived back at Southampton where I left the ship and then had two most enjoyable train journeys. After the intense heat of the Australian summer (when the countryside was brown and there were the worst bush fires on record) and the Egyptian desert, it was a great delight to see the green verdure of the English fields in spring.

On arrival in London I went to the head office of Shaw, Saville and Albion to thank them for the privilege of the trip. The report on my performance appeared to be favourable. I was seen by the manager who gave instructions for me to have a ticket to Glasgow on the newly-introduced prestige train the 'Coronation Scot'. This train had a streamlined locomotive and the coaches were painted in a striking blue and silver livery. The carriages were beautifully appointed and each passenger had a booklet which had a diagram indicating the main places of interest. In addition there was only one stop at Carlisle and the journey time had been reduced from the usual eight to six and a quarter hours. To a lover of train journeys it was a great thrill and – an important addition – I was going home with so much to tell!

And so the two train journeys, one of which determined my eventual career in medicine and the second which gave me a most pleasurable experience arose out of essentially unfavourable circumstances. The first occurred because of the Depression in 1932 and the second because of the loss of a job in the Royal Infirmary in 1938.

There must be a quotation about good coming out of a situation which at the time seems irreparable. I have observed this on several occasions – and, remembering my own experience, I have encouraged colleagues, when all seemed lost, with words of hope but, it must be admitted, usually because I had nothing better to say. This line from *As You Like It* seems appropriate – 'Sweet are the uses of adversity.'

And finally a quotation from Churchill's *The Second World War*, when the 1945 election results with the Socialist victory had devastated him, 'At luncheon my wife said to me "It may well be a blessing in disguise." I replied "At the moment it seems effectively disguised!" '

FOLLOWING a period in the University of Glasgow's Department of Medicine in the Western Infirmary under Professor Sir John McNee, in 1945 I was appointed Deputy Physician Superintenent at Belvidere Infectious Diseases Hospital. That was the time of the beginning of tremendous advances due to the advent of antibiotics, immunisation and therapeutic techniques – advances which were almost unequalled in any other specialty. And today, because of all these achievements allied to the important contribution of improved housing and nutrition, a child death due to infectious disease is a comparative rarity.

During my thirty-three years in Belvidere there were certain problems of infection which in their time were dominant – as each receded (either for reasons outside our control or as a result of therapy or immunisation) another came to take its place. *Seriatum* most of the important phases were poliomyelitis, tuberculosis (especially tuberculous meningitis), epidemics of dysentery, hospital infection due to the resistant organism (the staphylococcus), herpetic infections in those whose immunity had been compromised as a result of chemotherapy for malignant disease. Obviously one cannot write in detail of these but I will concentrate on the achievement of the development of a unit for the treatment of respiratory failure which arose from our experience in poliomyelitis.

The late summer and autumn of 1947 was marked by a great epidemic of poliomyelitis. It is now almost a forgotten illness in the developed countries of the world, but it is probably timely to remember the great anxiety this crippling disease brought to all sections of the community. Epidemics in the past have usually been associated with poverty, overcrowding, squalor and general deprivation. The story of poliomyelitis is quite the opposite. These epidemics have occurred in countries where the standards of hygiene were the highest, witness the fact that in 1916 in the USA 27,000 persons were paralysed and 6,000 died – New York City alone reported 2,000 deaths. And the importance of this new scourge was further reinforced in 1921 when Franklin D. Roosevelt, who was later the wartime American President, contracted poliomyelitis and was left with almost complete paralysis of both legs.

In 1947 Belvidere had 186 cases and there were ten deaths. Prior to this, polio had only occurred sporadically but this epidemic caused great alarm and no less than 400 cases were admitted as suspected poliomyelitis. And the anxiety and fear in the public mind was not lessened by the death of Nancy Riach, the most talented and popular swimmer that Scotland had ever produced. She had been taking part in the European Swimming Championships in Monte Carlo and, as reported in the press, had been taken ill with infantile paralysis on Saturday, September 13th and died within forty-eight hours. There were unprecedented crowd scenes at her funeral in Airdrie.

At that time there was no means of immunisation against polio and two of our nurses developed it. One recovered completely but the other had residual paralysis of one of her lower limbs. Indeed that autumn was the time of great endeavour by the medical and nursing staff with long and continous hours of duty but it is a time Belvidere Hospital can look back on with pride.

Fortunately the experience of 1947 was not repeated although there were significant outbreaks in 1950 when Belvidere had 68 cases with three deaths and in 1955 when there were 71 cases with one death.

The deaths in poliomyelitis were invariably due to paralysis of the muscles of respiration and when this occurred the patients were treated in tank respirators popularly known as iron lungs. Attached to the tank was an electrically-controlled pump which resulted in air being drawn into the lungs via the mouth and then being expelled by positive pressure. That sounds easy, but the management of these tank respirators required skilled nursing. In many cases the respirators were life saving but there were still many in whom the treatment was unsuccessful.

In 1953 there was a great outbreak of more than a thousand cases of polio in Copenhagen and in that epidemic a Dr Ibsen, an anaesthetist, spotted the fundamental reason for the failures in the tank respirators – the lack of a clear airway. These patients in addition to their respiratory failure were unable to swallow. As a result their saliva was puddling at the back of their throats. (Two pints of saliva are produced and swallowed each 24 hours). In the tank respirators this saliva was being sucked into the lungs and Ibsen made the cardinal observation that they were literally drowning in their own saliva. The situation was combated by doing a tracheotomy and introducing a cuffed tube to block secretions from the mouth, and a mixture of oxygen and nitrogen was pumped into the lungs by a 'hand bag' at normal respiratory rate. The mortality in these cases had been almost 100%, but with this new management it was dramatically reduced to about 10%. All the medical students in Denmark were commandeered to manipulate the hand bags in eight hourly shifts.

I visited Copenhagen to observe this amazing exercise. Obviously the students had to be replaced, and just before I left a small mechanical respirator was being tried out. I showed interest in it and one morning several months later two gentlemen from the Aga Cooker Company in Stockholm turned up at Belvidere with a prototype respirator. That very evening I took it to the Royal Infirmary and it was tried out by an anaesthetist Dr – later Professor – Alec Forrester (who had also been to Copenhagen). It worked! With basic equipment and a great deal of optimistic enthusiasm a unit was set up in Belvidere and the first case of respiratory failure associated with failure to swallow was successfully treated in 1955. It made history, for it was the first case in Scotland to be treated by tracheostomy and mechanical intermittent positive pressure ventilation. With our experience of treating polio, (which disappeared due to immunisation) the unit was able to deal with all types of respiratory failure – including polyneuritis cases (who were often totally paralysed and were sustained by artificial ventilation until the muscle power returned), tetanus and porphyria.

All the success was achieved by team work, medical, nursing and physiotherapy and there was always the ready help of senior members of the Royal Infirmary Anaesthetic Department. Special mention must be made of the quality of nursing. It was really superb and in all the years in these severely paralysed patients there was not a single bedsore! These units for the treatment of respiratory failure were the forerunners of Intensive Care Units. Indeed Belvidere provided this service for seven years before the IC Unit was established in the Glasgow Royal Infirmary. It was a very demanding but satisfying commitment but it was a special privilege to be the leader of a team of so many talented and fine young medical men and women. A very considerable number of them are now leading consultants and three of them have professorial chairs. Also in Belvidere there was a nursing staff second to none. There was a tradition of nursing excellence which had been handed down from the many years when nursing was essentially the only therapy in Infectious Diseases. And I must also add a tribute to the loyalty of the domestic staff which was an essential part of the whole set up.

I have always been keen on teaching nurses and medical students. In the fifties and sixties there was an avalanche of new antibiotics and they were a main topic in all the medical journals. Of course, in my speciality I had a particular involvement, both in the wards and in the laboratory, and all over the country I gave lectures on the use and abuse of antibiotics. I was also in considerable demand as an after dinner speaker at medical occasions.

A few years ago, I became interested in video photography. In addition to ordinary use, I began making short interviews with those who had personal reminiscences of previous members of the Belvidere staff. This was most useful as material for the history of Belvidere that at present I am engaged in writing. It is a quite remarkable story. However, I then did two full length interviews with Professor Charles Fleming and Dr Robert Hutcheson, both of whom had long association with the 'office' in Glasgow University. These two interviews were such a success that I extended the scope to my senior colleagues and the video interviews became a project which revealed a background of the history of Glasgow Medicine. Thirty-four of these video tapes have been presented to the Glasgow University Archives

Department and are also being typescripted with a view to publication of the highlights.

It has been a privilege to have so many people of high calibre for interview and to become privy to so much University and medical history which would almost certainly have gone unrecorded. It is a story in which we in the Glasgow Medical School can take great pride. Indeed, I have first hand experience that there are giants in the land.

In June 1992 Glasgow University conferred on me the Doctorate of the University in recognition of distinguished service to Medicine and for contributions to the Archives Department of the University considered to be of historical importance.

Doctor in the Antarctic

SURGEON CAPTAIN DAVID DALGLIESH
LVO, OBE, OStJ, MRCS, LRCP, MFCM, DPH

Formerly principal Medical Officer
on Her Majesty's Yacht *Britannia*

I CALL myself a Cockney as I was born in East Finchley.

My father had an arm shot off in the First World War, and was then sent out to Egypt as a censor of correspondence – he couldn't be a combatant any more. My mother had been an army nursing sister and they met out there. She was in a hospital ship during the landings in Gallipoli looking after the wounded men and cases of cholera. She was awarded the RRC and, most unusually for a woman, received a Mention in Dispatches. They used to talk a lot about Egypt and the War and I think that was why as a family we all had the travel bug. For instance, once in the 1950s when my parents were on holiday in Gibraltar, my youngest sister was on holiday in Sweden, the eldest was in South Africa, the second in Kansas, my brother in Hong Kong, and I was in Antarctica.

When I was a year old, my family moved to Kent where I later went to a preparatory school and then on to public school, Merchant Taylors. I had put my name down for St Thomas's Hospital before the Second World War started and as I was in a reserved occupation I wasn't allowed to join up. I did my medical training at St Thomas's.

In passing I should say I enjoyed my prep. school very much. I had a marvellous headmaster with very good and fair standards. I learned Latin there and as a prep. school boy was translating Virgil. I enjoyed public school without achieving very much and left at eighteen, having done what you were allowed to do then: my first MB instead of Higher Certificate, the equivalent of what is now I suppose A levels. I went straight into St Thomas's.

Any holidays I had I worked as a farm labourer at two pounds a week and thoroughly enjoyed the open air.

Having qualified, I got a job briefly at my Alma Mater, St Thomas's. I had the MRCS and LRCP and half the MB.BS (London) when my father asked if I was qualified to practise, because he was rather hard up. So I didn't finish the MB.BS and it hasn't really mattered. It meant I qualified when I was twenty-three.

Then the Central Medical War Committee decided jobs in the teaching hospitals should go to doctors returning from the forces so I had to leave. I found a very rewarding job in the County Hospital at Farnham. It's quite frightening to look back to those days when within a month of qualifying I was running a 250-bed hospital. This was because the house physician was often sick so I had to do her job, and the resident surgeon had ulcers and sometimes I had to do his job, too. At that time I was working 110 hours a week regularly for a salary of £2.5s. a week. I didn't mind for I enjoyed it.

That was in 1946. It was a terrific experience which stood me in good stead afterwards. You were sometimes suddenly confronted with an emergency which you would never have seen as a student or in your teaching hospital. On one occasion I delivered a baby. I handed it to the midwife and, before I turned back to the mother, heard the haemorrhage before I saw it. I had to do a manual removal of the placenta and I suppose that I saved her life. I remembered what my teacher had told me about the necessary movement of the hands. It was frightening for me but I had to hide that and get on with it, or I'd have been no use to the patient.

I always thought I'd like to be a GP in Devon, and I didn't want to specialise. I dreamed of Devon because when I was only six, and my father was enlarging our house in Kent, he sent the whole family to a farm there. It was only a mile from the sea, and I thought it absolute heaven. From then onwards I wanted to come back to Devon.

I joined the RNVR in October 1946 to do my National Service

and enjoyed the first year so much I decided to straighten my wavy navy stripes and make it a career.

I became attached to HMS *Superb* which took me to North Africa, Copenhagen and Stockholm. I enjoyed the life. There was a certain amount of medicine involved. My assessment is that in the Navy there is as much or as little medicine as you care to find and you also travel and are paid to do so. Then, when I saw the man who did the appointments in the Navy and who seemed in a chatty mood, I asked him if they had any expeditions nowadays – for I had always wanted to travel. Both my brother and I had agreed we wanted to go to places where no one had ever been before. When I asked this chap he looked at me searchingly and asked "What have you heard?" I said "Nothing." – "Well," he said, "I was asked only yesterday if I could find a Surgeon-Lieutenant to go to the Antarctic. Will you go? You leave in two weeks' time." That was in 1947.

I joined the Royal Research ship *John Biscoe*, a wooden boom-defence vessel, for a remarkable voyage, for the crew were among the sweepings of the London docks. Two joined by rowing boat as we sailed down the Thames – we reckoned they were one jump ahead of the police. We had an Estonian who was slightly mad and tried to knife someone. The second officer was a peer of the realm, who had a marvellous way with the men. The Estonian complained to him that one of the men had called him an Estonian bastard. The officer said "Well, you are an Estonian, aren't you?" – He said "Ja, ja." – "And you are a bit of a bastard, too?" The Estonian roared with laughter and calm returned. But eventually he went berserk with a knife in Montevideo, the Uruguayan police got him and we never saw him again.

Going down the Thames at five o'clock on a December morning, fumbling in the potato locker, I wondered what on earth I had let myself in for; I and another chap had the job of peeling the potatoes for twenty-five expedition members and twenty crew. But we got used to all the other jobs, painting the ship and, soon after, acting as stevedores in the Antarctic. We went from London to Cape Verde Islands and on to Port Stanley.

When we arrived at Port Stanley in the Falklands the first job I did was to conduct a post-mortem. There had been a death on the operating table. The local doctor, who became a good friend of mine, asked me to do the post-mortem. He explained that if an outside doctor did it the locals wouldn't feel there had been any cover-up. The patient had had a weakened heart from undiagnosed pulmonary tuberculosis which was rife in the Falklands at that time.

On the ship I was both doctor and dentist. Before I left HMS *Superb*, when I knew I was going to the Antarctic, I asked the dentist if he'd show me how to pull teeth. He'd have the wretched sailor in the chair and then bang on the bulkhead and in I'd go and remove the tooth.

In Antarctica we went to Graham Land. It is the peninsula south of Cape Horn and is part of the chain of mountains that eventually curves up and continues north as the Andes. Our voyage ended at Marguerite Bay, which is a thousand miles south of Cape Horn. We couldn't get into Stonington until some American ice-breakers broke the sea ice, but we finally got there, where I was to spend two years. Our job was to do a coastal survey for the Falkland Islands Dependencies.

Our transport was supplied entirely by dogs – about eighty huskies. We bred our own, killing off the weak members or the old ones and training the suitable young ones. Nowadays they use skidoos as they proved to be more economical. We were desperately fond of the dogs. There were nine dogs in a team and I had my own, of whom I was in charge. You really had to drive them. They fought like mad, a natural pastime as far as they were concerned, and I had to stitch up their torn noses and ears.

We only meant to be there for a year, and at the end of that time a ship came down. It got as near as 250 miles but couldn't get in as the frozen sea didn't break. They radioed to say "Sorry we've tried to get in but don't worry; we'll come back next year." So we took a deep breath, demolished a bottle of whisky very quickly and thought about what we'd do for the next year. There were eleven of us. We were a bit amused to hear that one Sunday newspaper referred to us as 'the lost eleven scientists' – for we knew exactly where we were and didn't think we were scientists! After that we always referred to ourselves as 'the Lost Eleven.' That was from 1948 to 1950.

Fuchs, later Sir Vivien Fuchs, our leader, had in fact made plans for this contingency before the news came that we would be there for another year. On a long northern journey during my first year we had found what was then only the third known rookery in the world of Emperor penguins. They are the largest and most primitive of all penguins. It was an exciting find. One of the things he said we should do was to take a series of embryos during the winter. They're funny birds in that they breed in the winter; the reason is that by the time the young birds' down has gone and they have adult feathers the ice is breaking so they can swim in the water and drift north with the pack ice. Three of us, a chap who later became a professor of zoology, plus the air mechanic and myself, spent the winter of 1949 in a tent measuring seven feet by seven, with eighty-four days in pitch darkness and temperatures down to the minus forties. But we did get a series of embryos, taking one egg a day and getting the embryo out and putting it in alcohol. The series of embryos are all now in the Natural History Museum. We did what Scott's party tried to do in 1911, but couldn't. Having taken the embryo out, we had the egg left. So what to do with it? We had it scrambled and it was extremely tasty. We are the only men living or dead to have wintered in the Antarctic, that is inside the Antarctic Circle, under canvas.

My first impressions of the Antarctic were awe-inspiring. I've always maintained that even if I had been an atheist, which I wasn't, I would have known I was in the presence of something much, much bigger than myself. I've regarded it sometimes as God's workshop, with the great glaciers grinding away, sculpturing the landscape. There are moments I can still remember vividly, years later. Once, when we did a winter journey, I had gone out in the morning. The sun was just due to come back but hadn't reached us yet except for the top of the peaks which were a lovely salmon, peachy pink. I stood and looked, and the world was silent. The sea was frozen, the glaciers were different blues and greens, and the mountain peaks immense: the beauty was so awe-inspiring that I found I had stopped breathing and there was absolutely no noise at all.

I remember the first iceberg I ever saw. There was no horizon, with fog over the sea. Suddenly there was an area of brighter light like washing powder in this fog and that was my first iceberg. You thought you could smell the ice. People have often said that. You don't actually smell it. What it is, is that it is so much colder, you can feel the coldness on the hairs in your nostrils.

When we got back to the Falkland Islands the Governor wanted me to stay on the *Biscoe* as the doctor and not return to Britain with the rest of the expedition members. The *Biscoe* had a final supply run to the Antarctic bases, which was extremely hard work but delighted me, and then a three week hydro-graphic tour around the Falkland Islands themselves – a fascin-ating and unique experience. I love the Falkland Islands; I like and respect the Falkland Island people – so generous, so hospit-able, so hardworking. I get very angry if people say they're not worth fighting for.

Topographically the Falklands are very like the Shetlands – moorlands with no high peaks, and the weather is never as hot or as cold as in this country. Round its shores are four hundred known wrecks. I loved my time in the Falklands; I was lucky enough to go back again for a few days in 1964 and three years ago I made yet another visit. I'd like to visit again.

My next job was in a hospital in Plymouth doing medicine and anaesthetics, because I wanted to specialise in the latter. But I was sent for by the Appointments man and he asked me if I'd go on an expedition up to Greenland. I said I was just back and really had to get on with my medicine. He was very angry and rude, but back I went to Devonport. However, two weeks later the Admiral-in-Charge sent for me to tell me I was off to Trincomalee in Ceylon. I had two years there in the hospital doing medicine and anaesthetics. I came to love the island. This was in 1954 and later in 1970 I took my wife out there, also.

When I was in the Royal Naval Hospital in Trincomalee in Ceylon there was a doctor in a frigate called the *Loch Glendhu* who was married but seldom saw his wife. I was then not married and he asked me if I would swop with him. So he came to do my job in the hospital and for five weeks I accompanied His Excellency the Governor of Mauritius round his Depen-dencies on a fantastic trip – round tiny islands miles from nowhere, to Chagos which is now a tracking station. It was about two hundred yards wide and twenty-seven and a half miles long.

After I returned, the Admiralty told me they wanted me to study skin. So I went to the Hospital for Skin Diseases off

Leicester Square. I found it extremely useful. Then I was asked
by Dr Fuchs if I would go to Greenland and buy huskies for
him to take on his famous Trans-Antarctic Expedition. So off I
went to Copenhagen to take a Danish ship up the west coast
of Greenland, stopping at all sorts of places on my way to
Jacobshavn.

When I arrived in Jacobshavn there was a scene I shall never
forget. The sea was dead calm and there were enormous icebergs
coming down the fjord; they were blue on the eastern side and
golden yellow on the western side – a magnificent sight. Then
round an iceberg came an Eskimo in his kayak, which made the
picture perfect.

From the Greenland ice-cap twenty million tons of ice carve
off into Jacobshavn fjord every day. Because of this there's a
very high fish population and a very high dog population: about
seven thousand huskies. I stayed with the local Governor, a
Dane. He put a notice up in Danish saying that on Saturday I
was buying twenty huskies. This produced a marvellous sight, as
two or three hundred huskies were brought, on bits of string
held by their Greenland handlers. I say Greenlanders for they
are not pure blood; they're a mixture of Eskimos and Norse. I'd
say "That's a nice one. How old is that?" And they'd tell me
and the dentist would ask to see their teeth. I wanted to buy
them at eighteen months, and I got twenty splendid huskies. But
they warned me I must get to know my own huskies and I
wasn't to trust these until they knew me, because old people and
children were killed every year. I didn't pay the owner until I
had inoculated each dog. Then I hired a schooner which took
me and the caged huskies to Egedesminde, a twelve hour trip
across Disko Bay, then transferred to a Greenland trading ship.
I watered and fed and cleaned them out every day so they got to
know me, and by the end of the trip I had them playing with the
children on board.

Eventually I got them back to Denmark and put them in a
police dogs' kennels overnight and asked the police to send them
off to the docks the following morning while I stayed with
Danish friends. But next morning the police phoned and said
"For goodness sake come quickly. They've all broken out!" I
went down to the police kennels. I put my thick gloves on and
windproof clothes which smelt of dog and seal and fish. I went in

and shouted at them. They recognised my voice and returned to their cages and I repaired the damage with a hammer and nails. The dogs went to the Antarctic and did the crossing with Fuchs in 1957.

Just before I went to Greenland I had a letter from a chap called Sir James Wordie, who had been a geologist with Sir Ernest Shackleton in 1915, asking if I would think of taking the Royal Society's International Geophysical Year Expedition to the Antarctic. I turned it over in my mind, thinking how much I'd love to do it, but not quite sure because it was such a hell of a responsibility – a lot of money was involved, with millions of pounds of equipment. Eventually one day I came back into the wardroom and was told I was wanted on the 'phone. It was Sir James. I said I was in agreement but I couldn't do much in preparation till I got back from Greenland.

We went to sea in the Motor Vessel *Tottan* with a Norwegian crew and a black-browed captain, a very nice man who spoke in monosyllables. His brief was to do what I wanted except in matters that might hazard the safety of the ship.

Fuchs himself was going in the Motor Vessel *Theron*, a week before us. He was to go into the Weddel Sea and I was to follow a week behind. He had aircraft to tell me and his own ship where open water lay. The plan was to establish two bases side by side. In the event he tried to cut a corner and got stuck in the pack ice for five weeks, held fast. We kept to the east, got into open water and kept to the coast. I was instructed to establish the base just south of 75°, for scientific reasons. We got down to 77° and found unbroken frozen sea except for one lead of open water. In the distance we could see what is called a water sky, that is, when water is reflected back on clouds and the sky appears dark. The opposite is an ice blink; if you see brightness in the clouds, the sun is bouncing off ice. But this was darkness bouncing from water. The Captain said he could go down that lead, but if we couldn't get through we'd have to come out backwards, which is the best way known of losing your propellor. So we turned and found a suitable site for the base at 75° 31' S, 26° 38' W. We effected a landing and I and my companions went up onto the ice shelf. That is where the ice sheet has come over the sea. It is 1,000 feet thick, as the Antarctic is in the grip of an ice-age. The ice sheet is formed by snow being deposited in the interior. It compresses and flows towards the coast. There it comes down over the sea: it was called in Scott's day the Great Ice Barrier – now Shelf Ice. It is, as I said, 1,000 feet thick and is slowly moving and breaks off as icebergs: large ones. I've seen one over ten miles long.

I and my companions found a way up onto this ice shelf and about two miles inland I said I reckoned this would do for our base. I took possession of it in the name of Her Majesty the Queen, having been sworn in as a magistrate in South Georgia. I am still a Falklands Islands Dependency's Justice of the Peace! I took possession because no one had ever landed on that 400-mile coast before. Then we made our way back to the ship for equipment and stores and we established our base, at that time the largest single building ever erected in the Antarctic – 120 feet long. It was to house twenty scientists, and there were ten of us to build it. Our job was to get it up, get it painted and get it ready, so that when the main party came they would have a running concern.

It was very hard work. I was accused, correctly, of being a slave driver. Only two of the men had been in the Antarctic before, not as experienced as me. That was my qualification for being there. I made us all work a seven day week and up to a twelve to fourteen hour day. My idea was to get the outer skin of the hut completed before the real equinoctial, autumnal or winter blizzards came, which might have torn it down or got underneath it and packed it full of snow. In the event we just did it, by a few days. By chance and, I suppose, partly by my determination and bloody-mindedness, I had ordained that we would not have days off until the outer shell was completed.

We finished the outer skin and at a slightly more leisurely pace did the inside. We had already started doing scientific observations, one of which is now of especial interest. Remember that this was 1956. We were the first people in the world to measure the ozone layer with a machine called the Dobson spectrophotometer. So thirty-three years ago we had the ozone layer under investigation!

Although the leader, I was also the doctor and dentist. There was a marvellous chap, a commissioned bosun who came with me – a charming chap who, sadly, was later killed in a car accident. George started out as a boy seaman, came up through the hawse-pipe as we say, and got a commission. When I was getting ready to go from Portsmouth barracks, this smart figure with a Captain Kettle beard asked me all sorts of questions about the expedition. One day I said to him "You seem to be very interested in all this. Do you want to go?" He said, "Of course I do." – "Right, you're on." He was wonderful, and never stopped working. He broke a bone in his wrist and I had constantly to put plaster of Paris on it. Believe it or not, he then used that as a tool.

On my first expedition I was also the veterinary surgeon, photographer, gardener, dog-driver and cook. We had a six by four foot double-glazed greenhouse. We grew radishes, spring onions and carrots. We had taken Falkland Islands soil with us. My greatest achievement in this area was to sow radish seeds one day and eat them twelve days later, because they had sun twenty-four hours a day.

For my work in the Antarctic I got a Polar Medal. This is not a campaign medal; it comes from a recommendation through the Hydrographer for the Navy, who makes recommendations to the Monarch. The award is made by the Queen. The medal has two and a quarter ounces of silver in it, with a bar saying where you were, etc. When I got back from the Antarctic the second time another bar was added to the Polar Medal. The OBE, which I got later, was given for diplomatic reasons. My Russian counterpart in the Antarctic with whom I had been in constant radio contact was made a Hero of the Soviet Union.

In the Antarctic I had been told to make contact with the other eleven nations there. My best radio contact had been with the Russian leader Mikhail Somov. He and I talked on the radio once a month. We had contacted England to ask them to tell the Russians we would contact them at a certain time on a certain day and wave length. And we did this once a month. I later met Somov at an international conference in Paris and later still I accepted an invitation to visit the Russian Polar Institute in Leningrad. He met me and I was entertained very kindly. He was wearing the Antarctic Club tie we had given him.

In 1959 I was working for my membership – for in the end I didn't do anaesthetics – to become a medical consultant physician. Then one day they sent for me and offered me the post of Principal Medical Officer on the Royal Yacht *Britannia*. I thought it would be a pity to turn that one down – and I was on the Royal Yacht till 1962.

It was a magnificent experience. HMY *Britannia* was the only vessel in the Navy that did not have a tannoy. All the people – I say this with awful immodesty – knew exactly what they had to do so they didn't need to be told. The sailors, who are called yachtsmen, don't have people shouting at them. They know where they ought to be and at what time. There was a system that if there was something urgent a red disc would go up above a 'red-hot' notice board and you read what was underneath. And if there was a white disc, it was 'white-hot'.

The first trip I made was when the Queen opened the St Lawrence Seaway. We went up the St Lawrence Seaway through locks rising hundreds of feet, and we did probably five thousand miles in fresh water, to the head of Lake Superior.

Going into the locks the Canadians and Americans were amazed to see the sailors in their white uniforms handling oily wire-hawsers without a word being spoken. The first Lieutenant being on the fo'castle and the second Lieutenant on the quarter-deck, they would simply clap hands and point: it was all done like that and the sailors knew when to pull, when to let go. As the vessel rose in the water, not a word was spoken. All the banks were lined with people watching us as we went up. The Royal Marine Band would be on the Royal Deck. As we rose up in the water, they would play Oom-pa, Oom-pa. You'd have people shouting for request tunes. Someone requested 'Sussex by the Sea'. The Canadians would shout perhaps "Anyone there frae Dundee?" One of the sailors would say yes, just to be kind even if it wasn't true.

I was a doctor on the *Britannia* for nearly three years. It was a fascinating experience to see how very hard the Royal family work. It was our job to get them from A to B and to see they could relax and literally kick off their shoes when they got back on board. I did a trip with the Queen's aunt, the late Princess Royal. It was a gruelling trip for an old lady in that heat. We went from what used to be called British Guiana through the chain of Caribbean islands to British Honduras. A few weeks later we were out there again for Princess Margaret's honey-moon. We did a trip with the Queen and Prince Philip to Italy; with the Gloucesters to Greece and Turkey, where they were doing a tour of the war graves which was fascinating. We did two trips round Scotland with the Queen and the children, which was very relaxed; and we went with the Queen to Ghana and West Africa. That was in 1961.

I went back to running wards in the Royal Naval Hospital, Gosport, near Portsmouth, subsequently doing a post-graduate course in public health, for a DPH. I asked if I could go to Hong Kong as PMO at HMS *Tamar*, the shore establishment there, so I went off via the Trans-Siberian railway in 1965 and stayed until 1967. I looked after the sailors and some of their families and was dermatologist to the Services. I also looked after the Chinese ratings and their families. I did voluntary work one day a week in a church clinic. I was put on the colonial equivalent of the General Medical Council in Hong Kong. It was interesting and quite responsible work: listening to cases, striking people off the list and putting people back on, remembering chaps' livelihoods depended on it. I loved Hong Kong, which was a most exciting place.

As I became interested in a tri-services approach to the medical services, I asked if I could do the Joint-Services Staff Course in Buckinghamshire. I was given permission to do it and found it instructive. Then I went to Dartmouth Naval College, where I stayed until 1970.

At Dartmouth, too, I had a very interesting job. The cadets were all young men who knew exactly what they were aiming for and were under terrific pressure both mentally and physically. It was my job to keep them fit and if they found the pace too hot, it was up to me to help them. For me it was a fine experience. I reckoned the two best jobs in the Navy for me were the Royal Yacht *Brittania* and the Royal Naval College.

In 1970 I asked if I could go out to Singapore and I went, the last Fleet Medical Officer to the Commander, Far East Fleet, Singapore. I covered the area from Hong Kong west to the Persian Gulf and was in charge of all the medical personnel in the Far East.

I would say the best part of the area is Malaysia and we used to go up the east coast to the islands which are lovely. I did a trip to Hong Kong on duty and took my wife with me. My wife and I also did a trip up into the centre of the Malayan peninsula, to what was called King George National Park and is now Taman Negara. You had to write to the chief game warden and say what you wanted to do. It was all arranged and we drove right up the centre of Malaysia to a place called Jerantut. I parked the car at the police station and got a lift down to the river Pahang in the state of Pahang. Our boat was about thirty feet long, no wider than my armchair, with a canopy, a Malaysian at the stern with an outboard and a Malaysian at the bow with a pole. We set off, my wife and I, feeling like Cleopatra and Sanders of the River, chug, chug, chug for four and a half hours up this vast jungle river past trees covered with blossom. And there round a corner on the cliff was the rest house where we stayed for a week. Another unique experience.

We did one trip overland wearing jungle greens which was a good idea, for on our first night, after a stroll without them, we came back with our ankles covered with leeches. Our other trips were all by boat. We went up some cataracts and we were told by the game warden not to try and help because the Malaysians knew what they were doing in this enormous river with these roaring cataracts. They knew which boulders to steer between, the chap at the stern steering and the chap at the bow fending off with his pole. When you got to the top you could feel the boat level out. After going up seven of these we landed at a village, Kampong Bantal. It was for only an hour but neither of us will ever forget it. It was so peaceful. The head woman, not man, greeted us in the traditional way, asking us to sit down, and a little boy was sent up a coconut tree and brought down two green coconuts. The tops were cut off and we were given a spoon and drank the milk which was thick and ate the flesh which was thin. It was pleasant and refreshing. We chatted away as I previously had taken some lessons in Malay while at Dartmouth. They all joined in; it was all very tranquil and unspoilt. Then we walked back to the boat and the children followed us and we suddenly heard them singing some English verses, a nursery rhyme that someone had taught them. We gave them boiled sweets, which I'm afraid would be bad for their teeth, but they enjoyed them. It was, as I said, a magical experience.

In 1971 I developed a frightful fever and that put the finish to Singapore. I was in hospital for five weeks and it was touch and go – but as my wife says, I'm a good survivor.

Back home in England I was asked if I'd become Deputy Director General to the Director General of the Navy, and Chief of Naval Medical Personnel and Logistics as Surgeon-Commodore. The following year I was made an Officer of the Order of St John of Jerusalem.

For ten years coming up for retirement I was Clinical MO, then Senior Clinical MO with Torbay Health District, which included weekly hearing assessment clinics. I retired in 1987 after a long, varied and fruitful professional life in medicine.

Both my wife and I are keen on travel and have travelled a lot since my retirement. We have been to the Virgin Islands and Madeira. We went as a family to Morocco. My wife had been there before as a friend of hers had set up a Cheshire Home at Marrakech. In 1986 I went to the Antarctic and my wife and family went skiing in Austria. In 1987 we went to Bermuda then on to the USA and Canada, staying at Gettysburg *en route*. Since then we have been in Egypt, Italy, Pakistan, Argentina, Chile, Sri Lanka, South Africa and also France, where we took my son Adam who wanted to learn more French. Our daughter Anna, having got her BA Hons degree in photography and graphic design, went on a tour of the Far East, as she had been born in Singapore. Travelling is in our blood.

I have had a most rewarding professional life in medicine. Looking back on it, there has been great variety and extremes of experiences, treating leprosy in Hong Kong, frost-bite in the Antarctic, and dealing with people from Eskimos to the Royal Family. You can't get further extremes than that!

Training as a Nurse at Plymouth in the War

BERYL SKIDMORE

WHEN I was sixteen years old, during my last year at school, I saw an advertisement for a probationer nurse at the Liskeard Cottage Hospital. I thought that would be a possibility for a job, although I knew nothing about the nursing profession. I contacted the matron and she agreed to accept me on a month's trial, to start in April, 1937. I was to supply my own uniform for that period and if taken on permanently I would be provided with the regulation outfit, my salary to be £20 a year plus food and accommodation. So I was to step onto the bottom rung of the nursing ladder, with no conception of what was involved or what my way of life would be.

It was at Passmore Edwards Cottage Hospital that I entered the nursing profession in April, 1937. I had never entered a hospital ward before and, dressed in borrowed uniform of long grey dress and apron, stiff collar and cuffs, and a butterfly cap, I experienced my first encounter of the sights and smells of the wards and with the patients and nursing staff, which was daunting to say the least. I was to work under the supervision of Sister Moon, who was in charge of the women's ward and operating theatre. I was soon to learn that I was indeed on the bottom rung of the ladder. I opened the door for any nurse who was senior to me, and that meant everyone. I sat at the bottom of the dining table and was the first to answer any patient's call.

There were three trained sisters, two working day duty and

one on permanent night duty. Matron, Miss Gilhespy, was in overall charge of the hospital. She was responsible to the local Hospital Committee for the general administration and to the local general practitioners for the nursing of their patients. Matron and sisters were all State Registered Nurses. Matron was an ex-Army sister with red hair and she insisted on strict discipline, as I soon discovered.

The hours were long. We were called at 6.30 a.m. and were expected to be in the wards by 7 a.m. At 8.15 a.m. we had breakfast and returned to the ward at 8.45 a.m. During the day we were given two hours off duty – either 10 a.m.-12 or 2–4 p.m. – and then worked until 9 p.m. We were allowed a half day per week; if the work was slack it commenced at midday but if we were busy we were lucky to be away by 2 p.m. We were also required to be back at the hospital by 10 p.m. A holiday of three weeks a year was arranged by Matron when it was convenient. The pay was £20 a year and with insurance deduction it was calculated to be £1 13s.4d. a month.

During my month on trial I became very interested in the basic nursing duties I was entrusted with. I had a desire to be of some use in the world and set out to help the patients. I observed that on admission the majority of both patients and relatives had mixed feelings, partly fear of the unknown, doubt as to how they would be received and treated and hope that they would be cured or relieved. The change from home to hospital ward, surrounded by other sick people, requires courage and the attitude of the nurse is all important. So much depends on her kindness and thoughtful sympathy. So, although I was young and capable of making many mistakes, I made a tremendous effort always to be kind and patient to the sick I was attending. A high percentage of my time, however, was spent on non-nursing tasks – the sort of discipline thought necessary to accomplish good teamwork. I acted as messenger and cleaner of cupboards, bathrooms and toilets in addition to my special responsibility, the sluice. Evenings were spent padding wooden splints to apply to fractured limbs, sewing tapes on gowns and swabs used during operations, making pneumonia jackets for the treatment and comfort of patients with pneumonia and any other mending as required. Generally speaking, I coped fairly well but came to grief with the electric iron. I was not good at

switching it off or standing it up. One day I was summoned to
the ward while ironing bandages. I answered the call immediately but when I returned found I had left the iron flat on the
bandages and had burnt a hole through the ironing blanket
onto the kitchen table. Unfortunately for me, Matron discovered it and I was severely reprimanded. I was so devastated
I wanted to go home but somehow could not leave my post.

The majority of patients were confined to bed and required
bed washing, bed pans and feeding. I was instructed how to give
bed pans and was told I was totally responsible for their cleanli-
ness and disinfecting and that the sluice where they were stored
had to be scrubbed daily; this also was my responsibility. I was
not used to having water on tap and at first frequently drenched
myself, making my nice butterfly starched cap all floppy. Feeding and washing patients I quite enjoyed as the patients would
talk to me, but I did wish that they would be more careful with
the jugs of water on their lockers as cleaning the brass corners
was one of my tasks and Matron always seemed to find a dirty
corner to complain about.

Economy was the key word. Nothing was wasted; everything
had to be accounted for.

Two local doctors were responsible for the medical care of the
patients. Dr Metcalfe was a surgeon and Dr Toogood a physician.
They visited the hospital daily and whenever required.

Following an operation a junior nurse would be instructed to
sit with the patient until he recovered from the anaesthetic in
case he vomited. It was also usual for the nurse to be given the
tray of instruments that had been used that day for drying,
following their washing and sterilising. I was very frightened the
first time this duty of sitting with the patient was assigned to me
and had all sorts of visions as to what could happen to the
patient. Another task for the junior was the washing and boiling
of the soiled swabs, then the drying and ironing of them ready
for re-sterilisation.

At the end of my trial period I was interviewed by Matron in
the day room, which also served as her office. She told me she
would allow me to continue my work at the hospital. I was
amazed and also pleased that I had not been a complete failure.
I could hardly wait to tell my mother on my next half day at
home.

Off duty periods were very precious to me. At first I tried to continue my music lessons with Mr Butchers and would sometimes play the old piano upstairs in the nurses' sitting room, but the physical strain of my duties, the tired body and aching feet, made it difficult for me to concentrate, and reluctantly I had to relinquish my lessons and played the piano only when at home.

When it was my turn for an annual holiday, arrangements were made by my mother for me to spend some time with her friends, Doris and Tom Smith, at Rugby. I had not travelled beyond Devon before, so it was a pleasant experience. The Great Western Railway (GWR) transported me to Birmingham. Doris met me and we transferred to another line, the London Midland & Scottish Railway (LMS) and continued the journey to Rugby. Doris and her husband Tom were caretakers of the Midland Bank in the centre of Rugby and they lived in the flat provided for them. During my stay I visited Coventry to see the Cathedral (later bombed during the Second World War) and Peeping Tom of the Lady Godiva legend. An excursion was also arranged to Bournville, the village where the employees of Cadbury's Factory lived. We also toured the factory which I found fascinating. The huge vats containing green marzipan, pink sugar, cream and chocolate looked colourful, but I wondered how those machines converted the sticky messes into attractive confectionery. The smell of cocoa made me long for a cup but it was an anticlimax when we were offered tea and a sample box of chocolates at the end of the tour.

I thought the countryside around Rugby was very flat but interesting, especially the Grand Union Canal. There were nice walks.

I returned to my duties at Passmore Edwards Hospital feeling refreshed and thinking that there is life beyond the hospital ward.

The days passed very quickly as I became more absorbed in hospital life. Another probationer nurse joined the staff, by the name of Lottie Keast. She had been working in Okehampton Cottage Hospital and as her home was at Darite, a nearby village, she wanted to transfer to Liskeard. There was a vacancy when Dorothy Eade left to commence her training at the South Devon and East Cornwall Hospital in Plymouth and Lottie was appointed to the post. This meant that I moved up a step and my duties carried more nursing responsibility. I was taught how to make beds with patients in them and to prepare a bed to receive a post-operation patient or an accident case. There were frequent motor bike accidents on the Moorswater corner (now a by-pass) which was an accident black spot. Fractures of the skull and limbs were likely injuries.In those days motor-cyclists wore leather helmets which offered very little protection to the skull.

Medical conditions admitted were varied and included heart and chest conditions, diabetes, sometimes with leg gangrene, rheumatism, arthritis, varicose ulcers and skin diseases. We were kept busy all the time. My first experience of a patient dying saddened me, but the sister soon brought me down to the practicalities and I was told to assist the nurse with the laying out of the body, known as the 'last offices'. There were tragic deaths, too, when we all were affected. I recall a child of two who had opened the car door of her father's sports car and had fallen out. She was badly injured and died soon after admission; we all shed a tear then.

I missed my connection with church or chapel as we did not have Sunday evenings off. Canon Mills, then Rector of Liskeard Church, approached Matron about this matter and Lottie and I were asked if we would like to attend confirmation classes. We very willingly agreed, and were subsequently confirmed in Liskeard Parish Church.

Liskeard was a friendly town and the townsfolk respected the nurses from the hospital. There were annual money-raising events such as flag days, garden parties and fêtes. The sisters and nurses were required to attend these functions in uniform, if duties permitted. At Harvest Festival time we were inundated with fresh vegetables, fruit and flowers sent by the churches of the surrounding area. Matron, in addition to being a State Registered Nurse, also held a Housekeeping Certificate. She was a marvellous cook and would produce some very appetising meals for the patients and staff from some of this food. We in turn would spend our spare moments in the kitchen preparing fruit and onions for preserving. Edith, our cook, was fully employed preparing patients' and staff meals and had no time for extra cooking. Although the nurses worked long hours they were expected to volunteer to help on these occasions.

The main meal of the day was always at 1 p.m., when Matron

presided and served the meal. She kept a watchful eye on whether we cleared our plates, and conversation was limited to a dialogue between her and Sister Moon who sat next to her. Occasionally Matron would take a day off to visit Plymouth on a shopping expedition. The atmosphere in the hospital changed the moment she disappeared. Everyone carried out their duties in a more relaxed manner and at lunch even the food tasted better, and we were free to chatter if we wished. Sometimes at tea time the sisters would treat us to an iced walnut cake baked locally, and this was much enjoyed. Matron returned in the early evening as we were preparing the patients to receive their evening visitors, but she would retire to her room and so the day remained a welcome break from her beady eye.

Christmas was always devoted to the patients. The Mayor of Liskeard visited the hospital at a time arranged with Matron, and visiting hours were extended. We were busy before Christmas Eve decorating the wards and assisting with the preparation of the extra food. The patients who were too ill to join in any of the festivities were usually moved to a private ward or screened off in a quiet corner. We were not allowed time off until after Boxing Day, but if Matron could, she permitted us to sleep at home one night during the Christmas period – a great privilege.

Life in the hospital was busy and well organised. The patients received excellent care and attention. There were very few drugs available then and it was largely due to good nursing procedures, conscientiously carried out, that the majority of patients recovered or were discharged. I remained at the hospital until I was eighteen years of age, and by that time I had decided that I would apply to undertake my general training. The question was – to which hospital should I apply? Nurses' training classes were contained in the larger general hospitals.

In addition to cottage hospitals there were voluntary hospitals and municipal hospitals. Voluntary hospitals were financed by public subscriptions and donations and the facilities provided varied. Municipal hospitals were financed by local authorities. They were the successors to the Poor Law Hospitals under the 1929 Local Government Act. The former Master was replaced by a Medical Superintendent as medical care had been established, and both the Matron and the Lay Administrator were responsible to him. There were both such hospitals in Plymouth, so I discussed with Matron Gilhespy which would be right for me. She advised that I should apply to the municipal hospital known as the City and now called Freedom Fields. I took her advice and applied to the City Hospital and in due course was called for interview with Miss Waterhouse, Matron, and Miss Bishop, Sister Tutor. Following questions and answers concerning my work at Liskeard, Miss Waterhouse explained to me that I would be required to pass an educational test set by the General Nursing Council before I could commence my training. She suggested I joined a group who were attending a revision class given by a retired head teacher three times a week to prepare myself for the next examination in July, 1939. I could, however, commence duty at the hospital as soon as I was released from my present post, and I started there early in April 1939.

Sunday, September 3rd, 1939, was a bright and sunny day. I was on duty and remember an announcement over the radio at 10 a.m. that the Prime Minister would speak to the nation at 11.15 a.m. We tried to finish our urgent tasks in order to listen to the broadcast and then positioned ourselves by the patients' bedsides to hear what the Prime Minister had to say. Mr Chamberlain was a man of 70 years of age. His voice sounded tired and sad. He spoke from the Cabinet Room at No. 10 Downing Street, saying that the British Ambassador in Berlin had handed the German Government a final note stating that unless the British Government heard from them by 11 a.m. that they were withdrawing their troops from Poland a state of war would exist between us. No undertaking had been received, so consequently we were at war with Germany.

The announcement was followed by the National Anthem and we stood to attention. Stunned by the news and having no conception of what might lie in front of us, we continued with our duties. The patients anxiously waited for visiting time so that they could talk over the events of the morning with their relatives. His Majesty King George VI broadcast to the nation at 6 p.m. For the past few weeks the hospital carpenters had been erecting wooden frames to the ward windows in preparation for the blacking out of the lights. The black-out was now put into operation. No one was allowed to show a light.

Black material was available for sale, so people could make their own black-out curtains. Cars, buses and bicycles all had to partially cover their lights, and trains were dimly lit. Street lighting was banned and people were permitted to use torches for walking, provided the beam was small and they pointed them down. The most popular torch was a small handbag size that used a No. 8 battery. I acquired one of these but found that the batteries were in very short supply. So if I could manage without switching it on I did. There were many accidents at first but gradually we became used to it. Air raid wardens of the Civil Defence were mobilised and they supervised the carrying out of the black-out regulations. Servicemen were coming to Plymouth with the mobilisation of the Territorial Army and the call up of young men and women over the age of eighteen for service training. Work at the dockyard increased as Government orders poured in, creating new jobs immediately.

The Ministry of Health took over the task of dividing the country into sectors and grouping and grading the hospitals for the reception of casualties. The City Hospital was graded to act as a casualty clearing station. In order to acquire beds for these expected casualties the hospital began to plan the evacuation of patients. A new block of small wards had just been completed but these were for use as maternity beds because the hospital was also a training school for Part 1 of the Central Midwives Board examination. The general beds were increased from 570 to 635. In addition, there was a sick children's ward and a nursery, the nursery being staffed by girls aged sixteen to eighteen who were taking their Nursery Nursing training.

The Medical Superintendent, Mr Larks, the doctors and sisters of the wards concerned decided which patients could be discharged and those who could be moved to other hospitals away from the coast were moved. There were tearful scenes as those who were to be moved were informed. On Ward 4 I remember Mr Morgan, a man in his forties, becoming very distressed. He suffered from ankylosing spondylitis and was so immobile that he was like a plank and was dependent on our administrations, even to our lighting and holding his pipe for a while. The day following the evacuation of patients, those of us remaining had the task of disinfecting bedsteads, lockers, bed pans, urinals and other patient utensils. The beds were then made up clean, fresh white paper was placed in the lockers and fresh charts and bed cards were placed on the bed boards ready for the next patients.

Lectures continued. I was attending those on anatomy, physiology, hygiene and general nursing measures. Miss Bishop, the tutor, was very strict. Lectures had to be written and submitted to her for marking. If she was not satisfied with your work you were told to do it again. You did it without question as you could not progress unless she passed it. The discipline sometimes irked me and I would feel frustrated and defeated, but somehow she spurred me on and I was eventually very grateful to her for the discipline. The lecture room was in the older part of the hospital. The seating was tiered and a lectern, blackboard and screen were placed centre front. The times of lectures were posted outside the door and we were expected always to be punctual. When on ward duty, time was given to us by arrangement with the sister, who also allocated off-duty times. On night duty we either stayed up or got up from bed, depending on whether the lecture was in the morning or early evening.

The older building also contained two three-storey wards, Nos. 14 and 15, where the chronic senile patients were cared for. The students took their turn on these wards but the patients were chiefly nursed by sensible women who were unable, for one reason or another, to undertake the general training. They were called assistant nurses and worked under a sister in charge. The majority of the patients were bedridden and had been for years. They were doubly incontinent, and frequent changing of bed linen and treatment of back and pressure points was the prime nursing care. Special feeding with nourishing food to these patients was essential to maintain their resistance to infection to heal any sores they might have and because many had no teeth as it was not safe to give them dentures. This type of nursing is rarely seen today as patients are more ambulant and there are better facilities and equipment available to take care of the incontinent patient. Ward 14 was a female ward and Ward 15 male. In the early days of the war, as one died so the bed remained empty. Consequently the numbers of these patients were gradually reduced. The male ward admitted vagrants who had got bronchitis or pneumonia or who had had heart attacks or strokes. In addition to being very ill, they were

usually alive with body lice and it was not always wise to carry
out too much cleansing treatment in case the exertion killed the
patient. A few of these cases survived but the majority died. A
male attendent was attached to these wards to give assistance to
the nurses when required.

A number of young soldier recruits billeted in Plymouth were
not familiar with the living conditions they found themselves in
and many became ill, some requiring minor operations and
other nursing treatment. There was also, I remember, a severe
out-break of influenza. We had empty beds at that time, so an
allocation was sent to our hospital. After forty-eight hours'
treatment of gargles, aspirin and bed rest they were fit to be
discharged, and were sent to join the British Expeditionary
Force to France.

At home my mother and grandmother had two evacuees
billeted on them. They were boys aged nine and seven called
Keith and Colin Wright. The evacuation of children was
entirely voluntary and parents had to register if they wished to
partake of the scheme, but the billeting of the children was
compulsory. Few people wanted to accommodate the mothers
but it was quite easy to find homes for the children. Keith and
Colin were from the East End of London and travelled to
Cornwall by train and then by bus to St Ives. The Billeting
Officer placed them with my mother and grandmother as they
had a spare room in their council house. The boys were clean
and adequately clothed. Keith was a quiet, thoughtful lad but
Colin was more active and full of mischief. We teased them by
calling them Keith Wright asnd Colin Wrong. They settled
down well and my mother counted herself very fortunate as
some poor children were rough, dirty and ill-mannered. Some
were bed-wetters and some had vermin-infected heads, and the
language in some cases left much to be desired. The official
billeting allowance for two children was 8s.6d. a week each. My
mother's only income was a widow's pension of 10s. weekly and
my grandmother's the Old Age pension, also 10s. weekly. So
they were grateful for the extra money. This arrangement lasted
for approximately six months. Then Mrs Wright, the mother,
managed to obtain a furnished cottage to rent, so she moved
from London and took care of the children herself. My mother
and grandmother did not have any more billeted on them.

At the hospital we were still standing by, waiting for casualties that did not come. Patients with serious illnesses continued to be admitted, chiefly those requiring operations and those in need of intensive nursing care. All the staff were given training in the use of stirrup pumps, and fire fighting exercises took place regularly. We were issued with gas masks and were instructed to walk through a gas chamber and were given a lecture on the detection of and danger from gas. We packed huge drums with gauze, cotton wool, rubber gloves and gowns to be sterilized for use in emergencies. When off duty in the Nurses' Home, instructions had been issued that in the event of an air raid we should take warm clothing and make our way to the ground floor corridor where stretchers would be available for us to rest unless we were recalled to duty. Sandbags were placed against ground-floor windows to prevent flying glass. The male staff acted as wardens of the hospital and kept vigilance at all times. Available to civilians were Anderson shelters that could be erected in their gardens and Morrison shelters which were large steel table-like structures, used chiefly by the elderly and infirm, where a mattress could be placed under- neath and the whole thing kept in the living-room. The Corporation built brick shelters at street level for people who were caught in a raid while shopping. In some of the parks there were large underground shelters.

Socially, the nurses would visit the dance halls and cinemas. There was no shortage of male escorts, so off-duty periods were generally very enjoyable. There were some new songs, for example, 'There'll Always Be an England', 'Hang out the Washing on the Siegfried Line', 'Run Rabbit Run', 'Roll Out the Barrel' and 'Kiss Me Goodnight, Sergeant Major'. These were very popular. Some cinemas had large electric organs which were played to entertain the audience at the opening of the evening performance and again at the close to play the National Anthem.

At Christmas members of the nursing staff got together a programme of entertainment and relatives were invited to a concert held in the recreation room. Staff Nurse Rothwell and I played the piano and I also sang. On Christmas Day we rose early to sing carols to the patients, the night nurses joining the day staff. The rest of the day was devoted entirely to the patients. No one had off duty on Christmas Day. Our Christmas dinner was held in the dining-room in the evening. There were two sittings. Matron sat through both, having her first course at the first sitting and her main course at the second. We always had a marvellous meal. A Nurses' Ball was organised during the Christmas period, when commissioned and non-commissioned officers of the forces were invited. They were happy occasions and no one gave a thought to tomorrow.

The winter of 1939-'40 was hard but spring eventually came. Within the hospital, staff and patients had fortunately been kept warm and reasonably fed. The wards were still only half occupied, and so those of us working towards the Preliminary State Examination were given more nursing tuition on the ward. I was working on a surgical ward, a new experience for me, which involved the preparation of patients for operations, accompanying them to the operating theatre and their post-operative care.

In the classroom we had nursing, hygiene and anatomy lectures. Miss Bishop supervised a practical session for two hours each week. We learned to become proficient at bed-making, bandaging and simple procedure tray-laying. The classroom's box of bones was also an enormous help in the learning of the anatomy of the body. As it was difficult to arrange visits of observation to sewage and water works, pictures of the workings of these systems were shown to us on an epidiascope as part of the hygiene lectures.

On May 10th, 1940, the Germans attacked and occupied Holland and Belgium and were marching towards France and the Channel Islands. France fell on June 30th. It was then tha Winston Churchill became Prime Minister and a Coalition Government was formed.

When France had fallen and the Channel Islands became overrun by invaders, Plymouth became the next target. A pattern of small raids developed over a period of a few weeks. Casualties were slight and the death rate small. During one raid a bomb was dropped on the kitchen and supplies stores within the hospital. A great deal of our provisions was lost. Valuable food was destroyed and could not be replaced. Food rationing was in force at that time but only for bacon, sugar and butter, but in March meat rationing began, although offal was excluded. The kitchen and store staff were under the supervision of a dietician, Miss Soper-Dyer. She was an excellent manager and throughout my time at the hospital I never knew a nurse or patient refused a meal, whatever the time of day or night.

Successive raids throughout the autumn months of 1940 convinced many families that they should leave the city for the comparative calm of the towns and villages around. November, 1940, saw the first major incendiary attacks. They swept through the city sending flames into the sky and through the streets. Several thousand bombs fell. Mount Batten, the RAF base, was directly hit and others fell on the Barbican and north of the city as far as Crownhill. One of our nurses, Nurse Bridgeman, was returning to the Nurses' Home after a period of duty when an incendiary bomb exploded just in front of her. Her face and arms were badly burned and she suffered severe shock. Fortunately she received immediate attention and eventually made a full recovery. So great was the task of the city firemen that they had to enlist volunteers to assist them. Towards the New Year the incendiary bombs were reinforced with bigger bombs. The hospital was again hit by a high explosive. Ward 7 and Ward 5, which was beneath Ward 7, were cut in half and some patients were left suspended on a platform, shocked but uninjured. One child patient died, it was thought, from shock.

Casualties were now being admitted fast. Incendiary burns were extensive and difficult to treat. In some cases their clothes had become adherent to the tissues and to cleanse the wounds the patients were put into a boracic bath. This method helped to combat shock and soaked the clothes off. The medical and nursing staff had to be ever watchful for sepsis. Limbs were suspended in saline baths and tannic acid sprays were used for those extensively burned. Sadly, some patients failed to recover and many others were permanently scarred.

I was transferred to yet another ward and there we received the casualties from a ship that had been torpedoed outside Plymouth Sound. One victim was a female African journalist who was working in France at the time of the invasion. She managed to escape from the country, embarked on a ship and was making for London. Her name was Paulette and her injuries were extensive, including a compound fracture of the femur. She

was a hysterical and demanding patient, and although we felt
sorry for her, well aware of what dreadful pain she was suffering
so that we gave her relief, there were others who required our
attention also. Although our patience became stretched to the
limit, Paulette was a fascinating character and we loved her. As
she grew stronger and her wounds began to heal she would sing
Negro spirituals to us. Her resonant voice and the moving words
of the songs brought tears to our eyes. Because of her long stay in
the ward we would sometimes shop for her. Her hair had been
straightened and it was gradually getting the curl back. She
disliked her curls and would command that we buy her wide
coloured ribbon to cover them up. The psychological benefit of
that ribbon and also her passion for coloured nail varnish, which
was not always easy to come by, played a big part in Paulette's
recovery.

On March 20th, 1941, I was summoned to Matron's office.
Matron told me that she required me, along with other nurses,
to form a guard of honour for two important visitors. I was to
wear clean uniform and white gloves which she would provide,
and I was to be in the Guildhall Square by 2 p.m. My fellow
companions were Nurse Gendall, Nurse Kelly, Nurse McGuirk
and Nurse Moffat, and we gathered together with nurses
from other hospitals and formed three rows. Matron joined us
later and we found we were in the front row. The people
of Plymouth, cowed and tired, donned their best clothes and
turned out to greet these visitors, who were no other than King
George VI and Queen Elizabeth. They were visiting their West
Country subjects to encourage and inspire us all to fight on. I
was thrilled to see them at such close quarters. The King spoke
to Nurse Gendall. I was standing between Nurse Kelly and
Nurse McGuirk. It was a glorious sunny day and the Royal visit
did indeed put new heart into the people. We made our way
back to the hospital, feeling hungry as we had missed afternoon
tea. We pooled our pennies and bought sausage rolls to sustain
us until supper time.

Two and a half hours later Plymouth was subjected to its
cruellest raid. Thousands of incendiaries and high explosive
bombs were dropped. The City Hospital was struck again. I was
working on Ward 15. The male nurse and I had moved all the
patients onto the ground floor. There were two floors of concrete

above us and sandbags protecting the windows around. We had the blue ceiling light on, normally used by night staff and known as the blue moon. We did this to preserve the blackout. I was terrified. The explosions seemed so near but I tried to appear brave. At least I was on my feet and not, like the patients, confined to bed. Eventually there was a lull and through the darkness I saw movement. Then I recognised Matron with her tin helment on and her warm cloak. "Nurse," she said, "we have been hit twice. The maternity wing, the children's ward and the nursery have been demolished. There has been loss of life but I cannot tell you to what extent." I was stunned. I could also see that Matron was deeply shocked. She refused my offer to sit a while and continued on her round of the wards. When the raid abated the night staff were able to take over ward duty. I made my way towards the Nurses' Home. Devastation confronted me everywhere. ARP wardens, stretcher bearers, ambulance men and many volunteers were frantically trying to free injured children. In a daze I reached my room and attempted to rest on the bed for a while, as I knew I would be recalled before long.

The night ended and gradually the results of the raid became known. Fourteen new-born babies had died on the maternity ward and two nurses, Nurse Kelly who had been with me that afternoon and Staff Nurse Rothwell, who was my co-pianist at the hospital's concerts. On the children's ward six children died and many were extensively injured. Nurse Willing and Nurse McGuirk, another nurse I had been with during the afternoon, were killed. Nurse Walters and Nurse White, two nursery nurses, also lost their lives. What a sad time it was for us! Other hospitals also suffered and the centre of Plymouth was gutted. 20,000 properties were destroyed or damaged, including St Andrew's Church, the mother church of Plymouth, and the Guildhall.

But before we could recover, even slightly, we were doomed to more raids – one the following night on March 21st and six more during April. 926 civilians are known to have been killed and many more were missing. Devonport fell, including the Royal Sailors' Rest, founded by Dame Agnes Weston, which contained over 700 beds, all fully occupied, and the canteens and kitchens that had been providing up to 2,000 meals a day. Bomb disposal teams were searching for unexploded missiles. The plight of the homeless people of Plymouth was heart-breaking and the city earned the title of being the worst blitzed city of Britain. Lord and Lady Astor still thought that the Government had not done enough to help. Churchill visited Plymouth, presumably to boost morale and to survey bomb damage, but the effect of the sustained bombing meant that the people required material help, and the visit had little effect in that respect.

Dancing on the Hoe continued under the protection of the barrage balloons and to the accompaniment of Service bands. The dancers came in the afternoons from outside and then stayed to prepare meals in makeshift kitchens for those who had been working on the bomb sites.

Amidst all this turmoil life continued as normally as was possible. I successfully sat Parts 1 and 2 of the Preliminary State Examination in April 1941. I had been working on casualty receiving station. We were very busy during the raids. ARP ambulances brought victims to us who were too severely injured to be treated at the first aid post. Doctors and nurses examined and assessed the extent of the injuries and labelled patients accordingly: red – urgent attention, blue – attention required as soon as possible, yellow – requires attention, white – remove to mortuary. We treated for shock and haemorrhage only. The patients were then removed to the wards. It was a grim and exhausting spell of duty.

I started the lectures in preparation for the Final State Examination according to the General Nursing Council's syllabus. These were to be given on medicine and medical nursing treatment, surgery, gynaecology, surgical and gynaeco-logical nursing treatment and general nursing. At the examin-ation there would be a one-hour paper on the first two subjects and a two-hour paper on general nursing. The medical staff lectured us and Miss Bishop gave tutorials, with the exception of the general nursing lectures which she gave in their entirety. All these lectures were compulsory and only sickness would excuse us. Many were given during our off-duty hours, which we grumbled about, of course, but would not dare to miss. Some-times we were so tired we found it difficult not to nod off.

I became a member of the Royal College of Nursing Student Nurses' Association and attended its monthly meetings. The

Royal Charter was granted to the College in 1939 for its work in promoting better education and training of nurses and the advancement of nursing as a profession in all its branches. We were encouraged to support the Royal College as our professional organisation. In 1941 I attended, as delegate, the annual meeting in London, with Nurse Underwood, who became the winner of the Gates Shield Speech Competition. On leaving the hall we rang Matron to tell her the news. She was so pleased she said we could arrange to stay another night and to attend a show at her expense. Expressing our thanks, we lost no time in selecting which show and obtaining the seats. We chose *The Dancing Years*, starring Ivor Novello, and I was enthralled by this spectacular show. Returning to Plymouth the next day, we found a reception had been arranged in our honour. It was to a large staff gathering I related the events of the meeting and our evening out, and Nurse Underwood delivered her speech. The break had been very refreshing and we felt our colleagues had shared it with us, if only in spirit. It remains a pleasant memory.

A clearing-up operation was in full swing at the hospital. The children's ward and the nursery had been transferred to the outskirts of Plymouth at Tamerton Foliot. The new maternity wing was being repaired and was then to be used for abnormal midwifery only. The mothers whose confinements were expected to follow the normal pattern were evacuated to Lord Mildmay's mansion at Fleet, Ermington.

Many of the medical and nursing staff who so bravely fought for their lives and those of their patients were ultimately honoured with awards. Dr McNairn received the George Medal. Nurse Clancy, who was badly injured herself, got the British Empire Medal, and others were highly commended for bravery.

I was transferred to the operating theatre to work as one of the junior nurses. My chief duties were to scrub instruments and wash utensils after operations, to re-load the sterilizers, keep them on the boil and to pass sterile equipment through the hatch when required. Dressed in white rubber boots, rubber apron and wearing a muslin cap, I worked in a steamy atmosphere most of the day. The large forceps known as cheatle forceps, used to lift articles from the sterilizer, were kept in a bowl of lysol. Rubber gloves were forbidden. When the forceps became warm the lysol would run down the handles onto my fingers, burning them, which was very painful. The dampness also gave me rheumatism, so I did not enjoy my stint in the sterilizing room of the operating theatre. However, it was not for long as I was soon required for night duty.

The following two months of duty were spent on the male ward of diseases and disorders of the urinary tract, known to the nurses as the 'water lilies ward'. I had charge of thirty patients from 8.30 p.m. to 8 a.m. In some respects it was easier than day duty, although there was only one break of half an hour for dinner at 12.30 a.m. or 1 a.m. I also had to keep an eye on the ward opposite, which was male surgery, when the nurse there went to dinner. A few of the patients were very ill and demanded attention throughout the night, but the worst period was the preparation of the patients for the day staff. Commencing at about 5 a.m. the temperature, pulse and respiration of each patient were taken, usually with the aid of a torch as, strictly speaking, the lights were not to go on until 6 a.m. Then followed patients' bed washing, collection of urine specimens, any treatments that were due and finally serving of breakfast and the collection of dirty dishes. A full report on each patient had to be written in duplicate each night. One copy was collected by night sister and the other copy was entered in the ward report book for day sister. Sometimes, especially if there had been an emergency, I would be so busy and pressed for time that I enlisted the help of the patients who were up to assist me in the collection of the dishes. I had one night off a week and one late night, when my duties commenced at 11 p.m. instead of 8.30 p.m. The extra time enabled me to go home more often.

My family consisted of my mother and grandmother, who were finding it very hard to manage financially on their pensions. The Ministry of Labour were appealing to employers to employ more women. So my mother eagerly scanned the newspapers for suitable vacancies. At the time I had become very friendly with a family called Harris, the same name as mine, though they were not related. They were devout Methodists and I was often invited to sing at the evening service of their local chapel at Greenbank. Mr Harris was an Inspector on the Great Western Railway and when I mentioned that my mother needed employment, he suggested she might like to apply for a ticket collector's post which was vacant at Saltash railway station. She was pleased to do this and was duly appointed to the post by the stationmaster, Mr Robertson. She lodged with a friend as a temporary measure but subsequently obtained the tenancy of a flat overlooking the River Tamar, and eventually my grandmother joined her. I was delighted with this arrangement as it meant I could go home each week – a wonderful privilege when so many young people were forced to be miles from home.

Railway journeys were a nightmare during the war. Because of the shortage of fuel many people had to use the trains to get to work, so they were always crowded. In the West Country we had two railway companies – the Great Western Railway and the Southern Railway. They had branch lines to most towns on the coast. Special trains were run when there was movement of a large number of troops but most long distance trains also carried the forces, chiefly those going on or returning from leave. Overloading was a problem for the railways and so was the blackout. The windows had black strips painted around the edges of them and blinds that could be drawn. The lights were dimmed unless the train was caught in an air raid. Then they were turned off. The carriages of the Great Western Railway were painted brown and cream and those of the Southern Railway a soft green. All the trains were pulled by magnificent steam engines but sadly, as the war progressed, the performance of these engines deteriorated because of the lack of maintenance and the shortage and poor quality of the fuel that had to be used. Travel was even more difficult at night as the station name signs had been removed and it was difficult to recognise which station the train had pulled into. Placards were displayed everywhere saying 'Is your journey really necessary?' Most people, whether patriotic or not, did stop and think but it was necessary at times, and was certainly an experience to remember.

My mother worked shifts – 6 a.m. to 1 p.m. or 2.45 p.m. to 10.45 p.m. She wore a navy blue uniform costume with yellow trim and looked very smart. She enjoyed the job very much and the £4 a week wage was wealth indeed to her.

In May, 1942, I took a fortnight's holiday and travelled on the train to Shrewsbury. It was full of people standing in the corridors and the vestibule – some even in the guard's van with goods and luggage. Having been advised, I was wise and took food and drink with me as refreshment was difficult to obtain. I travelled happily enough. The purpose of my journey was to meet a young man I had become very fond of. He was serving in the Navy and was on convoy from Liverpool to Londonderry. He had written to me saying he had leave and if possible would like me to meet him at Shrewsbury so that he could introduce me to his family. Fortunately, Matron agreed to grant me my holiday.

His name was Ivor Lewis and the family were from Brecon, Wales. His parents welcomed me warmly. I had not been to Shrewsbury before and was fascinated by this attractive mediaeval town. Ivor and I enjoyed our holiday and before we parted we had become engaged and I was the proud owner of a diamond ring.

On my return to the hospital I found the wards very busy. I was anxious that the General Nursing Council syllabus of training was being covered in preparation for my Final Examination in September. I was now regarded as a senior student and took more responsibility on the ward. I also returned to the operating theatre, this time working within the theatre and taking responsibility under Sister's supervision. I packed drums for abdominal operations ready for sterilisation, assisted in the preparation of the operating trolley and counted swabs and checked instruments and needles before the surgeon closed the wound. I was also sometimes required to scrub up, that is, to do the surgical cleansing of the skin and the donning of the sterilized gown, cap, gloves and mask, and then assist the surgeon at an operation.

The X-ray department was another interesting assignment, particularly when the radiologist visited to diagnose or carry out special screening. In the lecture room our theory was concentrated – no slipshod written work. Miss Bishop became very strict indeed. I am afraid we did not always appreciate it then, but she was only anxious for our success.

War conditions increased the danger of the spread of the venereal diseases syphilis and gonorrhoea. Local Authorities, namely County Councils and County Boroughs, were required under the 1936 Public Health Act to make provisions for the diagnosis and treatment of these diseases at hospitals or other institutions. The City Hospital had a large out-patient clinic with a ward overhead for patients requiring bed rest and treatment. There was strict confidentiality of the identity of the patient. Student nurses were required to cover night duty on the ward. My six-week period coincided with important lectures on bacteriology and specific infections. I knew that syphilis could be congenital or acquired and that babies a few months old could develop signs of the disease. I became very interested in the treatment given to the patients confined to bed. Intramuscular injections of arsenical preparations were given weekly and this course could last up to a year. Attention to the general health of the patient was also important, so an adequate diet was essential. Gonorrhoea was treated with sulphonamide, a powerful drug, and the patient given plenty of fluids.

Other specific infective diseases which were admitted and barrier nursed on general wards were erysipelas, tetanus and bovine tuberculosis, which is caused by milk from tubercular cows. It was essential that a nurse should be well instructed in the signs and symptoms of all these possible inflammatory conditions and in the nursing treatment to be applied. The conditions are not often seen in this country today, thanks to modern vaccines and immunisation programmes and antibiotics.

After America joined the war the number of air raids on Plymouth began to change. There were further intensive raids causing damage, injury and death in 1942, but they were infrequent and appeared to be aimed directly at a specific target.

I was off duty one day with a sleeping-out pass and was at home with my mother and grandmother at Saltash. The air raid siren was sounded at approximately 10 p.m. and was followed almost at once by heavy gun fire. We gathered our handbags, grabbed some food and made our way towards the air raid shelter across the back lane. The drone of the planes and the noise of the gun fire made us dive for the cupboard under the stairs. We had only just made it when – crash – the outside wall of the house caved in and we were trapped. My mother had caught the blast of the bomb and, I thought, had sustained fractured ribs. She was in pain and found breathing difficult. She had also been anointed with camphorated oil, a smell she disliked intensely. A bottle on the shelf had been knocked over and the oil spilled all over her hair. Gran and I were shocked but unhurt. After a period of what seemed hours but was actually only about a quarter of an hour there was a shout "Anyone there?" It was an air raid warden. "Yes," I replied. "Please send a stretcher. My mother is injured." In no time the rescue team was there and my mother was transferred to the local hospital. The raid had abated but the All Clear had not been sounded. However, Gran and I were taken to a nearby school. We learned that the house next door had had a direct hit and that one man was killed. A time bomb had also been dropped in the garden and until it had been defused we were not allowed to return. I remember the kindness of the people around us, how we were taken into a lady's house and given refreshment and a bed for the rest of the night.

The next day my uncle at St Ives took care of my grandmother and I returned to the hospital. The consequence of the time bomb was that my family's furniture and other belongings were removed from the flat by the Army and taken to a depot for storage about three miles out of Saltash. When my mother recovered from her injuries she managed to obtain the tenancy of another flat and the furniture was eventually moved back. A number of personal things were missing. We never knew quite what happened to them but to my mother and grand-mother they were only possessions. They counted their good fortune that we were still alive.

September arrived and I sat my Final State Examination. There were three written papers, an oral and a practical examination. I quite enjoyed the experience but was appre-hensive about whether I had made the grade. In November I received confirmation that I had been successful and was now a State Registered Nurse. One by one the candidates saw Miss Bishop, the tutor, to inform her of their results and to thank her for her help. Home Sister then measured each one of us who had been successful for a blue petersham belt. We had to provide ourselves with a buckle. My mother searched the secondhand shops and eventually found a suitable silver one which was sewn on to the petersham, and I wore the belt with great pride. The General Nursing Council issued a Certificate on November 27th, 1942, which gave my Registration No. 117912

and was stamped with the seal of the Council. An annual
retention fee of 2s.6d. (25p. new money) had to be paid to retain
my name on that Register, but in October, 1950, I was asked
to pay £2 12s.6d. for entitlement to use the designation of
Registered Nurse, without limit of time. I decided to purchase a
uniform badge which should have been silver, but because of
the war silver was unobtainable, so chromium had been sub-
stituted. In order to wear the official uniform a permit had to be
obtained and produced on purchase of the registered uniform
prescribed by the General Nursing Council.

Matron held consultations with all the successful candidates
with regard to the continuation of our careers. I decided to
commence midwifery training as I felt that without some experience of midwifery my training would not be complete. Matron
agreed with me and arrangements were made for me to join the
next training school which commenced in January, 1943.

Having completed my Part I midwifery training, I moved to
Leicester for Part II, where I could get training in the use of
equipment not available at Plymouth. I then took the post of
District Nurse and Midwife at Thurmaston, near Leicester.

Marriage and two children after the end of the war led to a
post as School Nurse, qualification as a Health Visitor, and in
1954 a return to the West Country as a health visitor at St
Austell. I moved on to Camborne/Redruth area as an Assistant
County Nursing Officer in 1962 and after other administrative
jobs at Plymouth and in Bristol, I finally retired, and returned to
Cornwall with my second husband.

I look upon my varied experience in the nursing profession as
a tapestry of care for the sick in hospital, for safe childbirth,
nursing in the community, preventative medicine, and finally
the counselling and advisory service given to nurses who were to
continue the care.

Public Health in Peace and War

DR HELEN R. BUCK

I WAS born in London within the sound of Bow Bells, a true Cockney. At an early age my family moved to a cathedral city from which my father commuted daily to the City for all his working life. Our home was comfortable but far from wealthy – no car, for instance – and provided a secure and Christian background for which I cannot be too grateful to my parents.

My sister and I first attended a local Dame school run by four spinster sisters who were kindly but demanded concentrated effort from all the pupils. At the age of eight or nine the week-end's homework took three hours. This was followed by our going to the local High School, which was luckily close to our home and had a good educational standard. For me the high-lights of that period were bicycle picnics in the surrounding countryside, usually on Bank Holidays, the annual summer holiday at the seaside and occasional visits on the train to London, when the adult return fare was 1s.6d., equal to 7½ new pence. I enjoyed visiting Westminster Abbey, St Paul's, Buckingham Palace and the Tower of London, and particularly the London Zoo.

Then came the 1914–1918 War, and in September we returned to find the school premises had been taken over by the military and the school was housed in very cramped conditions in the local museum, among the glass cases of specimens. One advantage was that our way took us past a local sweet shop where you could still buy chocolate drops, one ounce for a ha'penny.

The town was full of soldiers, mostly London Territorials in training as rapidly as possible for transfer to France. Every household had to take either two officers or a group of men. As we had a lounge with direct access to the garden, my parents decided to take the men. They used to go on long marches every day and came in so exhausted and footsore that they dropped down on the straw-filled paliasses on the floor and slept for hours. Their food was liberal at that time, drawn from a central mess, but had to be cooked by the householder. They were lovely lads and we kept in touch with the few who remained after the end of the war.

When food became scarce, in the school holidays I used to go to do the queueing for butter or meat or whatever, often to be told as we reached the head of the queue "Sorry all gone." There were ration cards, but the rations didn't always materialise. I helped at a Red Cross Centre (rolling bandages) and at a soldiers' canteen: cup of tea, a doughnut, and a packet of five woodbines for five old pence.

Halfway through the war in 1916, I went to boarding school on the south coast, a lovely area, overlooking the south downs with the sea not far away. During the summer term we were allowed two or three bathes a week instead of lessons, provided we could get down to the sea, undress in a bathing machine at the water's edge, bathe, dress and get back to school in three quarters of an hour. It was a happy time, with bicycle picnics on the downs to celebrate half-holidays. I do remember towards the end of the war feeling the pangs of hunger when our allowance of bread and butter was reduced to three slices each (previously, unlimited!) but in general the diet was good, ample and palatable. Anyone suffering from hunger at bedtime could ask for a ship's biscuit but to my knowledge no one ever did!

In 1918 the terrible 'flu epidemic struck the school, when 96 of the 100 girls and some of the staff fell ill. Thanks to emergency nursing arrangements and perhaps to their previous good health and feeding, no one died or suffered serious complications. It was very different in the general community where many even young and vigorous people died, probably debilitated by their often inadequate diet and exhausted by the long strain of war.

I was not involved in any enemy action (though some south coast resorts were machine gunned occasionally) but my father sent me a vivid account of the bringing down of the zeppelin at Cuffley on the outskirts of London, which my parents had watched from their home.

On leaving school I decided to study medicine and did my training at the London School of Medicine for Women and the Royal Free Hospital, commuting daily from my home by rail. This involved early rising and often late arrival home, but I was amply compensated by the relief of stepping out of the train for a twenty minute walk in the fresh country air, after a day spent in London with its winter fog (called the 'London particular') or the oppressive heat of a hot summer. There were compensations, too, in the accessibility of entertainment: cinema, theatre or concert (for which free tickets were often sent to hospitals for use by students and nurses) and particularly Covent Garden opera house where gallery tickets were obtainable and cheap. In those days it was usual for opera-goers in the more expensive seats to dress and a common sight was to see people in full evening dress at 4.00 pm on a summer day. Most colleges had their own sports grounds within reasonable distance where hockey, cricket and tennis matches took place on Saturday afternoons or swimming contests in the various London public baths.

Hospital practice was rather different in those days: insulin had just been discovered, revolutionising the treatment of diabetics, who had previously seemed to live on lettuce, and enabling a fuller diet to be allowed. There were no antibiotics; pneumonia cases and other acute infections depended largely on good nursing for their recovery. No intensive care units existed nor modern technology such as scans, and physicians depended largely on their skill in interpreting the physical signs of illness to make a diagnosis. Nevertheless, much good surgery and medicine was achieved. Consultants to the teaching hospitals were unpaid, giving their time and skills free and depending on private practice for their income. Newly qualified hospital resident doctors could expect to earn £50 a year for their full-time services, with board and lodgings provided.

During my student days in 1926 the general strike took place, affecting all public transport – many young men volunteered to drive buses, and even trains, sometimes at risk from attacks by strikers. Private car drivers picked up people waiting at bus stops.

After qualifying as a doctor, I took various hospital jobs to get experience and also a variety of locums in general practice. One I remember was a country practice in Norfolk during a particularly widespread though not deadly influenza epidemic. In some of the cottages the whole family was in bed, with the key left in the door for a doctor or nurse or a neighbour to let themselves in. The patients were 'Panel' (if employed) or 'Parish' (paid for by the Parish Council) or private, including most of the mothers and children. Many of them could not afford to pay, so were not charged. The treatment was never refused and I'm sure the doctor was out of pocket. He was highly respected, trusted and much loved by patients.

In 1935 I wanted to get married (in those days married women were ineligible for most hospital jobs!) and was also attracted by the prospect of a non-resident appointment, which involved working thirty-nine hours a week (five days of seven hours and Saturday mornings) instead of all the hours of the day and night usually worked in hospitals, especially maternity ones. There came a time when one had had enough of it!

I was lucky to obtain a permanent post as an Assistant Medical Officer in the public health department of a West London borough, dealing mainly with women and children, and this was to be my life's work until retirement.

Parts of the district were very poor and in such areas the infant mortality rate (deaths of infants under one year per 1,000 live births) could be 30 or more annually, frequently from infant gastro-enteritis. So much effort was directed to the instruction of mothers in hygiene and the care and feeding of young babies. The value and safety of breast feeding was heavily stressed. Every child born was visited regularly at home by a health visitor, working from the Local Authority's Welfare Centre, which was situated in the area, and few seemed to slip through the net, though 'night-flitting' practised by some families who couldn't (or didn't) keep up with the rent was a problem.

Maternal mortality was high by present standards (contributed to by back-street abortions, with often fatal results). But it was beginning to respond to regular supervision at ante-natal sessions, available free to all. Contraceptive advice was given free when necessary on health or social grounds; something of an innovation in those days. Many mothers were under-nourished; the weekly wage could be as little as £2.10s. and free dinners were available for the necessitous expectant and nursing mothers, as well as free milk. Public health departments were much concerned with the control of the common infectious diseases, measles being the most widespread and deadly. Pulmonary tuberculosis was prevalent, especially among young adults, and it was treated in numerous sanatoria where patients spent long months in the fight against their disease, followed by years of strict supervision at the Local Authority's TB clinic.

Infestation with head lice was common and the nit-nurses' visits to schools were regular and frequent. Body lice occurred in a few cases (usually in the elderly and eccentric) and bed bugs, residing in the fabric of old buildings, were a scourge to the occupants who were often forced to sleep in the street on hot summer nights. Delousing procedures and fumigation of clothing and bedding at the medicinal baths formed a considerable part of the work of the Health Department.

Alcohol problems existed in some families, contributing to their poverty, but not I think causing widespread cruelty to children, though mothers would sometimes appear after the weekend with a nasty black eye. NSPCC Inspectors were always available to be called on, with their expertise, but there were no safe refuges for mothers and children then. Alcoholism did not occur much in young people who hadn't the money and virtually no drug problem existed; I was never afraid to walk in the streets, even after dark.

I myself was working in a welfare centre. We had an office where the medical officers congregated every morning. There was one senior and three full-time doctors called Assistant Medical Officers of Health, covering a number of infant welfare clinics and ante-natal work.

Over us was the Medical Officer of Health himself. He was older and a more experienced person. As you worked alongside senior people like the Medical Officer of Health and his deputy you came into contact with other aspects of the work like the delousing procedures. I've mentioned the work of the nit-nurses. Parties of children were brought from schools to the cleansing centre to have their heads cleaned or there were visits to the schools by nurses. Heads were washed with disinfectant and combed with a nit-comb, a very fine steel comb, and the nurse removed the nits with that. Most of my work, however, was with the mothers and young children, and the Welfare Centres were the hub of the work.

The department as a whole of course had other matters to look at, e.g. housing. The Housing Department worked closely with the Health Department; for example, when priority had to be given to a certain family for health reasons. The Medical Officer of Health was responsible for the general state of sanitation including premises where food was prepared, with a team of sanitary inspectors working under his direction.

The Public Health Department had to keep a constant look out for infectious diseases. The Medical Officer of Health was top-notch at the diagnosis of unusual infectious illnesses, for instance, smallpox; not that there was much of it, although there was always the danger it would be brought in from abroad. Doubtful cases could be referred to the experts at the School for Tropical Medicine. We also had occasional malaria cases, among people from abroad. The Medical Officer of Health would be called in to advise the elected borough council on all health matters. I think then there were about fifteen of them in the whole of London.

At this time a part-time doctor, who was one of the pioneers of immunisation against diptheria, was working in the department. He had done much research on the subject and had worked out a plan for general immunisation of young children, which he was anxious to put into practise. This he was enabled to do in our district. Before this, not much was known about preventive measures, although the disease caused around 300 deaths a year. He liked all the children to come to his own clinic so that he could follow up their cases closely. He was a dedicated man with many ideas he wanted to prove, which I believe he did. He was certainly an influence on me, reinforcing my developing interest in preventive rather than curative medicine.

Later, of course, this scheme became accepted as routine procedure. The 'jabs' were given at all welfare centres, and protection against whooping cough and tetanus was added.

Another advantage we had was that the headquarters of the North Kensington Women's Welfare Centre, a pioneer of the birth control movement, was situated in our area – thus enabling our medical and nursing staff to keep in very close touch with them, as well as being easily accessible to the mothers referred from our Welfare Centres.

The use of the recently discovered sulphonamide drug known as M and B was being researched in special centres during the 1930s for the treatment of severe puerperal sepsis (child-bed fever – previously often fatal). Penicillin was to follow in 1940 but this was not available widely to the civilian population until after the war.

Neville Chamberlain's visit to Munich in September 1938, bringing back his over-optimistic message 'Peace in our time', nevertheless provided a valuable breathing space for the local authorities to prepare their plans for setting up civilian rescue and casualty treatment services, air-raid shelter arrangements, gas cleansing stations and, perhaps most important of all, the Air Raid Wardens Service. The street warden had to familiarise himself or herself (many were women), with the normal occupancy of every house; invaluable information when bombs started to fall in 1940. Street wardens were responsible for ensuring satisfactory domestic blackout precautions, and woe betide anyone showing the smallest chink of light! They provided a splendid service, being the first on the scene in an incident, a source of great strength and comfort to their area.

When it became apparent that war was inevitable the plans for evacuation to country areas of all inner London schools were put into operation – a massive undertaking, by the mainline railways, movingly described on the radio one night by Howard Marshall. In spite of immense difficulties faced by reception areas, the scheme worked well on the whole, and pupils and teachers settled down to at least part-time education in their new environment.

Less successful was the voluntary scheme for all mothers with children under five years. Many went but few stayed long. It was either too quiet, or there was no fish and chip shop. As no raids appeared to be happening they soon returned home. Expectant mothers were offered facilities for confinement outside London with a stay of about six weeks, and many, especially those having a first baby, with perhaps husband in the forces, took advantage of this.

There ensued the period of the phoney war when the expected air raids on London did not occur. The main danger was due to the black-out and of being knocked down by a car whose masked headlights, later modified, made it almost impossible for the driver to see anything, or the pedestrian to avoid it.

It provided further breathing space to bring the Civil Defence Services (partly full-time, but largely provided by members of the British Red Cross and St John Ambulance Brigade and others in a voluntary capacity) up to a reasonable state of training and efficiency.

The issuing of gas masks to the general public was undertaken, with appropriate instructions in their use. The gas mask was a rather fearsome-looking object contained in a cardboard box which had to be carried at all times. A smaller size suitably decorated (the 'Micky Mouse') could be fitted to children over a year but was not suitable for infants, and I remember the agony of mothers when told this. Later a contraption rather like an iron lung was issued, in which the baby was put and air provided by manual pumping – mercifully these precautions were never put to the test of real use.

A big expansion of day nursery provision for children under five was required to help those mothers willing to undertake war work or to replace men called into the services. Fire fighting routines were established at all offices and institutions and one or two nights a week duty had to be undertaken by all staff in addition to their full day's work. A stirrup-pump and bucket was issued to householders to deal with incendiaries.

During the summer of 1940 air activity consisted mainly of 'dog fights' with enemy aircraft and defending Spitfires and Hurricanes visible high in the sky. In September nightly raids began – at first, on the East End of London and dock area. Thousands were made homeless and were catered for at temporary rest centres until other arrangements were made.

The LPTB, as it was then, had not intended the underground stations to be used as public shelters, but the public thought otherwise and flocked down. The Board capitulated, fitted up three-tier bunks along walls and marked out spaces on the platforms to be allotted to local residents. Sanitary arrangements (Elsans) were installed, an area reserved and equipped as a first aid post and later even canteen facilities at some stations. Shelterers brought their bedding, which had to be removed by morning, but as many went straight from the station to work this produced a problem and many bedding stores sprang up in nearby houses, bringing the inevitable result of infestation with bedbugs. This was countered by permitting the stores to exist only if the owners and customers agreed to a weekly fumigation routine. It was a strange sight to see the platforms covered with people peacefully sleeping, while trains roared by every few minutes (they stopped from 1.00 a.m. to 5.00 a.m. only) and travellers picking their way through them as best they could.

If a raid occurred, an additional influx appeared and a large station could contain about 7,000 people until the raid was over. The lifts were stopped during raids so anyone wanting to get to the street had to tackle the emergency spiral staircase (175 steps at my station!).

Gradually one became accustomed to war-time routine and fortunately most people were tired enough to sleep soundly through sirens, gunfire and bombs, unless very close. One man I knew infuriated his wife, who had been awake all night listening to the racket, by waking up when a bomb exploded just outside the house asking "Is that the All-Clear?" There were quite long periods when raids on London ceased temporarily, to be followed in the last year of the war by self-propelled 'doodle bugs' (V1s) when the engine cut out and one had to wait for a terrifying few seconds for the explosion to know how close it had fallen. Finally the enemy sent over the very powerful and damaging V2s, and then the war was over.

What are some of my most vivid memories? The presence of King George VI with the present Queen Mother who remained at Buckingham Palace (in spite of a direct hit) throughout, often visiting badly bombed areas the following day. Winston Churchill, whose inspired and inspiring leadership and magnificent speeches left me in no doubt that victory would come in the end and the belief, whether justified or not I do not know, that we were being told the truth, in bad times as well as good.

The remarkable absence of serious epidemics – the only really widespread one I recall being of scabies, brought under control eventually, with the aid of legislation by assiduous tracing, treating and follow-up of all family contacts.

The reasonably good state of health of the general population must be attributed largely to the efficiency of the rationing system, which continued with modifications until 1954. Dental caries in children actually declined, attributed to sweet ration-ing. When orange juice was in short supply, evacuated school children collected rose-hips to produce rose-hip syrup (a good source of Vitamin C) for issue instead, but most wartime children would not have recognised a banana! All in all, the Public Health Service came through the war with great credit.

The BBC must be given credit, not only for the news bulletins, but for keeping our spirits up with radio programmes (television was not widely available then) such as Tommy Handley's *Itma*, *Much Binding in the Marsh*, and the like.

I admired above all the spirit of unity and neighbourliness, all grades of society working together towards a common end – tinged with a modest pride in being a small part of the 'London can take it' slogan that London earned for itself – an experience that I would not have wished to miss.

After the war the immense task of reconstruction had to be faced and slowly this began. Partially-destroyed buildings were repaired or, more often, demolished, leaving bomb-sites where wild flowers quickly took over before new blocks of council flats, including some monstrosities of fifteen or twenty storeys, were built. One could not pass some of these sites without memories of the tragic events associated with them coming to mind, and I remember one cinema that had had a direct hit with many killed and injured, which I could not bring myself to enter for some years.

There were rewarding moments, too, when one met someone last seen being dragged from a collapsing building going about his business fully recovered from his injuries.

The outstanding event of the post-war years was the birth of the National Health Service in 1948, based on the Beveridge Report, giving free general practitioner service to all, including the mothers and children previously ineligible.

During the post-war period, responsibility for the care of mothers and children under five years was transferred from the local authorities in London to the London County Council, together with the personnel of the Welfare Centres *en bloc*. It was probably beneficial, as it meant that work with children of all

ages was under one authority – the LCC having always had
responsibility for the health as well as the education of children
of school age. It made no difference to our work and the Welfare
Centre continued to attract a majority of mothers to the existing
premises, with the staff unchanged.

The availability of antibiotics revolutionised treatment of
many acute diseases. Diphtheria had virtually disappeared,
tuberculosis had become treatable by chemotherapy. Immunisation procedures against diphtheria, whooping cough and
tetanus had become an established routine, and the scope was
widened to include protection against polio and TB, and later
measles.

Scientific advances were many and with their aid, and
continuing watchfulness over the health of mothers and
children, the infant and maternal mortality rates began to fall.

I continued to work in Public Health until retirement in 1963,
and consider myself fortunate to have lived long enough to see so
many dramatic victories in the battle against disease.

I retired to Cornwall, which I had known since 1934. I enjoy
the country life, gardening and swimming and exploring this
lovely county. Anyone coming here connected with the medical
world is usually invited to join the Cancer Research Campaign,
if they are interested; and they usually are. I was secretary of
the local branch for eight or nine years, then chairman and
president.

One of the most interesting features of my retirement was
meeting and developing a friendship with Dr Edward Griffith
and his wife. He had many years of general practice in Devon
and Hampshire and then as a consultant in London. He became
very interested in the subject of marriage problems early in his
practice, when he was moved by the situation in which many of
his women patients found themselves. He felt so many of them
needed instruction in contraception and sexual matters generally – not only among the poor for many of his patients came
from comfortable suburban backgrounds. He was determined to
do something to help them.

Much of this was disapproved of in many quarters in the
1920s and 1930s. In fact he lost a number of his patients to other
practitioners on this account, but he felt there was a need and
he could supply it. He was a founder member and one of the

great supporters of the Marriage Guidance Council and wrote several books, many having world-wide circulation. It is a privilege to have known a man of his distinction and commitment.

It is over fifty years since I got my first job in the Public Health Service and it has been interesting to watch its development. It has been a valuable part of Britain's health service.

Psychiatric Hospital Attendant

ROBERT ROWE

IN 1918, when I was nineteen years old, on the battlefield at Cambrai, I was walking with a full-size pickaxe slung across my kit-bag, its points resting on top of my pack. The pick pressed heavily on the back of my neck. I came under fire from machine-gun bullets and was wounded.

One bullet passed sideways through my pack, hit the canteen, went through my bread and cheese and passed out on the other side. When I heard the ping of that bullet, I was down on the ground in a flash, otherwise I would have been wounded more seriously. When I went down, the pick hit me on the back of the neck and nearly knocked me out.

When I was demobbed, I got a job as attendant in what was then St Lawrence's Asylum in Bodmin, Cornwall, where I was to devote the next thirty-six years to caring for those who, certified by two doctors and a magistrate, were classed as insane. At that time there were 1,300 patients, about 700 men and 600 women. Today that number is greatly decreased. In those days little research was done into the efficacy of drugs or electrical treatment, and the word madness covered a depth of ignorance. Also, the training of nurses for mental institutions was in its infancy. For three years I studied mental health, sat and passed the necessary exams and qualified as a staff nurse. I became deputy-in-charge, then charge nurse and finished, forty years later, as assistant chief nurse of the hospital.

I had joined the service in 1919 with some apprehension because I knew I had to qualify in three years, which was not easy for someone with an elementary education. I was, however, thankful to have a job at all, having just returned wounded from France. I was one of over two million unemployed.

Looking back today, it all seems primitive, for the methods were those of mechanical restraint, strait-jackets, dungeon and padded cells, with shower baths each morning as punishment for wetting the bed. Unexpected things were always likely to happen when you were dealing with sadly deranged people. I recall an incident when a completely naked patient clambered through an open window and climbed up a drain-pipe onto the roof of the Kendall building where he remained for three hours. He was as agile as a monkey and the damage he did was considerable. Cars were stationary in the Dunmere for three hours as people watched this incident. The patient stood in the guttering and if this had collapsed he would certainly have crashed to his death. A pair of trousers were placed on the fire-escape ladder for him and it was this that finally induced him to come down. One of the staff managed to grab him by the ankle. Needless to say, he was placed in a strait-jacket for some period after that.

I remember when the only way to deal with violent patients, before drugs were discovered, was to put them into strait-jackets. The sleeves came down over the men's hands and the tapes on the end, like sail-cloth, were pulled across the body in front and tied behind so that the man couldn't move. That's all gone now. In my early days there were also the padded rooms where the walls were padded with leather so that a man couldn't hurt himself. Even the floors and ceilings were padded. The strait-jackets and padded rooms show how ignorant we were then about the violent mentally handicapped. It was a great step forward when drugs became available.

Before I retired they were trying many new techniques: for example, they were operating on the brain, doing pre-frontal leucotomies, in which they separated the frontal lobe from the rear lobe. They experimented with prolonged narcosis, that is putting people to sleep to lessen anxieties, and the application of electrodes to administer violent shock. At one time, general paralysis of the insane was practically incurable. It was tragic to watch. When a man died, he looked like a trussed up fowl. His bent legs came up to his chin, his arms were bent too and his eyes would stare upwards at the ceiling, quite helpless.

It was a great day when they learned how to help the paralysis by the introduction of what we called malaria blood, which they injected. I saw it at first up in York where a man was being bitten by a mosquito. That was the initial phase. The malaria germ was stronger than the germs which caused the paralysis; it induced a high temperature of 105°. But it did the trick and I think it was one of the most advanced treatments that came along during the time that I was looking after these patients. There was nothing like it before.

I spent fifteen years of my service on permanent night duty – twenty-eight consecutive nights on duty followed by five off. We did a sixty-hour week and during night duty pegged a clock on the hour and half-hour to show we were alert and not asleep. If you missed too many times you were dismissed for neglect of duty. We had our meals on the ward and the total of our pay was £10 a month. However, in those days you had some cheerful episodes. I remember there was a prolonged drought about 1922. The Medical Superintendent thought it best to sleep the patients of some wards out on the lawn by day and night. I remember asking one old patient one morning how he was getting on. "Bloody awful," he replied, "they left the bloody window open all night."

There are some patients that should never be released. It is better for them personally and for society that they stay where they can be cared for. I remember a man who the medical superintendent thought should be allowed home to stay with his sister. I had been close to him and I knew, and the staff knew too, that he was very unpredictable. He wasn't a suitable person to go home. One day he was put out in the yard chopping sticks. I suppose his sister must have said something to him and he reacted violently. He had the chopper in his hand and he chopped her down. He was brought to court and judged insane and sent to Broadmoor. Now, I knew Harry and he knew me and I could treat him according to his needs. But he was sent to Broadmoor for twenty-five years. Twenty-five years after his conviction I had retired but I went back one evening to see a friend who worked at St Lawrence's. He

told me Harry was back from Broadmoor and asked if I'd like to
see him.

I went along and there was Harry with a nurse in charge. He
peered at me and said "I know you, you're Mr Rowe." He
looked much older, as was to be expected after twenty-five years
in Broadmoor. I shook him by the hand and told him if he
should want for anything to let me know. "No thank you, Mr
Rowe", he said, "I don't want no money. I've got everything
here." He was a bit breathless but in his day he had been handy
with his hands; he could have been a professional boxer. The
years in Broadmoor had taken their toll. The sad thing is that he
should never have been let out of here in the first place and we,
who had been in close contact with him, knew better than
anyone what was best for him.

There's the other side of the coin. There were some who I
knew were artful and shouldn't have been here in the first place.
They enjoyed what in fact was good living. But as time went on
and we learned to understand people better, I think most of
those who were taking advantage were weeded out. But you've
got to get to know people and make friends before you can come
to a judgement about them.

A lot of credit for the progress at St Lawrence's in recent years
should go to Mrs Banham who became chairman of the
Cornwall and Isles of Scilly Area Health Authority. The food
and furnishing, the well-being and care of the patients is
excellent. Indeed, my wife and I have expressed the view that
we wouldn't mind spending a month's holiday at St Lawrence's.
The old twenty foot long bare tables with basins for tea have
gone. It is now really like a first-class hotel service. In my early
days, every patient was certified. Some arrived handcuffed to a
policeman. Everybody had a fear of being taken to Bodmin
Asylum as, once admitted, they were seldom visited by relatives
as many could not afford to travel from distant parts of the
county. Some patients never returned home but died in the
hospital, some of them after fifty or sixty years here.

Since the last century the Clifdens have given generously to
the development of Cornish hospitals such as Redruth, Bodmin,
and East Cornwall Hospital, the foundation stone of which
was laid by Lord Clifden. The interest from investments
by the Clifdens was allocated to the League of Friends of St

Lawrence's, who used it to have an extension built onto the hospital.

When Viscount Clifden became ill and needed constant nursing, he turned to me. Although I had retired from St Lawrence's I was glad to serve him. Although I constantly emphasised to the Viscount that I was a nurse and not a doctor, he often turned to me for advice. When we were together, there was no side to him. He used to say "Where there's sickness, we're all the same." It was a rewarding experience and I developed a great respect for the Clifden family.

Thirty-four Years in Midwifery

CLARICE KING

I WAS born in Winterslow in Wiltshire, about eight miles from Salisbury. My father worked on a farm. There were nine in the family, some born in Winterslow and some near Wimborne where we moved when I was seven. I went to school in Winterslow which I enjoyed very much.

One memory I have of Winterslow is going to a Methodist church. The seats had open backs and I fell through one of them. Perhaps I fell asleep during the sermon! I left the village school at fourteen.

When I left I helped with children; a paid job, but I was not paid much. Then I decided to go in for nursing. I began my training in April, before war started in 1939. This was the start of four years' general training, which I enjoyed very much. There was very little social life as there wasn't much time off. At this time my pay was £12 a year. We were living in but we had to pay National Health Insurance and we had to provide some of the uniform ourselves: aprons, flat heeled shoes with laces and lisle stockings.

The discipline at Southampton was strict. The Sister Tutor was in charge of training and you could go to her for advice. There were twelve of us starting our new career but we didn't start off in the training school as they do now. We went straight onto the wards where we had to learn how to clean them, among other things. We were quite happy about this but it was changed soon after that when they started with the training school.

fessor Sir Thomas Symington

Young Thomas Symington's first
mpse of his university at Glasgow,
behind the statue of Lord Kelvin.

lasgow Royal Infirmary, where much of Sir Thomas's research was carried out.

Dr Peter McKenzie, OBE

as Assistant Surgeon in
SS *Jervis Bay*, 1938–'39.

Merchant ships including SS *Jervis Bay* with **HMS** *Hood* behind.
Both ships were sunk in the 1939–'45 War.

Surgeon Captain Dalgliesh, LVO, OBE

in the Antarctic.

Antarctic mountains photographed by David Dalgliesh.

The Passmore Edwards Cottage Hospital, Liskeard, where Beryl Skidmore
began her training in 1937.

Probationer nurses
with their Sister, Liskeard.

Nurses and babies at the Ealing
Maternity Hospital, where Helen
Buck was Resident Doctor, 1933–'35.

Then came the bombing, when the nurses' home at the hospital was hit by an incendiary. The patients were transferred to a hospital outside the town and we went to a hospital in Winchester to continue our training. We stayed there about three months, then went back to Southampton.

At that time nowhere was safe. We had had to be moved because the Southampton hospital had no windows. Actually when the fire bomb dropped there were no available supplies of water to put the fire out. Later, all the hospitals had water tanks and they also appeared all over the town in case of fire. Fortunately during the fire, no one in the hospital was hurt. The bombing happened just at the change-over period. Staff who had been off in the afternoon were just getting the reports of those off duty at six o'clock. There was no one in the nurses' home.

I finished my training at Southampton and became a qualified nurse. Then in 1943 I decided I would move into midwifery so I joined Plaistow Maternity Hospital in the East End of London. At that time we had about fifty beds and clinics. There was an annexe out in Epping Forest. As I arrived the doodle- bugs were beginning to come over London. My part-time training was in the annexe. I very much enjoyed the maternity work and in fact remained in it until I retired in 1977. I preferred midwifery to everything else. In Plaistow I did my training, then I was a staff midwife, then a sister, then a nursing officer.

During the first year's training in Plaistow, I went back to five shillings a week. This was because I was beginning training again, training as a midwife. But at the end of the year, 1944, I got a little bit more money as a state certified midwife. I could now take a pupil with me when caring for the patients. This would be a girl just starting midwifery. Of the girls just starting some had gone straight into maternity, others like myself had gone into a general hospital first. I worked as a midwife for three years before becoming a sister.

When I was doing my training in midwifery, I spent the first six months in hospital and the second six months out on the district. Part of this time I was in Stratford on district work. We weren't allowed to look after a maternity patient without being a trained midwife. In earlier times people without training delivered babies and looked after the mothers.

I have many memories of Plaistow Maternity Hospital. We had branch homes in Stratford, Barking, Forest Gate and the Docks. After working as a midwife in the hospital I was put in charge of the Stratford branch home. I was called out one night and there at the door waiting for me was a black maria. There was a policeman with the driver. He told me he was very sorry, it was the only vehicle he could find to come and get me! It was dark and I'm glad the neighbours didn't see me! As it turned out I was being fetched for a policeman's wife who was in labour.

When I was training there was a pregnancy in the Docks area. Before the baby was due, I visited the house to make sure the wife had everything – saucepans, bowls, etc. that would be needed. Then I visited one day and found nothing – not a bowl in the house. They had all been given back to the people who owned them. They had only been lent for my visit! But when the baby was on the way suddenly people from all the different houses came running with pans and bowls: anything I needed for the delivery.

Another time I remember a husband who was really very kind. He appeared with a mug of beer and a jar of winkles. His wife had had her baby. Perhaps this was a celebration offer. I had to ride a bicycle back so I thought I'd keep off the beer and I couldn't eat a winkle if I tried.

When I was on the district in those days there were many home births but later there were more women coming into maternity hospitals like Plaistow. In hospital as a staff midwife I was now working under a sister. I would be in charge on night duty. There was always a sister in the hospital but she wasn't always on night duty because it was a small hospital. But as a staff nurse you were always able to call on a senior member of staff.

To start with in 1947, I was Sister in charge of a branch home. I had two midwives with me and four nurses in training. Ration books were one of the first problems I faced. We kept the ration books for all the staff so I did the shopping for the unit on my bicycle.

We visited the homes before the babies were due, hoping to get things straight. Sometimes you arrived to find things were in the pawn shop. My friend Beryl Armstrong was very good. She used to knit baby jackets for me. Sometimes the mothers hadn't a thing. There was a lot of poverty then. We had to collect money from the patients. If it was their first baby they paid twenty-five shillings. That was for all their ante-natal care. They would start their payments when they came to book. They perhaps paid one shilling each time they came to clinic. If they couldn't pay it there was a fund I could apply to, which also gave so much towards baby clothes. I would choose the clothes when necessary. You got to know who needed them.

The National Health Service came in the following year, in 1948. The women did not have to pay any more. Before, on clinic days we had had to collect the money, so it made a difference for us. I think it made even more difference to the patients. Ours were a special kind of people. They were always ready to help each other. There was a good community spirit. All the neighbours rallied round when a baby arrived. I was in charge of the branch home for about six years working among those people.

About the middle fifties I went back into the Plaistow Maternity Hospital because the branch homes were closed and the districts changed. The district midwifery was taken over more by the local councils. Before, the hospital committees helped to run it. When I went back to the hospital it was as a ward Sister in charge of another ward as well as the labour ward. It's different nowadays. Now, if you're in charge of a post-natal ward, you've nothing to do with a labour ward.

I started duty in the ward at eight o'clock and took the reports from the nurses and detailed the day staff about what they should do. There were six of them. If they needed advice they would ask for it. The staff midwife would give the women whatever medicines were required. Should a particular situation arise we could always call on the houseman, in our case, a lady doctor. She in turn could contact the patient's own doctor or consultant. There was a good sense of co-operation.

Quite early in our work at Plaistow we were quite happy for fathers to come and be around. I knew there was a certain amount of opposition in the early days, but they were welcome at Plaistow provided of course they were clean and tidy, for many of them worked in dirty jobs.

Men had different reactions. One I had to drag out because he fainted, another came in with his wife. He wanted to be present. I told him that would be all right so long as he went home and changed. When he came back, after cleaning up, I didn't recognise him. The important thing about the men coming in was that it was all right if the mother wished it. Quite a lot of men didn't want to be present anyway. We always asked the mother first.

There were some early problems with immigrants. Many mothers found difficulty with English. The fathers probably could speak it better because they were working among English-speaking workers. There was one immigrant who turned up first with his wife and then at different times with different women. If I asked questions about a lady's condition and background he knew the answers. He was the one who had the language and presumably was able to help all these women in the neighbour-hood. He made things a little bit easier for us.

There was one occasion when a coloured student was working with me. A mother had her baby and we got them tidied up before asking her small daughter, who was waiting outside, to come in and see the new arrival. When the little girl saw the baby, she burst into tears and asked the student who was with me "Why didn't you bring me a black one?" You never knew the reactions the other children in a family would have to the new baby. I think that's why I most enjoyed working in the district; you saw more of the families' reactions in their homes.

I remember when I was on the district there was a little boy who brought me some money. He said "I've only got tuppence but we want two babies. I want one and she wants one." He was referring to his sister. I said "That's asking an awful lot." His mother who had just been X-rayed had been told that in fact she was carrying twins, but she didn't want the children to know just in case something went wrong. Anyway we delivered these two. In those days we were allowed to deliver twins at home but not now. The kiddies were out in the garden playing and their grandmother called them in. Then we gave them each a baby to hold and the little boy turned to me and said "So we did have enough money for them!" But children nowadays seem to know everything beforehand.

Another time I went along to a house – this was also when I was on the district. There was a furniture van at the door and there was my patient about to have her baby. The furniture men put a bed up in the room downstairs and that was all that was immediately available. Whatever else I asked for was in a packing case still to be unpacked. The family had just arrived from the north, and the removal men were moving furniture and things upstairs while we were delivering the baby in the front room.

I had some wonderful nurses living in the home with me in those days. One Christmas I had a parcel of toys sent to me to distribute. Two of my girls came with me to one mother who was a patient. The four children had gone for a walk. There was nothing in that house and although it was Christmas Day she had no dinner for them. The nurses knew what I had made for their own tea. They had already had their Christmas dinner on Christmas Eve because we couldn't manage it on Christmas Day. A coloured girl asked me "Couldn't we give them our tea?" I said "If you take them your tea, there will be nothing for you." She said "That's all right, we're not hungry." We went home and got the cakes I had made, took them round, laid the table and were just finished when the four children came in. You should have seen the looks on their faces when they saw the table. My nurses came home with me and had a piece of toast for their Christmas tea.

I retired in 1977. People were very sorry for me at the time. They thought I'd have nothing to do, but I was retired only a fortnight when I was asked to help with meals-on-wheels. I went back to Dover because I had friends there and a home. I do canteen work at the mental hospital and collect for Christian Aid. I am a pastoral visitor in the Methodist Church and of course I have a lot of visitors to my home. I enjoy my retirement very much because I am free to do whatever I want to do. My years in midwifery were always happy ones, for there, too, I was doing what I always wanted.

A Queen's Nurse Looks Back

JESSIE BARRON

I WAS born in Keith in Banffshire near the end of the last century. My father had been a meal miller but when he was out of work he got a job in a distillery and he was working there when I was born. Then he got a job again as a meal miller out at Crooks Mill in the country. Later he went up near Dufftown to the mill of Towey and he was there till he retired.

I was educated in the primary school at Keith, then went on to Keith Grammar School. I liked it fine there. My sister was the clever one, always at her books. I wasn't as clever. There were seven of us in the family but we didn't all come together. I had a sister about twenty years younger than I was.

I worked at home for a bit, then worked for a lady and it was while I was with her that I realised I wanted to be a nurse. During the First World War I was accepted by Aberdeen and did three years in the hospital doing fevers. After a holiday I went right on to my general nursing. I was living in the hospital but I went to Edinburgh to become a Queen's Nurse. This was after the 1914 war.

The headquarters were at Castle Terrace and I began to learn the job of district nursing and had six months training there. I was proud to be a Queen's Nurse.

When Queen Victoria had been fifty years on the throne, they collected money to recognise the occasion. She didn't know what to do with this money. It was suggested to the Queen that she might give this sum of money for the nursing of her sick poor who couldn't afford a nurse. So William Rathbone, who had been interested in getting nursing care for those who couldn't afford it, started the Queen's Nurses with other people.

The story of the Queen's Nurses is told in a fascinating book, *The History of the Queen's Nursing Institute over the Last Hundred Years*. The Queen appointed well-known people to act as a council for what she called Queen Victoria's Jubilee Institute for Nurses. Princess Christian, Princess Louise and Princess Beatrice were members of the Council and William Rathbone was its Vice-President. This Council designed a Queen's Nurse uniform. Gold and silver badges were given for distinguished service and the bronze was awarded to a Queen's enrolled nurse.

Nurses in ordinary hospitals of that time concentrated on treating diseases by medicines or surgery. But a Queen's Nurse's training concentrated on subjects that were not taught then in general district hospitals, things like sanitary precautions, ventilation, drainage, water supply, diets for sick people, special care of babies, the monthly attention for pregnant women, and so on. At that time infant mortality was high. So Queen's Nurses were doing a very important job for the country. Another idea that came in about the end of the century was that there should be a separate corps of women trained as health visitors. But at this time the job of the district nurse was a heavy one because she was doing the duties of a home nurse, a school nurse and what was called a sanitary missionary. The next century was to see a separation of these different jobs.

At one time we were called Jubilee Nurses. I always remember the first time I saw a Jubilee Nurse doing her job. My mother was always kind to anybody who was ill, giving them all the help she could. I was sent to Mrs McKenzie, a lady who had a very sore leg. I told my mother I didn't like going as I didn't like the smell of her house. Her legs were full of ulcers; terrible legs. Mother was fair annoyed at me saying that. While I was there, in came a tall nurse. She took off her cape and to my surprise she took off her skirt and she had a big apron on that went right round her. Out of a great big pocket she brought out a pudding dish. My eyes must have been popping out. This was a meal she had brought for this old lady. I went home and told my mother who was always horrified at the stories I told her and who used to impress on me never to repeat them. She made me promise I would never tell about the pudding dish as it would have embarrassed old Mrs McKenzie.

You had to have your general training in nursing and also to have done your midwifery before you applied to be a Queen's Nurse. I was proud to be one. People I visited were so grateful. I operated from the headquarters, 29 Castle Terrace in Edinburgh. We got lectures there and went out and did the work in our district.

We went to Atholl Crescent, which was known as the dough school, to learn to cook the right kind of meals: simple meals. I never did much cooking in the houses I visited. I preferred to take something with me. We were supposed to be able to cook a simple lunch for a working man.

The households I visited in those days were very poor. One thing made an impression on me. Very often the poorer they were, the cleaner the house. At Christmas at Castle Terrace they gave us rabbits to take round. That would be our patients' Christmas dinner. I particularly remember visiting one bed-ridden old lady. The head superintendent happened to be with me. The patient had a son who was nearly always drunk. I hoped he wouldn't come in when I was there as he used to come in and fling himself down on a settee and would be snoring before long, while I just had to carry on with my work, and I didn't like that. I introduced the superintendent to the old lady and she said "Wha is she?" "That's my superintendent." "Ah", she said, "She must be a nurse or you wouldn't have had her with you." She was very poor and her son used to drink all their money.

There was another family that was very, very poor. The mother was a wonderful woman and she was ill. Their house was spotlessly clean. When I visited her, she would send her husband and children out so that we could talk together. There were many fine people in those days despite the poverty.

I had years of practice in using the syringe. I used it in the early days as a staff nurse when I was in fevers, to give a serum for diphtheria. Later we used it for giving insulin in diabetes. I remember one incident with a young nurse who had never used it before. She was literally shaking. I thought she would have the poor man in hysterics before he got his injection. She couldn't face it and it was her first injection. So I did it for her. But she got over her fears.

When we were going round our district we learned a lot about our patients, and worked closely with the doctors who were very helpful. In those days you felt families were a real support. Usually when you visited there would be someone with the patient. Often a daughter would come in or other relatives would look after the patient when we weren't there.

People didn't have to pay but they were encouraged to give donations if they could to the Queen's Institute. Of course if they wanted to do this, they took it to the office at Castle Terrace.

We weren't supposed to get presents and in this connection I remember one incident. I had been nursing a lady for some time. Her son said he would like me to have some handbag or other. I remember I was called to the office. I didn't know what was going on. Our head, who was a very nice lady, asked me about all that I did during my training. Then she told me what this man had left for the Queen's Nurses at Castle Terrace. Then she said "And there's a present for you, this handbag, and you're to keep it." She gave me the bag and I still have it to this day.

I did visiting along with a health visitor and I got a certificate for that. At the time we had many TB patients. Then I was sent to Perthshire where I did a mixture of Queen's district work and welfare health visiting. It was hard work.

I was in the city of Perth. There were three of us in the Home there; the head, an assistant and myself. At this point we were operating here as public health; not as district nurses who went out doing the actual nursing with the patients, doing the dressings and so on.

From Perth I went to Bridge of Earn where I was put onto a district as a Queen's Nurse visiting the people. But I did welfare work with it. I was really kept at it. I had a nice cottage in Bridge of Earn and was there for a number of years.

Then in the middle of the war, I heard from my aunt who was a matron in a children's home in Aberdeen. She had forty children to cope with. She pleaded with me to come and work there. So I handed in my resignation at Bridge of Earn and went off to Aberdeen.

The mention of looking after children, as my aunt did in Aberdeen, reminds me of another good piece of work by the Queen's Nurses. By the end of the nineteenth century there were just under 1,000 nurses on the roll of the Institute. People began to think about school nursing and a system of school nursing was started at a school in London. A nurse, we were told, visited the school in Bloomsbury every morning and examined about forty children and took care of cuts and bruises, burns and abscesses. She also examined them for lice or vermin. Two years before I was born over 1,000 school children had been examined in Liverpool, thanks to the lead given by the Queen's Nurses. The Queen's Institute had really shown the way. When I was a district nurse people were very poor and children had not the constant care they have nowadays. As time went on and after my day, I believe people had to pay half a crown for the services of the district nurse and then of course with the introduction of the National Health Service in 1948 all that stopped and the service became free.

The home in Aberdeen where my aunt was matron had, including the staff, boys and girls, about forty people. I enjoyed helping her there. The inmates were the children of widowers. Many fathers came at weekends and took their children home. There was a great stir on Saturday mornings getting the children ready. My aunt was a big woman; she had only to put a hand on a child's shoulder and he would be quiet. As I said, it was pandemonium on a Saturday morning. They had a bath the night before but in the morning they had to be washed again, with faces and hands clean, all dressed and ready. Lunch was usually between 11 and 12 each day, for we were up early in the mornings. On Sunday mornings they all had to get on their Sunday clothes. Very few stayed in the home at weekends. The children left the home to go out into the world at fifteen. It was a private home. The lady who took a great interest in it was Princess Diana's grandmother. She was Mrs Ruth Gill and her husband was one of the Gill paint family firm. Mrs Gill was our secretary and a constant visitor, a fine lady.

During that time I went back to Queen's work for I loved it, but at the same time I was helping my aunt part-time. Then I heard they were short of a nurse at Mulben, a little place in Morayshire and so I went there. It was a farming area. After that I went to Knockando and was there for seventeen years as a Queen's Nurse. It was in the Keith, Elgin, Dufftown part of Scotland.

While I was there I went down to an inspection of the nurses in Edinburgh by old Queen Mary. There was a double row of nurses in the form of a square. This was in 1935 when she had been Queen for twenty-five years. The King was a modest man but Queen Mary could put everybody in their place if she wanted. But on that day as she went round she gave a little nod to every nurse. What I remember were her very blue eyes and that she wore a lilac dress.

Then again when I was in Knockando I went down to London to receive my gold medal for long service in the Queen's. That was in 1952, the year King George VI died. The Queen Mother presented me with it. She looked sad at the time, for her husband had just died. This trip to London was a tonic for I had been feeling a bit down through the deaths of my uncle and a very old friend.

I retired in 1962 after thirty years as a Queen's Nurse. I had the chance of an estate cottage which was very cheap and near Kingussie. It was a patient who had suggested this some time before I retired. She said "What about taking the cottage? It would be a fine holiday home for you." So I came to live in the cottage about two miles from Kingussie, which was all right as by that time I had a car of my own.

I thought I had retired but I wasn't there long when a gentleman who said he knew my family came to the cottage and asked me if I'd come to look after a lady who needed care. I said I wasn't wanting to continue as I had retired. However, as she was old I hadn't the heart to see her left alone and, believe it or not, I stayed seven years nursing her and looking after her. She died and again I retired to my cottage. I enjoyed myself visiting relations all over the place. I still have over forty relations in Scotland and I did the rounds in my car. I would put soup in my thermos and off I would go.

About 1977 when I had been ill my doctor suggested that I should consider going into a home. I went down to Colinton in Edinburgh for a wee holiday and when I was there I went to the headquarters of the Queen's Nurses at Castle Terrace in Edinburgh. They were very nice to me, and helped to get me into Strathmore House, which is a home run by the Benevolent Fund for Nurses in Edinburgh.

I have had a long and happy life. I am proud to have spent it as a Queen's Nurse. It is a privilege to have been one of them.

Founder of St Columba's Hospice

ANN WEATHERILL

I WAS born in West Hartlepool in 1914 and when I was about six the family moved to Redcar. My father was sea-going. He was a brilliant engineer and after the First World War he gave up the sea and was test-house manager to Cargo Fleet. I didn't go to school until I was six because of the move. Eventually I went to a school in Redcar till I was sixteen and I may say I hated it.

My mother was of Scottish descent, married to a Yorkshire-man, and she always liked to come to Scotland. Originally I believe I would come wrapped in a Shetland shawl. My father's ship was in Leith. Mother used to say it was a long walk from Leith to Comely Bank, where we stayed. There wasn't transport in those days and they had to carry me.

I always wanted to be a nurse so when I left school at Christmas I started the following January at Kirbymoorside. I was two years there and left as Nurse of the Year. But I was still too young to do my training for I wasn't nineteen. I applied to Edinburgh Royal but they wouldn't take me till I was twenty-one. I wanted to go to a London hospital but my older brother wouldn't let me go; so I went to a local hospital.

Meantime my father died and the matron of the local hospital got me into the Royal Infirmary at Stoke-on-Trent. Matron there said she wouldn't normally have taken me because I was only nineteen but because I had my children's training she

would take me. In the first year I was paid £12 less insurance.
That was in 1934. I was doing general nursing and it was there
I passed my finals and became a State Registered Nurse.

My brother sent for me to come home and help there.
Although he was only seven years older than me, in those days
his word was law. So I went back and started in the local
hospital in Middlesbrough and I was made a Sister there.

I saved enough to come up to Edinburgh to do my midwifery
training. In Middlesbrough it had been jolly hard work but
I had managed to save £24 a year to do my training in
Edinburgh. I started at Simpson's Maternity Hospital in March
1939. In those days you had to pay fees to do your midwifery
training and you had to keep yourself for six months. I am still
friendly with a girl I did my midwifery with.

I can't tell you how old I was before I had time to go out
with boys but I had certainly done my children's training, my
general training, midwifery training and I had been a sister
before this. We had to be in by 9 o'clock in the evening or have
a late pass for 10 o'clock.

The war was now on and I wanted to join up, so I joined
the Queen Alexandra's Nurses in 1940. I was sent to military
hospitals in Bath and York. Then we went out to India in 1942,
and I was there till 1946. I had a busy and wonderful time
in India. There is a tremendous atmosphere in the QA's. I felt
they were the élite in nursing. In my day we were all completely
trained nurses. Now they train people while they are in the QA's.

I was first in Ranchi. We were nursing Indian troops who had
been fighting in Burma.

During the Bengal famine while we were in Dacca I set up a
malnutrition kitchen. There were only five QA's and we had
a thousand beds in the hospital. We were in the university
buildings in Dacca and they were huge long wards. Despite the
circumstances, experiences in the kitchen I set up were not
without fun. I had to concoct food from local sources with such
unusual mixtures as toffee with cheese in it to achieve very high
protein. At first I couldn't get the mixture to set, but I used an
old toffee recipe of my mother's which set it. One day General
Sir Neil Cantlie who was over from Delhi put his head round the
kitchen door and asked what was going on. I said "Some silly
bugger from Delhi has made this recipe and no way will it set."

He sampled my recipe and liked it, so after that I used to get an empty tin every month sent from Delhi and I used to fill it with cheesy toffee and send it back to him.

I knew Lady Louis Mountbatten, who used to call me Ann. She was a wonderful woman. She would never give in and worked and worked. We all idolised her. She knew we were a very small unit in this huge hospital and it was appreciated. We were literally never off duty. One would say "Right, you take over my work and I'll go and get a shower." We had a man's bicycle so we'd cycle over to the mess, have a shower, put a clean dress on and come back. When we were operating a friend who was theatre sister and I would get up at 6 a.m. The Colonel and the Quartermaster were white, but apart from them all the staff were Indian.

I returned home in 1946. I was all lined up to go to Australia because the friend who had been through the war with me was going to Australia and she was keen I should go too. But just as it seemed all settled I came home one day to find my mother had had a stroke. I nursed her for fourteen years, until 1962. But I wasn't earning and there wasn't any money coming in.

Just before she died I had a chance of becoming Matron of Berwick Infirmary so she said she would give up her house and come up to Berwick. She was three months there when she died. I was matron there for four years.

Once again I contemplated going to Australia and had things all lined up but fate intervened in the form of a cousin who said he thought I was making a mistake in going to Australia. I said "Everything's organised." But he drew my attention to an advertisement for Matron of Corstorphine Hospital. So I applied for that and got it. Corstorphine Hospital is now a convalescent home, but it wasn't in those days.

I was there a couple of years when the Matron of the Royal, who was the superintendent, said I hadn't enough to do so she gave me Beechmount as well. They were near each other, on either side of Edinburgh Zoo.

But I found I still had too much time on my hands and that started me thinking. I had been thinking about the idea of hospice work and I thought the Royal would be interested in my ideas but they weren't.

I happened to mention this to my rector at old St Paul's and he said "Cecily Saunders is coming up to Edinburgh; why don't you see her?" She was the London doctor who started St Christopher's Hospice in London. It wasn't the first because some nuns had opened one at St Joseph's in London, but hers was the first of the modern hospices. So when she came up to Edinburgh I met her and she suggested that I should come down to her hospice to see it for myself and perhaps get a few ideas.

At the time I had some summer holidays and went to London and did a post-graduate course and came back full of the intention to start a hospice in Edinburgh. In the end I went to see the Bishop of Edinburgh. He agreed to have a meeting in his house and from that meeting we decided to invite Cecily Saunders to come up from London to give a lecture on the hospice movement at the Royal. There were about 250 people there, a cross-section of the community. Later some of us went to Tom and Anne Bell's house, along with Lord Birsey, and Margaret and John Strathdee. Tom Bell was an Edinburgh lawyer and Anne was a speech therapist. When I was off duty, I used to go to their home in Murrayfield Gardens. They had a big old-fashioned kitchen, a huge place with a big dining-room table where I used to sit and write. It was the only peace I could get. There was no use doing it in the hospital. Harold Leslie would come in sometimes, and later they interested Dr Doyle: he was my doctor, a very nice fellow.

I started all this in 1968 and we opened Challenger Lodge, the first hospice in Scotland in 1977. I had spoken all over Scotland to raise funds for it, for no way was I going to have any debt. I went as far north as Thurso, to Dumfries and Galloway, Glasgow, the Borders, Northumberland, as far south as Kent. From 1974 I devoted all my time to St Columba's.

To start with we had an office in the attic of the house of one of the Governors of the hospice. I spent time there. Then we had the offer of Challenger Lodge, if we could pay for it. The down payment was to be £50,000 and we had only £40,000. John Simpson said they would have to take my chapel fund, which they all knew about. This was a threepenny-bit fund I had started to furnish the chapel so that it wouldn't be a cost to the hospice. I said they couldn't have my chapel fund. "You can go

down on your knees and pray for it," I told them. Would you
believe it, we had the £10,000 within a week and we were able
to put down the £50,000 deposit, and we paid off Challenger
Lodge in just over a year.

Now we had to get the money for the alterations. It was in
a pretty grotty state when we got it. In the meantime my
night-porter at Corstorphine said if he could have the cottage at
the gates, he would help to put the garden to rights. He used to
work late at night at Corstorphine, go home, go to bed at five in
the morning and then come to us. I'd give him his breakfast and
he'd work all day in the garden. We never spent a penny on it
and he went on to produce vegetables for us. In time we had the
kitchen all done up beautifully to the standards the health
authorities required. We had the whole house painted. We did a
lot of the painting ourselves and I scrubbed floors. By this time I
had moved from the attic to the schoolroom that used to be at
the front of the hospice and I used that as a workroom. I had a
Singer sewing machine and people would bring me sheets and
things. All this time I was living in a flat in Granton, not very far
from the hospice.

There was a lady whose husband's mother died and left him a
house and a lot of household goods that she wished to dispose of.
The next thing I saw was a furniture van arriving and all the
stuff they didn't want they brought down to me. A lot of people
brought stuff and I never refused anything. What we couldn't
use for the hospice I'd take to Stockbridge to sell to the junk
shops there.

With material I got I made nighties and draw sheets. From
Yorkshire I got linen sheets, linen pillow-cases. I made open-
back gowns for the patients. I knitted shawls and crochetted
knee-rugs and made sure the windows had curtains. I furnished
the chapel and made the vestments. The Church of the Good
Shepherd gave me half a dozen hassocks. A friend gave me a
beautiful damask tablecloth, pure Irish. It had been a wedding
present and she hadn't used it. Her people were linen manufacturers in Ireland, so it was the very best. I cut this up and
made altar cloths with it. Another friend in Yorkshire had a
coffee morning for me. They gave me cushions.

The main furniture for the chapel was bought from someone I
had met years ago and who was an ecclesiastical carver. He is

well known in the north of England for his trade mark was a
mouse on all his work. One of his apprentices signed his work
with a beaver. I went to the beaver man, and when I met him,
he remembered me and took £200 off the bill.

When the hospice opened we started with fifteen patients.
We outgrew these beds within three months. Dr Doyle picked
the patients and interviewed them all. We didn't take long-
term geriatrics; it is for people who are terminal, who are in
real need of nursing care. We went on to take thirty patients,
which was the maximum. We didn't like waiting lists. What
we did was to have a home-care system and a day-system.
Under the latter, the patients came in for the day. It meant
the relatives who normally looked after them could go out
for the day and get a break. The home-care system involved
sisters fully trained and qualified who went out to people's
homes. They advised people in all sorts of ways and linked up
with the patient's own GPs. They were the support group. A
rapport develops between patients and nurses, which builds up
in a very solid foundation for the time when and if the patient
needs to come into the hospice. Some of course never need to
come in for relatives find with this home-care support they can
manage.

There have been many changes in the hospice itself. We built
the nursing unit, which is a separate building connected to
the house. The house is now the day-hospice and offices and
kitchen. There is a covered corridor to the nursing unit, so there
is no need to go outside. Then a few years ago we built a big
education unit and conference room.

We have developed an education system at St Columba's
where people can come from any where and learn what we are
doing. Then they can go out and start new units. In fact people
come from all over the world. Dr Doyle has a very heavy
programme between looking after patients and being involved
in the education side. We have three doctors.

People ask me why there is a need for the hospice movement
and how does it differ from the other health facilities. Three
words, it seems to me, are at the heart of the hospice movement;
these words are love, support, care. Hospitals do wonderful work
but in a busy hospital ward you just have not the time to give to
individual patients. In a hospice there *is* time because we have a

bigger staff ratio. There are not so many patients, so you have the opportunity of giving more to each one.

I think I started the hospice because I thought things weren't being done as I thought they should be. It is a dream come true.

District Catering Manager

EILEEN LENNON

I WAS born in Blantyre and my father was Headmaster of a High School in Glasgow. There were five children in the family. I had two elder sisters and two younger brothers. All the children except myself studied medicine.

The great hope of my life was to be a doctor. I couldn't get into Glasgow University at the time I applied, because all the places being allocated were given to people returning from active service. In the first year I applied I was just seventeen and they were only taking people from seventeen and a half. The following year was the one when returning service people were given priority. I think, too, that the powers-that-be in the faculty thought that two members of the family was allocation enough. So my father decided that I shouldn't waste my time any longer. As an interim measure I went to the Glasgow and West of Scotland College of Domestic Science. That interim measure lasted four years!

When I finished I did a year's teaching but I really didn't care very much for teaching. As I had a great love of medicine I thought I'd try to get a job in a hospital and at least be nearer the thing I had always wanted to do.

I went first to the schools meal service to get a grounding and knowledge of catering for large numbers. I didn't spend very long there before I applied for and got a post in West Lothian, as catering superintendent in a small hospital. From there I went on to become kitchen superintendent of the Royal Edinburgh Hospital. It was a larger establishment and catered for over a thousand patients. This gave me my first experience in preparing meals for large numbers of patients and in controlling large numbers of staff.

Then I was appointed assistant catering officer, as it was termed in those days. It was during this time I was picked by the Home and Health Department to go up to the Island of South Uist in the Hebrides to Daliburgh Hospital. It was a general and maternity hospital run by nuns. The Queen on her visit to the Western Isles that year was to visit the hospital and they were hosting a lunch for her. I went up and helped to cook the lunch for the Queen. Since then I've had a long association through the years with the then matron of the hospital who was also the Reverend Mother. I remember that incident with great delight. I went up on holidays later on and loved the islands and the island people.

From the Royal Edinburgh Hospital I went on to the Eastern General and Leith Hospitals, which came under the jurisdiction of the Northern Board. I was appointed as catering manager. I gained a lot of experience there as I was in complete charge. I must say I learned a lot from the head chef at the time, a little man called Charlie de Placeido. He was a rogue but I learned a lot from Charlie, especially what I had to watch out for. Charlie was a man of great character and experience, and I liked him very much.

When I came to the Eastern General Hospital, there was a very small dining-room, which was divided into three separate sections; a large one for the nurses, another for the senior nursing staff, and another for resident doctors and consultants. It was a case in those days that never the twain shall meet, and as they were all eating the same food it was absolute nonsense. So after long trials and tribulations I managed to get the dining- room integrated.At that time too I introduced a waitress service. I got the dining-room upgraded with nice tables and table cloths for the staff. We made it more like a restaurant than a cafeteria.

I introduced a choice menu system for all the staff which they had never had before. I also introduced it for the patients. It was at that time the pilot scheme in Edinburgh. We introduced it very successfully without incurring any extra cost and there wasn't the wastage that some people said there would be. If I remember correctly, the allowance for patients was two shillings and a penny per head for three meals per day.

I remember the time when the staff had to buy tickets for their lunch. I think in those days a three-course meal was half a crown (2s.6d.). They bought their tickets from the house steward. I got a call one day from the ward sister to say that they had a patient and they couldn't get him to eat anything. This young man was a resident houseman. They were very anxious about him because they thought that by this time he ought to be on the mend but he wasn't making any effort. They thought if he could only get something to eat that would interest him, it would help a lot. So she asked me if I would come up and see him, which I did. We went through everything I could think of. I said to him, "There must be something you would really like?" Smilingly he said, "Yes, I'll have some oysters." I just laughed and said "Is that so?" I ordered up oysters for him. We got them prepared and sent up to the ward. I think the poor fellow was so shocked that he ate them and enjoyed them. From that day on he started to eat.

This ties in with what I was saying about the staff having to buy tickets at the steward's office. Two days after the young resident had his oysters, two of the consultant surgeons were buying their tickets. One turned to the other and said, "Oh, well, maybe we'll get oysters today." So I knew there had been a bit of a laugh about the oysters.

I went on holiday in Spain with my sister once and came home from holiday really quite ill. I was on sick leave and confined to bed when the post of Catering Manager at the Royal Infirmary of Edinburgh was advertised.

I had heard all about the Royal Infirmary. I knew it was a vast place, with over a thousand staff. I had never been in it but in my job at the Eastern General I had been asked to look over the staffing rotas of the Royal to see whether I could produce better ones than those in operation at that time. This I did. All I knew about the Royal was by repute, and I thought that because it was such a vast place it would be an almost impossible job. However, I remember saying to my mother "Ah, well, I may as well try for it. There's no harm done and I'm happy enough in the post I'm in."

I applied and got word to go for an interview on the very first day I was out of my sick bed. I remember that there were three men on the list besides myself. One was a young Jewish man from London. One was a Scot whom I've known ever since and who was, and who may still be, the District Catering Manager at Raigmore Hospital in Inverness. The third man I think came from Glasgow. I can even remember the coat and hat I wore that day! The three men and I were first shown round the department. The kitchens were old and I was aware of what seemed a great many chefs. The kitchens themselves were very clean.

The interviews started at two . . . I was the third to be interviewed. Each candidate seemed to be away for a long time. Really they were only away for twenty minutes or so, but it seemed much longer. While sitting in the secretary and treasurer's office we were given the Royal Infirmary magazine to read. I remember thinking to myself that I didn't want the job at all. When I went in for my interview all I seemed to see at first was a sea of faces though probably there were only about eight people. Professor Romanes, who was Chairman of the Board, introduced himself and then introduced me to the committee. The first man to question me was I think a man called Sir John Storer. He asked me to answer a question and I was halfway through my answer when I knew I was giving him the wrong one. So I stopped and apologised and said "I know I'm giving you the wrong answer." I always remember Professor George Romanes saying "Miss Coneghan, please just take your time. You know, you may be nervous but we're all nervous too." I thought how kind that was. I thought the questions would never stop. After I was shown back into the secretary and treasurer's office, I hoped they wouldn't think of offering me the post. The next thing was that they called me back and offered me the post. When I came out my knees were shaking.

I started in November 1961, responsible for catering for over a thousand staff as well as all the patients in addition. I was really sorry to leave the Eastern General and Leith Hospitals. It had been a great unit of hospitals but I thought 'Here we go: here's a new challenge.' When I started there was a kitchen superintendent, Bert Smith, who had been there a long time, a very nice man. There was also James Bagan who was his

assistant kitchen superintendent. There were fourteen assistant
head chefs. The Royal Infirmary had always appointed assistant
head chefs because by so doing they hoped to be able to employ
a better class of chef. This was to the consternation of other
hospitals in Edinburgh who only employed cooks and head
cooks. However, I think in those days what was done by the
Royal Infirmary did pay off.

For the first two or three years it was very hard going. I made
up my mind that I would just stop, look and listen for the
first month without changing anything. By November all the
orders and preparations for the Christmas fare should have been
done and the Christmas cakes and Christmas puddings should
have been made. When I went in nothing had been done. The
dates of all the functions for the nurses and patients over the
Christmas period should have been entered in the official
diaries. However, when we looked for the official diaries I was
told by Mr Smith that my predecessor had destroyed every bit
of information about the things that were arranged. I had to go
to each head of department to get the information I needed.

In the first few weeks I was taken to be introduced to Miss
Taylor who was then the matron of the Simpson Memorial
Maternity Pavilion which was linked to the Royal. She was a
very strict person and most of the nurses were in fear and
trembling of her. I remember being introduced to her and
she turned to the Administrator and said "She's far too young.
They'll eat her. I'm sure she can't have the experience
necessary." I told her I was sure that I had enough experience
to get the results everyone wanted. The happy outcome was that
I became very friendly with 'Tubby' Taylor, as people called
her, and she and I were great friends always.

Something which helped me a bit was the Christmas functions
in December for the nurses. They all had to have different
Christmas dates for their Christmas meals. They had them in
sections in those days, no junior nurses mixed with the staff
nurses or the staff nurses with the sisters. The hierarchy was
sacrosanct.

I remember a phone call on the day of the second of our
Christmas functions for the staff. This was from Miss Taylor to
say she hadn't seen the tables in the dining-room set for her
nurses' Christmas dinner. I had not been given that date and it

wasn't down in my diary. I had only about six hours to prepare it, but we got it done and those nurses never knew that it had not been pre-planned.

Then an important thing happened. When I took up the appointment, I didn't control the dining-rooms. I only produced the food to be taken from the kitchens to the dining-rooms. The actual distribution of the food was under the jurisdiction of the Home Sister. The main nurses' home was the Red Home and the Sister of the Red Home controlled the dining-room staff in the RIE.

The dining-rooms of the Royal Infirmary were in a large area which was divided in two. The larger section was for the nurses and the staff nurses who ate at different times or in different sections of the large dining-room. The sisters and senior administrative staff had the smaller dining-room.

The dining-rooms were dull. There were wooden floors and all around the perimeters on the walls were little lockers, all in dark wood, in which the nurses had kept their rations during the war. There was a huge statue of Florence Nightingale on a pedestal and all round were photographs of previous Lady Superintendents of Nurses. The whole place was formidable, not a place anyone could have relaxed in.

There was no cafeteria service for the nurses and no place in the dining-room to keep the food warm. The food had to be brought down from the kitchens in large containers and placed on wooden benches and the dining-room staff dispensed it to the nurses. There was a jug of milk on each table and the nurses were allowed as much milk as they wished.

The food often became cold because the dining-room staff were not allowed to serve the food to the nurses until the Home Sister from the Red Home had arrived. The girls all had to stand behind their chairs and the sister then said grace. Only then were the girls allowed to sit and have their food.

If Sister was late – and she often was, at least five minutes – the soup and everything lay there getting colder and colder. I don't remember how long it took me to discover this, but I thought it was terrible. I discussed it with my assistant and my kitchen superintendent who told me it had been going on as long as they could remember. They got complaints that the food was cold, but nothing was done. These young nurses were treated like children. They were afraid to say anything but stood to attention when the sister came in. Bearing in mind that these young women were dealing with life and death, it was really terrible.

So I went to the dining-room on the following day when we had introduced a new soup, and we all waited while the food got cold. After five minutes when the Sister didn't turn up I told the dining-room supervisor to tell the nurses to sit down and start serving soup. She said it would be more than her job was worth. I said "The food is getting cold." She said "I'm sorry but I couldn't do it." I took a spoon and got the attention of the nurses. I said "The food has been sitting here for at least five minutes. It is getting cold so would you please sit down and say your own grace." As soon as they sat down the Sister walked in and there was a hush. When she heard I had ordered the soup to be served, she stamped out in anger.

The next thing, I was summoned to go to the Lady Superintendent of Nurses to get what I supposed was to be the telling off of my life. I let her go on and then I said, "Yes, that's right, I did do that." "And why did you do it? That's not how things are done according to the rules here." I said, "I know how things are done here. But I wonder whether in fact *you* know. I am aware of the fact that the nurses have to wait for the sister to come into the dining-room to say grace, but would you like to wait for ten minutes on numerous occasions while your food is sitting there getting cold? Is that what *you* want for your nurses?" She began to say, "But I don't think . . . " when I interrupted. "I am telling you now why I took the action I did. After all, why should we in the catering staff do our very best to give a good catering service when as often as not the food is served nearly cold because someone is late coming to say grace? I am not against the saying of grace, but if the meal is planned to be served at a certain time, it has to be served then. These girls surely can say their own grace. They are not in boarding-school." That ended the interview. Soon after that I was asked to assume control of the dining-room staff and the dining-rooms themselves.

Later I conferred with the Royal Infirmary architect, Arthur Dixon, and with his help and expertise plans for the dining-rooms to be upgraded were drawn up. We put in a cafeteria service, a self-service system, and a choice menu scheme for all staff who up to then had been allowed to dine in the dining-rooms. After a long and weary battle I got a fully-fitted carpet put down. This made it look beautiful and it was really a great up-grading. Even then there was no real integration in the dining-room. The sisters still continued to occupy one side of the dining-room and the nurses the other side. There had been no provision for non-medical resident staff to have dining-room facilities. There was a little cupboard of a place with an old hot plate and about ten of the consultants dined there. The facilities were shocking. I put forward a proposal that we open up the dining-rooms to the consultant staff and the non-medical resident staff. This caused furore amongst the senior nursing staff. Where were they going to dine? They said it would cause a lot of trouble in the nurses' dining-room. Some of the younger nursing sisters thought it a great idea, but the older sisters didn't want it at all and said, among other things, that those who wanted to smoke shouldn't be allowed to. However, by sheer persistence we got the medical staff into the dining-room. Then when the rest of the disciplines in the hospital saw that the medical staff were being allowed in, I was asked if I could provide meals for the physiotherapists. After a good deal of thought I decided to start. I couldn't take both staff and students. Initially we took in the senior staff of the Physio Department – for a trial period! Not long afterwards the students were allowed dining-room facilities.

There had been space in the dining-rooms but it had never been properly utilised. The nurses had had set times for their meals – but in consultation with the Lady Superintendent of Nurses and others their meal-times were staggered betweeen noon and two. Later with more space available the maids were allowed to dine in the dining-room, and later the gardening staff and tradesmen of the hospital. Resistance came mainly from the senior nursing staff who had been used to being a privileged section. They were marvellous nursing sisters in their wards, but in those days the old senior sisters had a great voice and say in everything. My own philosophy was that all who worked in the Royal Infirmary should enjoy the same facilities for eating.

My next job was to find a coffee lounge. I found a place which was too small for the numbers which I could foresee would want to make use of it. I suggested it should be extended, before it opened. It wasn't extended and the coffee lounge became full to overflowing. That was one problem we didn't get over at the end of the day. I think they've now built something else on the piece of ground that was available.

I was happy to take part in integrating the dining-rooms and extending the catering facilities to all those working, even remotely, for the patients. At the same time a lot of thought was given to improving, through selective menus, catering for the patients themselves. It came about through the use of modern techniques in which I had been trained, and with the help of a then very understanding and supportive Board of Management and Catering Staff.

The Simpson Memorial Maternity Pavilion nurses used to dine in the Simpson's dining-room over in the Florence Nightingale nurses' home which was far distant from the main kitchen. This caused problems. Eventually all came over to the Royal Infirmary and it worked very well. The SMMP consultants didn't want to come at first but at the end of the day they came too.

In the Royal itself was the Royal Infirmary mess, which was for resident house doctors in training. They stayed in the residency and had their own dining-room with a butler. They always maintained they would never give up their dining-room, but just before I left there was talk of their coming to the main dining-room. The scattered service points had always been a costly business.

I remember one day I got a phone call from the ward sister from one of the surgical wards to say she had a very ill patient who had a birthday in a few days' time. She had one or two children. She was a young woman and she wasn't expected to live long. The ward sister thought it would be nice if she could have a birthday party in a side-room with her husband and her parents. That was the first of the birthday cakes we made for patients in the Royal Infirmary who were gravely ill. We sent up a lovely spread for this lady and her husband and family. I remember receiving a delightful letter from her surgeon thanking myself and the catering staff for the efforts we had made to make this lady's last birthday a very happy one. To show this kind of letter of appreciation to the catering staff worked wonders. It made them realise they were part of a service which was primarily for patients who could be their mothers or sisters. I kept telling them this. Don't ever send anything up to a ward that you wouldn't serve to your parents.

We had a very nice man called Alec. He was actually a patient for the skin department. He spent his life swathed in bandages and he was emaciated. He was a cheery little man. The personnel department had found him a job with the gardening department. He used to sweep up sites in the Royal. I got to know him and found out that he had great difficulty in swallowing food and this was probably one of the reasons why he was so thin. I think it was Professor Hare in the skin department who told me about Alec's feeding difficulties. Alec all bandaged up would not come into the dining-room to face the others. I said I would get his food and he could come into the food stores and ask to see the menus for that day and make up his mind what he wanted. The head storeman would then see the kitchen superintendent who would make sure that everything requested was liquidised. That was taken into the store where Alec could take his food in peace. Professor Hare got to know how well the staff had helped in some respects to make Alec's life more comfortable. I was up in the skin department one day and the sister told me that Alec was next door. He had been getting treatment from the Professor and was shortly flying off to Canada to see his sister whom he hadn't seen for years. Alec never forgot us and he used to send me a card every Christmas. These were the sort of things that made the whole thing worthwhile.

While I was at the Royal Infirmary I was asked to take students from the College of Domestic Science for their outside experience and took HND, Institutional Management and Dietetic students. I also took students from Ireland. The medical missionaries and other orders of nuns would send people over for training and experience.

Chefs are notorious for their language in the kitchen but after I took over seldom did I ever have cause to reprimand them. It was quite fantastic, funny in a way, when the nuns were there. The chefs never even raised their voices.

I took over responsibility for all the old Southern General group of hospitals; that was Astley Ainslie Hospital, Sick Children's Hospital, Musselburgh, Longmore and Liberton.

There had been a lot of problems at Elsie Inglis with sky-high costs and an appalling standard of food, which we sorted out.

Then I was appointed District Catering Manager. The district was one of three within Lothian Health Board. It is a large teaching district with a population of 318,000, a complement of 5,500 beds and over 10,000 staff. The annual budget was thirty-six million pounds. The district was organised into three management Divisions plus a Community Health Service. This meant I had about 20 hospitals and over 500 staff of whom about 240 were part-time.

Looking back over the years some things have given me satisfaction, especially the knowledge I have made some contribution to the advancement of the quality of meals in the Scottish hospital service. While at Eastern General and Leith Hospitals I brought in a choice of menus to all patients and staff. I introduced choice menus into the dining-rooms and wards of the Royal Infirmary. The pay-as-you-eat system in the dining-room was inaugurated by us on the day it had been recommended, April 1st 1969. Previous to that all nursing staff had had their meal costs deducted from salary at source so we had no control of money coming into the dining-rooms. I implemented the forty hour, five-day week for the catering staff in 1976. These are some landmarks I remember with satisfaction.

I took early retirement in 1985. My main interests are my husband, my home and my garden and doing things that please me. It is a relief not to have to answer the phone constantly between eight o'clock in the morning and nine o'clock at night!

Hospital Pharmacist

RENEE CARRUTHERS

MY MOTHER liked the smell of chemists' shops and, funny as it sounds, I sometimes think the idea of my becoming a chemist came from her because of this.

I live in Edinburgh now, but I wasn't born there. I was born in Newcastle, where we lived for all my childhood. My father died when I was ten, and I was brought up by my mother. I was educated at *La Sagesse* convent in Newcastle. It was a French convent and the name stands for the daughters of wisdom. I never did chemistry at school. Later at the first lectures I had in chemistry when I started studying for pharmacy, I didn't know what they were talking about. In the 1930s if you wanted to become a pharmacist you served an apprenticeship and went to day-release classes.

I went straight from school to work in a chemist's shop at sixteen. That was in 1935. It was Taylor's big shop in Newcastle. It wasn't too bad as the staff were very helpful. I did my four years there and attended night classes.Then I came up to Edinburgh to Heriot-Watt college for my final year and took my MPS Diploma, which made me a fully-fledged pharmacist.

There had been six of us girls in the laboratory class. One of them, a very bright girl, had arranged to take on several locums when she finished her final exam. She was very quick and always looking for short cuts. In the final exam she had to make a solution of potassium permanganate. She should have added water to the crystals and dissolved them and then poured off the water, but to hasten the process she got a bottle, put the crystals in, put the stopper on and gave it a shake. The result was an excess of solubility in the crystals and she failed her exam which meant she couldn't do the locums she had arranged to do. She phoned me and asked if I could take on any of them. So I had my first real job. It lasted a fortnight and was a holiday locum. Then I had one at the City Hospital and another at the Sick Children's Hospital in Edinburgh. I was unemployed for a bit, then I got a job as locum over in Dunfermline in Fife. That was awful because for the first time in my life I had to work on Christmas Day. It was a retail one-man shop owned by the Co-op. That job ended after two weeks.

Later I got a job in public health and here it was a case of putting up medicines for all the child welfare clinics. When I worked in the hospitals, the main job was preparing medicines for the wards. In a small hospital there was usually just one pharmacist who sent an indent to the main hospital for all the things she needed.

Some events stand out in my memory from those early days. In Dunfermline I remember two naval boys. It was my first day with the Co-op. It was Christmas time and I had to leave in the early winter morning in the dark and come back at night, also in the dark. I didn't know how to get home as the trains were all haywire. By good luck these two boys turned up, one an officer and the other a rating. The rating carried my bag for me and we got on a bus to Inverkeithing, which was its terminus. Then we waited hopefully for a train which eventually arrived. It was eleven o'clock that night before I got home from my first day's work in Dunfermline. After that I found my way around in the black-out. I had to get away from the shop promptly at half-past seven to get the last possible train to Edinburgh.

I much preferred hospital to retail shop work as the hours were so much better. It was nine in the morning until five in the afternoon, although it may have been six o'clock before you finished. In retail you usually finished about half-past seven. As an apprentice it was sometimes after nine before I got away. In the beginning there's always the fear you might make a mistake with medicines so you check and recheck. Of course before you qualify there's always somebody checking what you do, but once you qualify you're on your own. One of the problems was

St Lawrence's Hospital, Bodmin, where Robert Rowe spent his career.

Clarice King in action.

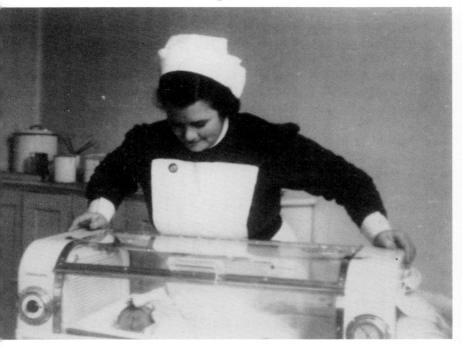

In 1939 Queen Mary sent this photograph to all Queen's Nurses, including Jessie Barron, with the message 'It is my constant prayer that God's blessing may be on the merciful work of all nurses throughout the Empire. Mary R.'

The Queen's Institute, Edinburgh

Challenger Lodge, the St Columba's Hospice founded by Ann Weatherill.

Weatherill (left) receiving the Good
Citizenship Award from Edinburgh's
Lord Provost, 1978.

Renee Carruthers, Pharmacist.

Eileen Lennon with her cooks, preparing for Christmas.

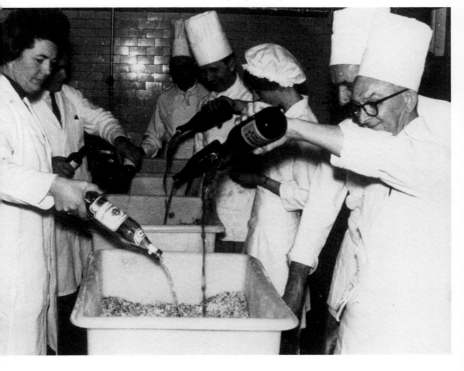

Professor Ronald Girdwood's hospi
the Edinburgh Royal Infirmary.

Lillie Dummer, starting her career in

Professor Girdwood in discussion w
King Hussein of Jordan.

interpreting writing in prescriptions. Sometimes doctors' writing was difficult and as time went on, with the extension of drugs and medicine there could be confusion, say about word endings where it was an -ine or an -en ending.

After Dunfermline I had another spell of unemployment until I got a job in a hospital at Craiglockhart. It had been turned into an emergency hospital with a lot of old people brought up from London. It is now an old people's home.

In those days when you started as a qualified pharmacist it wasn't a case of getting a permanent job right away. Before you could get slotted into the system you were dependent on getting temporary locum jobs. That's why I went from one to another for the first years. However, my first permanent job was just round the corner.

A woman who was working as a pharmacist at the Southern General Hospital in Edinburgh had to go for an operation. She asked if I could do her locum, which I did for three months. Then one morning I was told that she wasn't coming back and I was offered her job permanently. I was the only pharmacist without an assistant in the Craiglockhart district of Edinburgh. They brought across to us old people from the Northern General and we had evacuees from London. At this time I had also to dispense for the Norwegians who had come over during the war. We had 600 beds available and there were only 150 beds to begin with. The Norwegians took over two wards and they kept coming across the sea from Norway, some of them in a very battered state. I remember one poor lad whose crushed legs were in plaster. He was a sailor off one of the ships. We used to put him on a wheeled stretcher and he'd row himself about with a pair of crutches. One day he lost control on the laundry slope and finished up in the laundry!

The system in hospitals was that the doctor prescribed for the patient. The ward sister kept a drug cupboard with everything she thought she might want. If the doctor prescribed anything new, she would send a requisition to the pharmacy. I made it up and supplied the ward sister. I had dressings to do as well as drugs and I was responsible for ordering instruments, too. We had to learn a lot and gain experience as we went along. It was quite difficult for the pharmacist, especially in war-time. Mr Hall, the chief pharmacist at the Western, was always a great help.

In addition to the Norwegians we had a ward for ATS personnel. By the end of the war I was looking after a 600-bed hospital as a single-handed pharmacist.

My mother died in 1943 and I was on my own in Edinburgh. I started learning the violin; my violin teacher had a little flat above her own, which was four storeys up overlooking Bruntsfield Links, and she let it to me.

After the end of the war I went from the Southern to the Western. Mr Hall was recruiting there, for he wanted to get his stores organised and a central dispensary built up to supply other hospitals, and that included the public health department which supplied all the clinics. This post-war reorganisation was quite a big job. There were six pharmacists at the Western. We worked in pairs. One week we'd work in public health with the medicine bottles, boxes of ointment, etc. and all that was needed for the children. Another week we'd work in pairs for medicines for the wards, and in the third week we'd work at sterlising for infusion fluids for drips. We used to make those before the commercial boys came in. We did a lot of research making these things and then commercial firms became involved.

When I began my career in pharmacy I was paid £4.00 a week, which increased as time went on. Right after school I went for an interview with Boots, who only offered me £3.00 a week. I remember thinking "why did I bother to qualify for this wage?" The hospitals paid a bit better and gradually the salary rose with the years. You had to keep costing in mind when you were dispensing. I made a costing for the medicines I sent to each ward; for example, when I worked in the Sick Children's Hospital in the early days, in one of my first locums. A sad memory of the Sick Children's is of a young boy who had tetanus. I had to make up a special medicine for him. First of all the Infirmary gave me a supply, then I had to do it myself, an anaesthetic thing, to prevent the spasms. He had had an injury to his leg which had been neglected. The poor lad was really a little ragamuffin off the streets. In the end we controlled the tetanus but he died from septicaemia: blood poisoning. It was very sad. I had had no previous experience with tetanus and I just had to follow instructions on the bottles. It was concentrated and you made it up in individual doses.

When the National Health Service was introduced I was in

the Western. There were no grades in the job. You were either a basic pharmacist or a chief pharmacist like Mr Hall. Then a deputy chief was also appointed. I was in the Western for about fifteen years. I found it interesting, for we did a bit of research on drugs. I remember one connected with liquorice. At one time they thought it might be a cure for duodenal ulcers. The liquorice was broken down into constituents and we made capsules and pills to make it palatable for patients. We had a good relationship with the doctors who were interested in our research.

I continued with my violin playing and over the years I've been in several orchestras including the St Andrews orchestra and one in Kirk o' Fields. I was also in the Students' University Orchestra for one season.

In 1964 I got a job at Leith Hospital. In the Western General there had been six of us. In Leith I was as you might say, cock of the walk, as I had a staff of three. It was a smaller hospital and we did our own medicines and dressings, ordering direct from the manufacturers and wholesalers.

At this time I joined Clive Jenkins' Union, the Association of Scientific and Technical Workers and within a year our salaries were doubled.

I was in Leith Hospital for sixteen years and retired in 1980. When I retired I was still in St Andrews Orchestra and I got a lot of pleasure out of that. We give two major concerts a year. I joined the Cramond old folks' club, which meets in a room at Cramond Kirk. It was really first initiated by Dr Donald, who said he wanted to get the old people out of doctors' waiting-rooms and interested in outside things. We have excellent talks every fortnight. One day a choir came to sing, the Ingleneuk Singers, also comprised of retired people and I was very taken with it. I joined it and it's been good fun. The average age is in the region of eighty-two. I'm also a member of St Kentigern's Church club which meets every Wednesday. Till last year I went to sequence dancing there, but I'm afraid my legs have rather given up for that. It's nice having enjoyable interests in your retirement after a busy life as a hospital pharmacist.

Anaesthetist

DR LILLIE DUMMER
FRCA

I WAS born in 1903 in South Queensferry on the Firth of Forth where my father, Dr Dickson, was a GP. I was brought up there and it was always assumed I was going to be a doctor. My father had been impressed by the fact that there were so many women who grew old and didn't marry: they were often left looking after their parents and when the parents died they were more or less penniless. He must have thought to himself "I don't suppose this one's going to get married!" So he was all for me having a career.

My father had a Model T Ford and I used to go round the countryside with him, even as a young girl. That was in the Edwardian days before even the first Insurance Act, when everyone paid something for the doctor and any medicine they needed.

We used to go round "the big hoosies", the great houses of Hopetoun where the Marquis and Marchioness of Linlithgow lived, and Dalmeny House belonging to the Earl of Rosebery. My father treated the staff of these houses. The servants were a happy crew in those days. The feeling was that if they were employed in a good house like those I've mentioned they were better than the people in the not so grand houses.

I went to the well-known George Watson's Ladies College in Edinburgh and then, because my father was anxious that I should go, to a boarding-school in Ripon. It was a waste of time educationally speaking. However, I managed to get through my entrance exam and started my medical studies in Edinburgh and qualified in 1926.

After I qualified in medicine I got some experience in the North of England. I did six house jobs as a houseman, and in Hull I was in the children's hospital. I was also in West Hartlepool as a houseman.

I had a great respect for obstetrics. I thought it was dramatic, but the idea of obstetrics at home was so terrific I didn't think I could ever cope with it. My father said he thought it would be a good idea to go in for Public Health because I could sit in an office, so I did a DPH. I must have done quite well in the exams as I was offered one or two jobs. But whenever they heard I was going to get married, they said, "Oh, we can't have that; go home, have babies, look after your man." I thought what a waste of all that education, acquired with such effort. But there was a good deal of feeling against married women working. I remember when I had given birth to three boys, there was a survey about working mothers. We had to ask our children if they thought they had been disadvantaged by having a working mother. One of my boys said, "Oh no, Mother, it's better for you to work so you can have a car to take us around in!" I may say I worked only in the mornings, and felt this was fair to the children. I did a few clinics in Public Health when I got married and had my first baby boy. Then I saw an advertisement for an anaesthetist, wanted in the Children's Hospital in Edinburgh.

I well remember the interview I had for that job. I was interviewed by a board of senior consultants. They seemed a little dubious about this woman with the strange name of Dummer. Eventually, in the course of the questioning it came out that my father was Dr Dickson of South Queensferry. That did it. The job was mine.

I enjoyed my time there very much. Anaesthetics at that time was just ethyl chloride and ether on a mask – nothing fancy at all. They used to do some operations in the outpatients department. There they were, these poor little children who had their adenoids and tonsils yanked out and were then put into a room with their mothers who were told to hold their hands. Then they went home on the tramcars the same day – some of them spitting blood and in great discomfort. Nowadays of course they're all admitted.

After the Children's Hospital Dr Hertzfeld asked me if I would work with her. She was a lady surgeon here in Edinburgh, a big bouncy woman and an excellent surgeon who had been trained by Sir Harold Stiles. She was in charge of a ward in the Sick Children's Hospital. She also worked at the Bruntsfield Hospital for women and children. Her work with little babies was excellent. She also did gynaecology. I don't think the men ever really accepted her. I won't tell you what they called her, as she did so many circumcisions! I enjoyed working for her.

As time went on I began to get more and more sessions. In the end I had a session every morning at Sick Children's, another at Bruntsfield Hospital for women and children, and two more at Chalmers Hospital and the Edinburgh Royal Infirmary. By this time I worked in general surgery specifically in anaesthetics.

The changes in drugs and anaesthetics have been phenomenal. Everything nowadays is carefully monitored. We used to monitor our patients by feeling the pulse. Now you look at a screen and get all the relevant details immediately.

Gradually, new drugs used in anaesthetics were coming in. Improvements were being made all the time. It was all very primitive when I started. Anaesthetics was the dogsbody in the medical scene. Anybody who was standing by might be asked to do the anaesthetics. There was no proper anaesthetist. Usually in hospital it was the medical houseman who did the job. We induced with ethyl chloride or chloroform and went on to ether. Let me explain: you could get the patients under with ethyl chloride and chloroform, but when you had done that, you went on to ether which was considered safer to keep them going.

You got no actual guidance from the surgeon except in a rare emergency case; if a patient stopped breathing you watched for signs from the depths of breathing. The deeper the anaesthetic, the quieter the breathing and the more relaxed the muscles. If the surgeon was doing a job say in the abdomen, and wanted the muscles relaxed, he might tell you to give a bit more. In an extreme case the patient might stop breathing. Then they would throw away the towels and the patient would be resuscitated by Eve's method and by lowering the head and lifting up the patient's arms to induce the drawing of breath, just like resuscitating a drowned person.

We did use machines to give gas, nitrous oxide, and oxygen and sometimes gas and oxygen laced with ether. You had to get cylinders and not every hospital then had a machine. But they gradually became commonplace and you could give a mask and a bag. In earlier times it was even easier; just a bag and a bottle of chloroform and a mask and ether. You could go into the nursing homes and that was all you would probably carry with you.

Then we got on to cyclopropane which was very expensive, so they had to use a closed-circuit method. The gases were led through a cylinder with crystals of soda lime which meant you didn't need to use so much new gas. You just added your oxygen and a little gas and it breathed through the soda lime into a bag and rebreathed quite a lot of the gases into the bag so that they could be used again with added oxygen. To us this was a Scotsman's dream!

We now realised that by pressing the bag and releasing it we could control the patient's breathing. This saved all the gymnastics and the towels all over the place in an emergency situation.

An important thing was to get the patient relaxed enough so as to let the surgeon get into the abdomen without the patient's muscles tightening up and yet not letting the patient get so deeply anaesthetised that they didn't go on breathing. So the next thing that was invented was curare. This was arrow-poison. What Bernard Shaw would have made of this idea I don't know. Probably it would have made an intriguing play!

This South American arrow poisoning could paralyse the patient. When a person is completely paralysed, the muscles and respiration are paralysed and he dies of asphyxiation. On the other hand if an insufficient dose is given the patient could come round again. But by this time the drugs were measured in very careful doses. Curare was administered intravenously. By now we had nice little needles we could pop into the vein.

New drugs keep coming along all the time. Halothine was one of them and there have been many since then. The progress in training, scientific discoveries, the prestige of the profession, the development of new equipment over the last fifty years have been phenomenal.

By the time the war came, I was married. My husband was called up to the RAF as an air-gunner and I moved with my three children to South Queensferry. I did my ordinary anaesthetic work and to a certain extent helped my father, who was still practising in Queensferry. He was quite busy because some of the Fleet would come in and there was a good number of Norwegians as well.

My father was in charge of the first aid post. If there was a yellow warning he had to be ready, and if a red warning came he went to the first aid post ready to receive the casualties.

I remember that one day my husband who had not yet been called up, myself, my father and a friend of my father went to play golf. There had been gunfire and I saw a plane falling and told the others, but our friend said if it had been an enemy plane there would have been an air-raid warning. Nobody believed me, so we went on playing. Then, coming home at the 16th hole of Barnton course, as we had just driven off, a low plane came over above us, just about tree-top height, it seemed. I said "Look, there's a swastika on it." But my father said "Oh, it'll be a mock air-raid and that's them just practising." By the time we got to the club-house some guns nearby were all firing off. I asked one of the gunners if there was an air-raid and he said "For God's sake get under cover." I urged my father to go home. We got to the top of Hawes Brae where a sentry stopped us and said we couldn't go any further. I told him I had to get home as I'd left my children with a sitter-in. When we arrived the children were under the dining-room table with a box of biscuits, having a high old time. Unfortunately there were several casualties in that raid. There had been a cruiser lying below the Forth Bridge and one of the pinnaces was hit.

Over the years anaesthetics was advancing all the time in knowledge, skills and equipment. Training and refresher courses were progressively developed. The Royal College of Anaesthetics, based in London, gave specialist courses which I attended for my Diploma in Anaesthetics (DA). Then they introduced a Fellowship of the Royal College of Anaesthetists. It really was quite a difficult exam. The first question was always one on anatomy and I hated anatomy because I could never remember it. So I thought I'd give it a miss and stick to my practical skills. But in the end it was handed to me on a plate.

Things were becoming very different from the early days. Then anybody could do the anaesthetics. There was no special training. Very few people specialised. Dr Gillies was probably the first. He specialised and got the job of anaesthetist to Sir John Fraser. He announced he was not going to do anything else and this was looked on as very eccentric. He was in Edinburgh Royal and if there had been a Chair of Anaesthetics he would have had it.

When the old King George V required an operation and Sir James Learmonth with his theatre team went south to perform it, he took Dr John Gillies as his anaesthetist. John was very amusing about that. There was an Equerry standing outside the room and the theatre technician later made a bit of money selling bits of the swabs and plaster. John gave the King cyclopropane and said he thoroughly enjoyed the experience!

I retired in 1965. By this time all my boys were off my hands and my husband had died. I played golf and gardened but felt a bit lost. Dr Dodd, a friend, asked me to do a list at the Deaconess Hospital. I did quite a bit of that after I retired for when people are on holiday it is quite useful if somebody can take over. Then Dunfermline and West Fife approached me and I did five or six years there on a part-time basis and found it very interesting. They got fully staffed and I was quite pleased to stop. Now I had the freedom to go on holiday whenever I wanted and Edinburgh is a splendid place to spend one's retirement.

Refugee, Nurse and Director of Research

DR LISBETH HOCKEY
OBE

I WAS born in the city of Graz in Austria in 1918 and went to school and university there. The educational system was a little different from the British one. In Austria most young people went on from school to university if they passed their final school exam. I went to the Karl-Franzens University of Graz and began to study medicine. But in the middle of my studies there was political upheaval in Austria which made it necessary for me to leave the country. Hitler took Austria in March 1939 and I left three months later.

From a very sheltered home life I suddenly found myself alone, confronted by a totally unknown future. My parents and sister stayed in Austria.

It wasn't so difficult to get out if you were a woman. I had to sign a paper saying I wouldn't come back and I was allowed to take ten Austrian schillings with me and my tickets to London. I was extremely fortunate to have the help of the Quakers and an entry permit for the UK. It isn't easy going to another country if you don't know the language and have no money. I had only done the pre-clinical part of my medical studies, the subjects I had wanted to finish as quickly as possible before getting to the patients. It was a bitter disappointment that I couldn't study medicine in this country but I had three major disadvantages. First, I was not a British subject; second, I was a woman and it was hard in those days for a woman to go in for medicine; third, I didn't have the necessary money.

When I first came to London I was to meet a lady from the Quakers at Victoria Station and the distinguishing feature I was to recognise was a white handkerchief that she would be carrying in her hand; not a very obvious mark on a busy station in the evening rush hour! But by a miracle we found each other and I was sent down to Devon, my first port of call, where I stayed with a charming family as governess to two little girls. The father was a Major in the British army. The mother was a daughter of the famous Wedgwood china family; they were also Quakers.

I was supposed to teach the children German which didn't do much for my English; however it helped me to get on my feet till I got the chance to train as a nurse.

I had no idea how I would choose a hospital for training. I looked at lots of newspaper advertisements and eventually chose one that had a swimming pool, having no idea that it was one of the major teaching hospitals in London. It was The Royal London Hospital in the East End of London and displayed this notice: "The Largest Voluntary Hospital in England". This of course was before the National Health Service. I was interviewed and was deemed educationally acceptable but I would have to learn English competently in three months. If there was a cancellation I would be considered. There was great competition to get into this particular hospital. I had to work really hard to learn the language and I was accepted at the beginning of 1939 before the war started. Soon after the start of the war we were evacuated from London to the South Coast.

I was billeted with a postman and his wife for we were all living out in private homes. They were worried because I wasn't British so I wasn't allowed to have a light on at night.

Because there was a possibility of having to nurse enemy airmen who had been shot down, the government decreed that only British subjects would be allowed to nurse because of the risk of spying, so a few months later I had to interrupt my training because I did not have a British passport. Eventually I came back to London and was accepted in a hospital for my training, in the nursing of infectious diseases, meningitis, scarlet fever, diphtheria and so on. The patients were mainly children.

On night duty we had to do our own fire-watching and wear tin-hats – not easy to cope with the work wearing a heavy tin-hat! In order to protect the children against bomb damage they were bedded down at night on the floor under their cots, so to nurse them or give them potties and so on you had to get down on the floor. That was one time in my life when I was really glad to be short. Most of my colleagues had more backache than I by the end of the night. I completed my course there in 1943 and went on to a hospital in Hertfordshire for the final part of my nursing education in 1945. Then I did my midwifery training in North London and Essex.

In those days most women were delivered at home. I enjoyed it very much and I still believe it is better for a family to have a baby at home. It was in Essex too that I did health visitor and district nurse courses and afterwards worked as a district nurse and health visitor.

It was now 1947 and the National Health Service came into being on July 5th, 1948. I remember it vividly. Before 1948 money was collected for district nurse services and people were charged half-a-crown per visit unless they were insured under the Provident Insurance Scheme. Some of our patients just couldn't afford the half-a-crown and there were many times when one could not expect them to pay. Yet we had to have the receipts to prove the patients had been visited and had paid or had been in the Provident Insurance Scheme. The only possibility of helping some patients was to put one's own money into the bag and pretend the patients had paid it. This happened quite often although on £80 to £100 a year it wasn't easy. But when the National Health Service came in we had a big party and burned all redundant receipt books in a bonfire. We were so happy. It had been wonderful being a district nurse and I had loved every bit of it. I had worked what was called 'triple-duties' for a while in an Essex village, which meant I was a midwife, a health visitor and a district nurse all in one. In the country villages you really did everything for the people, unlike the pattern in the built-up town areas where the different duties would be separated. It was a wonderful life because everybody trusted you. You were, you might say, the queen bee of the area. You had a tied cottage. You would open your cottage door in the morning and find a gift from a patient lying there, maybe a couple of cabbages or half a dozen eggs. It was the patient's way of saying thank you.

Later I became a full-time health visitor and worked from a clinic giving advice to families. It didn't involve hands-on nursing as before. It was important work but perhaps not quite as satisfying because one couldn't identify the benefits to the families quite so easily. Certainly you were in contact with schools and with mothers and babies and old people and you gave talks on diet and so on. I found that part of the job fascinating. A few years later I was appointed as Deputy Superintendent of District Nurses in North London.

Then I took a year's course at the Royal College of Nursing in London to become a nurse teacher. For this, I was awarded a scholarship of £400 by the Queen's Institute. I was then employed at the headquarters of the Queen's Institute, first as a Tutor, then as a Research Officer. This post led to the setting up of a research department and we began to publish studies on many aspects of the service. At that time research in nursing was almost non-existent.

Perhaps I should have said that alongside that work in London, I went as an evening student to the London School of Economics to read for a degree in Economics. Those five years took every bit of my energy as my work during the day had to go on and was very demanding. During this period there was also a strike at the London School of Economics. It was a major battle to get to the library, and one was a 'black-leg'. For the whole of the five years I had known little sleep and during the last year I went to bed regularly at 2 a.m. to get up on the dot at about 5 a.m. In those days you couldn't resit exams at the LSE. I would have wasted those five years if I hadn't got my degree at the end. Fortunately I did, and a few years later I managed my Ph.D. for a study of the District Nursing Service.

In 1971 I was appointed to direct a new nursing research unit, the first in Europe, at the University of Edinburgh. I was there till 1982 when I retired.

While I was working at the University I was invited to pay regular professional visits to Sweden to conduct seminars and courses on research methods. It was a great honour to help another country in this way and I also enjoyed it immensely. The Swedish University of Uppsala most generously made me an honorary Doctor of Medicine. At the graduation ceremony they gave me a lovely traditional top hat and a beautiful ring with my name on it. The ring is placed on one's wedding ring finger as a symbol of commitment to science and scholarship. Some years earlier I had been fortunate enough to get an honorary degree of LLD at the University of Alberta in Edmonton, Canada. There was an amusing incident at that ceremony. I am very short and although they had shortened the academic robe, the sleeves had been forgotten and were far too long. Parading up to the platform with the Vice-Chancellor and to the sound of fanfares, I swept the floor. I had to shake hands with the Chancellor but I couldn't find any way to get my hand out of the sleeve. Eventually in the nick of time my hand appeared through a slit. There was laughter and applause. Another time at a major conference in Vienna I disappeared behind the lectern – embarrassing at the time, amusing in retrospect. A sense of humour is a great help.

My retirement at the end of 1982 marked the beginning of one of the busiest periods of my life. Nobody gives you a holiday when you are retired and even free weekends are hard to come by. Yet I seem to thrive on it and would not like to have nothing to do. I was pleased to be entrusted with a research project for the Hospice here in Edinburgh as my voluntary contribution to this worthwhile work to help people in the last stages of a terminal illness. For many years, I worked in a Save the Children charity shop, a total change from my professional activities. I am also quite busy with local citizenship affairs. Having been so fully and generously accepted as a British citizen, I want to do my bit. Trips abroad for lectures, conferences and consultations have continued, although travelling is becoming increasingly exhausting. A couple of months ago, I had a nine hour delay at the airport in London, causing me to arrive in Vienna at 2 a.m. with a teaching commitment later that same day. My Guest Professorship in Austria was a lovely surprise, as it is in the University at which I began to study medicine over fifty years ago. Committee work, writing professional 'bits and pieces' and trying to help research students are other enjoyable but time consuming activities. There is never a dull moment!

My career was neither easy nor straightforward but it had many highlights. To be given an OBE could not have featured in my wildest dreams. Of course, I would have liked to have finished my medical education. I had always wanted to become a general practitioner, so I was thrilled to be awarded an Honorary Fellowship of the Royal College of General Practitioners – a very great honour. I now have my Doctor of Medicine and my General Practitioner Fellowship, but both honorary. Actually, I now feel pretty certain that I was able to do more as a nurse than would have been possible as a doctor. Also, I loved nursing and am really grateful for the experiences and opportunities it gave me. When the Royal College of Nursing awarded me one of its prestigious Fellowships, I felt quite overwhelmed.

Without many marvellous people to help me and without faith I could not have achieved anything. I think that an experience like mine either breaks or makes one. I have been one of the fortunate ones. When I look back to July 13th, 1938, when I stood at Victoria Station in the rush hour, with ten schillings in my pocket, looking for a lady with a white handkerchief, I can only marvel. My heart goes out to the millions of today's refugees. I feel humble and profoundly grateful.

Research in War and Peace

PROFESSOR RONALD H. GIRDWOOD
FRCP (Edin.), FRCP (London), FRCPI, FRC (Path.),
FRSE, Hon. FRACP, Hon. FACP

I WAS born in Arbroath in Angus in 1917. My father wanted to be a doctor but family finances didn't permit that, so he was the nearest he could be, a pharmacist, and he had a pharmacist's shop. I actually remember when we left Arbroath, which was when I was two and a half years old. My father had bought a business in Edinburgh at that time.

At the age of five I went to Daniel Stewart's College and stayed there until I left to go into medicine. I had to stay on an extra year at school to be old enough to start medicine. I enjoyed school itself but I was unwell almost all the time. I had my most complex illness when we lived next door to a doctor who had been a missionary in Calabar, West Africa. It was partly his influence that made me take up medicine, but he was an old-fashioned doctor and he thought I had what he called 'threatened tuberculosis'. In addition to being off school almost every year with measles, mumps, whooping cough and so on, I was away at a rather critical time in my education because of this 'threatened tuberculosis', but I wasn't X-rayed as he had no experience of this new form of investigation. Of course it was nonsense; you can't have 'threatened tuberculosis': you either have it or you don't. I didn't have it, but unfortunately my father died of it at the age of forty-nine in 1933 when I was sixteen. He had it in a very nasty form in that his larynx was affected. He couldn't swallow and could hardly speak, so they had to make a hole in his trachea.

I had never thought of doing anything else besides medicine but that was due at least partly to the influence of the doctor next door. He and his wife had one adopted daughter, but no son, so in a sort of way they adopted me and I used to hop over into their garden and play there. Mrs King, who had been a missionary and had nursed Mary Slessor in Calabar, used to take me out for walks. It was just like another family. Strangely enough, years later I was asked if I would like to be Vice-Chancellor of the University of Calabar.

I started my medical studies in Edinburgh. In school, despite my illnesses and frequent absences, I had done quite well,and got ten prizes. It was rather strange that they gave me *Coral Island* when I was six, and then they gave me the same book as a prize at the beginning of the senior school! Then about five years ago the Headmaster heard about this, when I was asked to give the Address on Founder's Day, and they gave me *Coral Island* again.

Soon after I started university, I had a sudden change of attitude. At school I had experienced a feeling of hopelessness because of my being affected by illnesses. However, in the second week of my medical studies, I thought that maybe my ill health was at last being overcome and that I should work hard, so I began to study hard and so effectively that I got a Certificate of Merit for every subject in the whole medical course together with a number of medals including that for the best student of the year in 1939.

I had everything lined up to be a neuro-surgeon. At that time you negotiated your jobs and I arranged posts with the Professor of Medicine and the Professor of Surgery. At that time Norman Dott was Professor of Neuro-surgery and I was going to be trained by him to be a neuro-surgeon.

The first time I had gone abroad in 1937 I had travelled with another student to Nuremburg in Germany, not knowing that the Nazi Party Conference was on there. We saw Hitler, Goering and Hess and we saw the SS Storm-troopers. We noticed Japanese there too and we knew that war was likely to come, except that we believed the British Government somehow would be able to prevent a conflict. We felt then that Austria was going to be invaded, as indeed it was the next year. Then of course Chamberlain flew to Munich. Just then by chance I was testing out a camera in a youth hostel and I got a picture of me reading a paper about Chamberlain's flight. That happened in a remote area of the Western Highlands of Scotland. Our group of students returned to Edinburgh to find that we were on the brink of war.

When I qualified in 1939 I went down with most of my colleagues and signed for military service. I volunteered for the RAF and resigned from my surgical jobs. This was in fact a mistake for there was a delay in the call-up for the RAF and I now had no surgical job to go to. There was a vacancy in the out patients department and I did that as a fill-in. Then I was directed to the Astley Ainslie Hospital, also in Edinburgh, which at that time was dealing only with the military. As this was also just a holding job, I asked for my call-up to be expedited and then went into the Army, where I was posted first to a field ambulance in Chester-le-Street. Somehow or other a fire occurred there and my recollection is of the quartermaster throwing his ledgers into the flames, while the CO sat on the lawn drinking whisky and directing operations. From there I went to be medical officer of the 2/4th South Lancashire Regiment. There was a problem of communication as they couldn't understand what I said and I couldn't understand what they said but somehow we managed.

I was posted to Catterick military hospital as a graded physician, in other words a medical specialist, not as a major but a captain. I had two experiences I remember in Northern Command. One was when two children got lost in a minefield at Redcar. There were no charts or plans available as the mines had been laid by Polish troops and they had moved on. This was when I was with the South Lancashire Regiment. Another officer and I went into the minefield and poked the ground with bayonets, hoping this might distance us slightly from any explosion. In fact, one child had escaped and we saw that the other had been blown to pieces.

The other incident I recollect was an army exercise. I was sent as a medical umpire. There was also a non-medical umpire who had been on for a couple of nights. He asked me if I'd take over and I agreed. Part of my job as umpire was to tell people that they were killed or wounded. I set out to kill in theory the first person I saw. This was a lieutenant of the 4th Coldstream

Guards who was crossing a river. I said to him "You're dead."
He was terribly annoyed, and refused to be 'dead'. I said "I'm
the umpire. You're dead." Then somebody told me "You've just
killed the Marquess of Hartington." He was heir to the Duke of
Devonshire. I said "I'm sorry; it's nothing to do with me. War
is war." Soon afterwards he married the sister of the 1960s
American President John Kennedy. He was in the Normandy
landings and sadly he was killed just as I had theoretically killed
him in the exercise. It was later said that the bad luck of the
Kennedys started with the death of the Marquess of Hartington.

I was sent on to 23 Casualty Clearing Station near
Chichester, in tents in the grounds of Goodwood House. I was
involved in the preparations for an invasion exercise which we
thought was the real thing, but it wasn't and I got rather tired
of hanging around. I did all I could while we waited for our
exercise. I did some work in the local hospital and I arranged
meetings with the local GPs, but then the invasion was postponed
and I volunteered for an immediate overseas posting. I hoped to
go to Italy, where all the action was, but late in 1943 I was sent
on a tropical medicine course before setting off for an unknown
destination. We zig-zagged across the Atlantic almost to the
mouth of the St Lawrence, for there were packs of German
submarines on the look-out for convoys. We got safely across
into the Med. and were just off Algiers with the RAMC band on
board giving a concert, when the alarm went and we took up
action stations. My station was on the top deck. As my sergeant
I had the leader of Victor Sylvester's orchestra. The two of us
could see German planes coming. There was something strange
about this attack. There were things, a kind of bomb, that were
released from underneath the planes. As they came towards us
we did not know what they were. On our port side was a ship
that had joined the convoy. We didn't know what the ship was
but it was close enough for us to see that it was full of American
troops. One of these bombs dropped right in the middle of
it. The convoy of course had to sail on and the ship was left
blazing. There were over a thousand casualties, this being the
greatest troop transport disaster of the war. It was the first
attack on a convoy by glider bombs.

My sergeant and I saw a bomb dropping on us but it fell close
by in the water. We were soaked but the bomb itself didn't

explode. We wondered at the time if workers in the factories in Europe, possibly the Czechs and others, were sabotaging the Germans' war effort by tampering with some bombs and making them useless. It was a possibility.

We sailed on and were bombed again near Crete. We landed at Cairo just around the time of the conference between Churchill, Roosevelt and Chiangkai-Shek. They were trying to get Turkey to join the war but the Turkish President was unwilling. Eventually we set off for India and went first to Deolali, on which, years later, the TV programme *It Ain't Half Hot, Mum* was based. I was the best part of a year there, very busy medically in a general hospital which took both Indian and British troops.

I was doing research on my own in my spare time because I was interested in anaemia. At that time there were many more medical casualties on the fighting front in Burma than there were surgical ones. A serious problem was a strange form of anaemia associated with diarrhoea and a sore tongue. The Brigadier discovered that I was working on anaemia at the very time that they wanted someone to investigate this disease which was causing such a vast number of casualties, so I was immediately attached to GHQ, New Delhi. They didn't know what to call me but gave me the title of Nutrition Research Officer. GHQ wanted me to investigate malnutrition and decided to call me and the sergeant the Forward Malnutrition Unit. I said this was stupid as it was giving propaganda to the Japs and they should call us the Forward Marasmus Unit. It would have been good propaganda for the Japs to be able to say that our troops were suffering from malnutrition.

From then on I was allowed to post myself wherever I wanted in order to do my research. I wrote my own movement orders and sent them up to GHQ, where they were initialled and returned to me. They had to choose somewhere for me to go to find the largest number of people suffering from this strange disease. The best place seemed to be Sirajgunj on the west bank of the Brahmaputra river in what is now Bangladesh. There were two lines of evacuation through Sirajgunj, coming by river from the fighting front in Burma, and via a transit hospital like the one in the TV programme *Mash*. I was warned there would be eccentrics there, because it was so isolated, an example being the CO who kept pigs and goats.

The hospital was right on the edge of the jungle. The place was a township with a local bazaar, miles from anywhere. The only entertainment was a little local Indian cinema. It was a busy hospital and I was on the look-out for this strange disease which caused severe anaemia. The trouble was that during the time I was there the epidemic had stopped and no cases came through at all. I was very busy doing other research for GHQ, but when I say research, nothing was done that would harm any individual. We didn't have any real scientific apparatus and couldn't do anything really major. My sergeant had been ill and I didn't see much of him at that time so I was on my own carrying out the research side and reporting to GHQ.

It may be thought there weren't any Japanese prisoners of war at that period but there were and later I was sent back to Sirajgunj to assess their medical condition and to do blood counts, as many were anaemic. There were also a larger number of JIFs (Japanese Indian Forces). These were Indians who had deserted to the Japs. We didn't blame them too much for doing that, knowing that many had surrendered to save their own lives and that at the first opportunity they deserted back to the British. There was no resentment and as far as we were concerned patients were patients, whether British, Japanese or Indian, but I may say that at the end of the war three of the officers of the INA (Indian National Army) were put on trial in Delhi and sentenced to deportation. However, Field Marshal Auchinleck commuted the sentences and no action was taken. The INA officer who had been leader of the Indian National Army, Sundra Bose, couldn't be tried as he was killed in a plane crash in Tokyo.

In 1945 I was sent to Dhaka (Dacca) in what is now Bangladesh where I was in a purely Indian hospital with a lot of Indian patients and Indian staff. I had to do all my research in Urdu for many of the patients couldn't speak English. At last I saw patients suffering from the disease that causes anaemia and diarrhoea. A condition called tropical sprue is fairly common in Europeans who go to India and the Far East, but up till then it was said you didn't get the condition in Indians. In fact I'm quite sure that the patients I was now seeing were suffering from tropical sprue in an epidemic form and I'm sure it was due to a virus but there was no way that could be investigated at that time. The patients responded to treatment with injections of liver extract which we now know supplies folic acid.

The epidemic passed and I suggested I could do better things as there were no more patients to investigate and treat. I called into Calcutta and Sister Williams with whom I had been on friendly terms in Sirajgunj was there. We went out to the Tollygunj golf course and on the side of the bunker on the 18th hole I suggested we should get married. We rushed off and got a ring and then I moved on to my next posting which was actually back to Dhaka. A fortnight later I got a message saying I should come back to Calcutta ready for overseas service, which was probably meant to be the invasion of Singapore.

I arrived in Calcutta on the Sunday morning, dashed to the hospital where my fiancé was and said "Let's get married." She said "I've got nothing to wear." To which I replied that she should get something. We grabbed a taxi, rushed to the church, had the banns called and were married on the Tuesday, which was possible in the Church of Scotland under a war-time dispensation. Then I was all ready to set off but on August 6th the atom bomb was dropped, six days after our wedding, when I was on my way to Rangoon. We didn't realise it then, but that changed everything. Incidentally, I think I must have been the only person in the British Army to get hardship allowance for his honeymoon, for I discovered if it was disrupted, I could get such an allowance, which I claimed and received.

I had set off for Rangoon but then the invasion of Singapore was called off and when the ship got as far as Chittagong it was turned back and I returned to Calcutta.

I set off for Rangoon once more, where I had to investigate people let out of the Japanese prison camps. I was still being controlled from India, which was unusual, as most people were in a different Command from me. The men from the Japanese prison camps included British, Australians and Dutch. They were evacuated fast; nothing was done to stop them going home.

I was given, along with an eye specialist, a ward full of people who were blind. There was some unknown vitamin deficiency which caused blindness. Because of my previous work I had with me crates of liver extract used for forms of anaemia. Before and after the blind people were treated with liver injections I had their eyes tested by the eye specialist and where the blindness had not gone too far, there was an improvement in their vision. We gave them other vitamins as well.

Eventually it was time to go home but I was first of all made officer in charge of the medical division of a British general hospital in Rangoon. It was really past the time for my release but officers in charge of medical divisions were delayed. Already I had been offered a job as a lecturer in medicine in Edinburgh, but there was a problem. I was in South East Asia Command in Rangoon and my wife was in India Command in Calcutta and there was a regulation that if you were in South East Asia Command you couldn't go home by India Command. I had been an independent unit so long I didn't pay too much attention to regulations and wrote my own posting order and got on a ship for Calcutta. But there was trouble there and I found that in the main street in Calcutta I was the only British serviceman in uniform. The whole place was out of bounds as there were riots going on. The 'quit India' difficulties had already started, for this was 1946. A truck-load of Gurkhas came along and I stopped them and asked them to drive me to the hospital. I got there, collected my wife and got movement orders to go to the Reinforcement Camp back in Deolali where I had to go for discharge.

We were sent to Bombay and I was put in charge of the train as, being a lieutenant-colonel, I was the senior officer on board. It was a shuttered train and the troops had their rifles at the ready lest we were attacked, for there had been riots in Bombay. They thought the train might be a target, but it wasn't and we got on board the Polish ship, the *Batory*.

On April 1st, 1946 I started my duties as a lecturer in Edinburgh. I was a lecturer, then a senior lecturer, then a Reader. Then in 1962 the Chair of Therapeutics fell vacant. (Therapeutics deals with the treatment side of illness). When I graduated there was almost no medical treatment as we know it today. Tender loving care was most often the thing. There was no treatment for tuberculosis of any value; there were no antibiotics; sulphonamides had just come in; almost none of the modern drugs existed. But they were coming in during my years as a professor, and the Department changed its name from Therapeutics to Therapeutics and Clinical Pharmacology. It wasn't enough to know about which drugs to use; we had to know how they worked as well. The Therapeutics name has now gone and the Chair is that of Clinical Pharmacology.

At first I was very much a laboratory research worker working mainly with matters I had been stuying in India. For example, sprue was a condition that still existed and you could get a similar kind of anaemia in pregnancy which had quite often been fatal before the war. We treat it now with a few tablets of folic acid. We got the early supplies of folic acid in Britain and tried that, and then vitamin B12 came in for pernicious anaemia. There was a lot of research possible at that time. In 1948–49 I went to the University of Michigan in America for a year and learned methods of measuring the vitamins in the blood and came back and applied this.

My son was born in 1947 and my daughter in 1949 when I was away in America. At that time (1948–49) they paid so little on research grants you couldn't take your wife but I doubt whether this would be acceptable now.

At that time, in fact, I was pretty well starving in America. The only time I got proper protein was when I got baked heart on the hospital menu. The other thing was that you weren't allowed to take any money at all out of Britain. I wasn't the only one with that problem. I remember wandering round with Professor Witts from Oxford at an international meeting, look-ing for some place cheap enough to eat at. While I wanted somewhere to stay, I saw a building on a wall on which it said '7 Up'; I thought that meant it was seven dollars and above and I couldn't afford that much! This was a rather trying time, financially, but scientifically it was very valuable.

In my professorship I was mainly supervising other people doing laboratory research, although I did some myself, but on top of that I became Dean of the Faculty of Medicine, which was in addition to my professional and clinical duties. This was in 1976. It was a three years stint but I did four years as there were all sorts of problems. Money was being redistributed from the medical faculty to other faculties: staff was being cut. A new curriculum was coming in yet again. There was a decision by one committee after another to have a new curriculum. The Dental School was another problem, and we tried to reorganise and arrange for a new one to be built. There were an awful lot of committees. On the one hand I had been a scientific worker, going abroad on certain occasions to give scientific lectures, although fundamentally I was a clinician looking after patients (I estimate about 250,000 during my working career). In the university, in the Faculty of Medicine I was on various committees and also on some at St Andrews House and elsewhere in Edinburgh and London. The Dean was virtually unpaid in Edinburgh. The Deanship was not a full-time post as in some universities. There was however an Executive Dean whose job is full-time. My departmental secretary had to do the filing for all the committees I was on and she told me I was on 120 committees! So on top of looking after my patients, giving lectures, being the Dean, being the professor, I was on all these committees. It meant working almost from morning until midnight seven days a week.

I came to a stage where, when I wasn't overworked, I took migraine: proper migraine. This does happen; it is an accepted thing. I had terrible migraine headaches if I had a slack period. This still happens although I am now constantly busy writing and using a word processor.

When I retired I might have had trouble through lack of work, but I became President of the Royal College of Physicians in Edinburgh almost immediately. If you are retired you can spend your whole day with this commitment.

I went in every morning at nine and came home at half-past four or five. With a treasurer who had been a student with me, we ran the College. Where the London College has a staff of about eighty we had a staff of about eight, although we were doing similar work. The most important thing, I had been advised, was to visit our overseas Fellows. Fifty two percent of our Fellows were overseas. Although people think of the Royal College of Physicians in Edinburgh as being a Scottish thing, it is not; it is international. We have more Fellows south of Watford than we have in Scotland.

The overseas visits became very important but when I went abroad it was only on invitation. I was invited to Pakistan, India, Bangladesh, Burma and so on. In 1983 I was in Kuala Lumpur and Calgary in the same week. In 1984 I was in Egypt and Burma and later that year in Singapore and Bangladesh and Montreal. In 1985 we organised our first overseas meeting of the Edinburgh College of Physicians, which was held in Hong

Kong, with an official visit to China as well. Later that year I was in Pakistan, Australia and Malaysia.

My task on these visits was left to the local people to organise. I had no idea when I arrived what I was going to do. On one occasion I would have to give a lecture and on another attend one. Sometimes I would have to go round a ward. Again I might be asked to inspect a hospital and sometimes to see outpatients.

I did no private work and have never seen a private patient in my life. I don't like the idea of people who are ill paying money, but don't see why they should not do so if they wish. I have always been willing to see them but I've not been willing to see them as private patients. It's just that I personally didn't want to do private medicine. The best service in Edinburgh for acute illness is through the National Health Service. But if people are suffering from pain in their hips – and this is the case I've come across most where there is a long delay, why should they suffer for two or three years when they can afford to get it done at once?

When I stopped university employment, I thought it was not right to interfere and I've never gone back except when somebody wanted to discuss something with me. Similarly when I stopped being President of the College of Physicians, although I go back to use the library and attend quarterly meetings, I have never interfered.

There are various *Who's Who*s for which I have to fill up forms, where I put myself down as a medical author, as I am still writing a lot. I've been editor and part author of *Clinical Pharmacology*, a book that is actually over a hundred years old and originally had a different title. I became editor about ten years ago. It was then becoming old fashioned so a group of us rewrote it. We didn't read the previous edition but we wrote a new book. It was terribly successful, so successful that it was pirated and is now floating all round the Middle and Far East. As a result, neither the publishers nor I get any payment for it, but I don't mind as we didn't write it to make money but to educate people. There's another, a *Text-book of Medical Treatment* which first came out in 1939 with a new edition recently, for which another professor and myself were editors. Another one, of which I have written part, is about the side effects of drugs in the blood. Then there was one about malabsorption, which was based partly on the work I had done in India. In addition I've contributed to about three hundred medical papers and journals.

More recently I have gone into medical history and have written quite a lot of articles which have been published in a variety of journals.

We have a son who is a lawyer and a daughter who is a doctor; a GP whose husband is an obstetrician. My daughter-in-law is a nurse, doing night duty several nights a week.

What has given me most satisfaction in a long life in medicine is the fact that I was able to do scientific research work and yet concentrate on the fact that patients are individuals and should be treated as such.

Royal Army Medical Corps

MAJOR-GENERAL F.M. RICHARDSON
CB, DSO, OBE, MD, FRCP (Ed.)

I WAS born in 1904 and went to a prep. school at St Andrews where I was over-educated in the classics and under-educated in everything else. I went on to Glenalmond in Perthshire from 1917 to 1921 and from there to Edinburgh University as a medical student. After qualifying, I was a house physician to Professor William Ritchie and house surgeon to Sir Henry Wade. In those days we thought Edinburgh was the only respectable place to do medicine, apart from Heidelberg. I was a medical student from 1921 to 1926, then did the house jobs and in 1927 went into the RAMC and was there for thirty-three years.

The first thing to learn was how to be an Army doctor. For me that wasn't so difficult as I had been in the OTC and knew how to form fours and play around on the parade square. I must say I wasn't so keen on that side as on doctoring soldiers. I had to learn how to organise medical services in war. I was posted to York where I enjoyed association with the 5th Fusiliers, then to India for about four years. I was first in Lucknow, and in Lebong near Darjeeling. I became doctor to the 1st Battalion of the Duke of Cornwall's Light Infantry, 32nd Foot. I enjoyed that and got to know them all very well. I went with them on a ten day march and it was there I took up polo and pig-sticking. Unfortunately it was to lead literally to my downfall. I was riding a pony that didn't belong to me, on a long trek in the

Himalayas with a Ghurka officer and a gunner. My horse fell and I suffered severe injuries to my neck which caused other complications, so I was invalided home. That was in 1933.

My work in India had been mainly looking after the health of soldiers and some locals. I didn't get to know the native population as I should have liked, as my job was primarily with the Army.

In those days in India we hadn't the antibiotics we have now. There were cases of typhoid and pneumonia which carried people off and on occasions the doctor would do no more than go into the ward and look wise. The patient was really healed by the nurses. The nurse should have had full credit for any who recovered from pneumonia or typhoid in those days. Then of course one had to look after the soldiers' families. You had to be very careful with the children: tummy upsets could have unfortunate consequences. If children got gastro-enteritis they could die like little squashed grapes. I saw very little of Indian soldiers. My work was mainly with the British Army.

After I was fit I went up to Fort George on the Moray Firth. It was here I carried on my education as a piper by going every weekend to the great John Macdonald. I had previously been learning pibroch under Willy Ross in the Castle. At Fort George I co-operated a lot with the local doctor who looked after the soldiers if I happened to be away. I looked after his patients if he was on leave.

Automatically after ten years service we became majors and we were very favourably treated. You see, we doctors had a trade union which nobody else in the Army had. That was the British Medical Association. Pay and promotion were good and they insisted on good conditions for doctors.

I was posted to the Territorial Army as an Adjutant as it was called in those days – to a field ambulance which was in Dundee while my quarters were in Perth. It was here I met my wife.

In India there had not been much entertainment for the soldiers and when men were convalescing I'd take them out shooting. That was after I'd got the use of a car which I hadn't at the beginning. There was one occasion when one of the soldiers inadvertently shot a peacock. That was all right in certain parts of India but in this village it was held sacred and we had to run for it. Sometimes, indeed, we used to have peacock instead of turkey for Christmas dinner. The flesh was rather dry.

By 1938 when the talk was of war, I was involved with the 51st Highland Division. I was dispatched to India, again as senior medical officer, at a station in Cawnpore. India at this stage was slow in coming to grips with the war and, as the months went on, although I applied every month to be employed more actively, I was able to take two skiing holidays of a fortnight each in Kashmir. Even though by now it was 1940, the Indian Government was unbelievably slow to make use of the people who wanted to get into the real war. However, at last I was posted to command an Indian field ambulance, and took it to the Sudan. That was Christmas, 1940. I had five British soldiers and all the rest were Indians. We did endless training and endless marching and then we joined the invasion of Eritrea, held by the Italians. I had to make the unit climb mountains as hard as I could. Years later one of my soldiers came to see me. He said he and another soldier had been on a three months' march in Poland as prisoners of war captured at Tobruk. He said he only survived his march in Poland because of his training with Frank Richardson. We really got them fit for the invasion of Eritrea, so that we were able to climb mountains and take casualties from the battlefield down to a dressing station. The forward collection of battle casualties and first aid was really our preoccupation.

The country where the fighting took place was very difficult. There was the battle of Keren on Mount Dologorodoc. It was part of the mountain range that blocked our passage to the main town of Keren. Opposing us were Italians, reputedly among the best regiments of Italy under the generalship of a general known as the Lion of Keren. They had also black Askaris, Eritreans I suppose, natives of Italian East Africa. We were part of the Indian 5th Division and had the Worcestershire Regiment and also the Frontier Force and the Punjabi Rifles, which my cousin Roland had served in when he was subaltern – but by this time he was a general. We also had the Third Punjab Regiment.

When we got beyond Dologorodoc I was given sixty stretcher bearers from our Indian regiments. Sad to say, some of them ran away. I've always taught soldiers there is nothing unusual or uncommon to be ashamed of in feeling fear. Once soldiers realise everybody feels afraid, there's a different attitude to it. I've lectured at Staff College at Camberley on this whole battle experience for twenty-one years.

Anyway we got the Italians out of Eritrea and I got a DSO after the battle of Keren.

Later, I went to the Western Desert in command of a field ambulance which supported a forward brigade, the 9th Armoured Brigade, which played an exceptionally valuable part at the battle of El Alamein. Monty, meeting me many years later at the disbandment of the 51st Highland Division, long after I had retired, asked me which part of the British Army I had been attached to. When I told him it was the 9th Armoured Brigade, he said "The 9th Armoured Brigade at Alamein enabled me to win the battle." He repeated it: "To win the battle!" I only wish our regimental commanders had heard him say this. One had lost both his legs. Another had been killed. A third, Sir Peter Parker, is still alive and kicking. He commanded the only regular regiment of the brigade at that time. That was the 3rd Hussars. The territorial or yeomanry regiments were the Royal Worcester Yeomanry and the Warwickshire, and that really comprised the 9th Armoured Brigade of the 5th Indian Division.

After Alamein it was decided we should retire to Syria and lick our wounds. We went to Aleppo and while we were there I had to deal with a train smash. We spent the time retraining, thinking we were going on to the Caucasus. But I was posted back to Britain. That was in 1944 and they were collecting people with combat experience to get ready for D Day.

The 49th Division wanted a field ambulance and I was posted to that and the unit became a member of the follow-up Division. We followed up on D plus six and didn't face the fierce opposition of D Day. Our first battle was in the general area of Caen at Fontenay. You had to learn who was going to be any good in battle. One of my company commanders was not and he was sent back to a hospital to carry out excellent work in anaesthetics. You can't expect every doctor to be any good in battle for they're not really trained for that grim experience. In any case it isn't proper to waste highly trained lives if you can avoid it. I think you do well in battle frequently to take the trouble to convince yourself you are not as frightened as you really are. It is not easy convincing yourself under fire and there's no point in pretending a person really likes it. There were two things I hated more than words can tell. One was mortars which can slip in with a slithery noise and the other was mines.

I was operating as a lieutenant-colonel at the time of the Normandy bridgehead, which seemed to go on for ever. But eventually we broke through. We went on to take part in the siege of Le Havre. The Germans put up a tremendous resistance there. With our shelling you wouldn't have thought rabbits could have lived in the ground. Latterly they withdrew and all we were shelling were their empty forward dug-outs.

The soldiers got very tired. No beer had come through and they were drinking local Benedictine liqueur. We drank it with all our meals until I couldn't have looked at another drop. It was not at all up the soldiers' street. We reached St Valery where I got some flowers to put on the grave of a cousin of mine who had been killed during the withdrawal. He had been second in command of the Lothian and Border Horse. He had a famous name in brewing circles – Harry Younger. He had been killed by our own soldiers, due to the kind of muddle that happened in those days. The Lothian and Border Horse Yeomanry wore a distinctive kind of uniform. They had lain up in the loft or attic of a barn and some Gordon Highlanders by mistake firing up through the roof, killed my cousin and blinded his commanding officer.

We went on through Belgium and Holland in beastly weather conditions and fetched up on what is called the Island of Nijmegen. This was after the battle of Arnhem. I'd take people who visited my unit to climb up the church and look across at the Germans walking about in Arnhem.

About the time of the Ardennes offensive there was a determined attempt to break through. This battle was a most unpleasant affair, for the shells opened up graves which were lined with stones on the recovered land and the bodies were thrown out of the cemeteries, an unpleasant spectacle. A very fanatical young German officer was admitted wounded to my unit and asserted that Germany was going to win the war. It wasn't up to me to disillusion him.

I was posted as ADMS (Assistant Director of Medical Services) to a Division that in my opinion was most distinguished, the 15th (Scottish) Division. This was, you might say, Monty's centre-forward in the attack. Our first job was to play centre-forward in the Reichswald and Rhine battles, the advance through Germany and the crossing of the Elbe.

The first devastated German town we saw was Goch. Our propagandists scored a victory there. There were signs all the way for the roads were all blocked. The signs were in English and German. They read 'Give me five years and you won't recognise Germany – Adolf Hitler.'

I'll tell you a story about the Germans scoring a minor propaganda victory. This was just after the war, when the fighting had stopped. Our chief engineer had cleared a whole village and was ready to blow up one of the bunkers. He had laid charges and everybody waited for the explosion. When that happened the building shuddered a little but stayed put. The next morning in ten feet high letters somebody had painted on it, MADE IN GERMANY! Don't tell me no Germans have a sense of humour!

We settled down to plan the next stage, the Rhine crossing. I was responsible for the medical services of the Division. There were three field ambulances under my command, providing casualty collecting posts, CCPs, from which the casualties were evacuated to advanced dressing stations and thence to the casualty clearing stations, CCSs.

During the planning of the Rhine crossing my Commanding Officer, Tiny Barbour, gave me leave to go back to Britain. Coincidentally I was able to attend the christening of my first child.

For the Rhine crossing I had an American battalion medical unit put under my command, the colonel of which kept addressing me as Sir and Colonel! I had to find them a place to cross the Rhine and plan for their crossing. I managed to get medical units across the Rhine to get forward positions set up overnight, to deal with possible casualties. There were very many vehicles crossing the river and a problem was to get casualties back without damaging the ramps which the Royal Engineers had built. With so many vehicles crossing, storm boats and God knows what, they had to stop work when darkness fell because they would damage the ramps. I happened to be absent from the left hand side of our attack where things were not going well and here the second-in-command of one of my field ambulances acted in a manner which would have won him a Victoria Cross in the last war and a Military Cross in this one. His name was Ian McCallum; he is now retired and living in Edinburgh, having been a skin specialist after the war. I was away when a DDMS of the Army arrived and said "Casualties must be got across." His order resulted in the breaking down and damaging of some of the crossing places. It resulted in him having to go later and apologise to the Corps Commander. This illustrates one small point, that in battle the doctor who says casualties must come first and must be given priority over every other consideration, is wrong. Attainment of the objective of the battle is the first priority and to damage these ramps, which were necessary to attain that objective, in a battle that had caused the loss of several men when they came under small-arms fire as they crossed the river, was wrong, even if the ramps were damaged under fire in getting men across the river. It may be all right in relation to doctoring but it is all wrong in relation to soldiering. If the objective doesn't take first place, there will be more casualties.

We advanced through Germany fighting battles all the way and dealing with casualties. I finished up at the Elbe with the 15th Scottish again. The job of crossing the Elbe was harder than the Rhine crossing. Germany was at its last gasp and was putting up the most tremendous resistance. They flew kamikazi-type missions from the Hamburg autobahn and perhaps the most stubborn opposition was shown by formations of young naval cadets. Our Division received the first offer of the Germans of surrender. Our Divisional Commander, Tiny Barbour, requested myself and the CRA, Commander Royal Artillery, to be present. He was the only man in the Division who wore a flat hat with the red band round: the rest of us wore balmorals. He and I changed hats so as not to be identified when the surrender party turned up. One was an admiral who eventually committed suicide. Later the overall surrender was taken by Monty on Lunenberg Heath at the scene everybody knows about. After that things were very ordinary.

I was on duty in Germany till 1948. The Division was disbanded, and I moved to be ADMS, Assistant Director of Medical

Services of the 51st Highland Division. Then for the first time I became Commanding Officer of a large hospital at Münster. After a bit there I was sent to command an even bigger military hospital at Hamburg, with two thousand beds. We employed a great many Germans. A German who played the violin co-operated with us. Another German, Peter Konstam, a Jew who had been an anti-Nazi, and who later became a very popular surgeon in Orkney and is now retired, played the piano. So we had Mozart's piano sonatas with Peter at the piano and this charming fellow playing the violin.

I was now ADMS of the district, which included Schleswig-Holstein. It was quite hard work and by this time my wife, daughter and son had come out to join me. My son is now in Kuala Lumpur and my daughter Jenny is a very capable artist in Comrie and is well known there.

In 1949 I was posted to Tripoli in North Africa, in those days under the rule of King Idris. I was with the 1st Infantry Division under the command of Sir Horatius Murray, who was once Commander-in-Chief in Scotland, a splendid man who is now blind and living in a nursing home. He was a distinguished athlete and a great tennis player and actually had kept goal for the Army soccer team. He was a very challenging person to serve with. I was in Tripoli till about 1951. My wife and family had gone home and I stayed behind to help with the planning of what we believed might lead to the Third World War. This was the dangerous situation in the Persian Gulf which had been caused by Mossadeq. Fortunately it never came to anything but there had been talks about possible landings up the Shatt-al-Arab waterway at the confluence of the Tigris and Euphrates rivers.

I was then sent home to do a job at the War Office as Inspector of Training, for which I became a Brigadier. That involved getting around the country and making contacts with invaluable people in the Territorial Army. Then I went back to Germany as head doctor of the 1st British Corps. After a short time there, my superior officer, Jimmy Hall who had lost a leg long before the war because of an explosion of an artillery piece, had to leave for fitness reasons and I took his job as DMS and became a Major-General. My post was in the town of Viersen close to the headquarters of the Rhine Army. I was in this job for five years.

When I retired in 1962, I organised the Army Benevolent Fund as District Officer here in Scotland. Then I became Medical Adviser for Civil Defence in Scotland, and was involved in lecturing to a wide variety of people: doctors, nurses and so on. We were located at Taymouth Castle, until Mr Wilson disbanded the Civil Defence Corps.

In 1965 I started writing books. I wrote two books on Napoleon, also *The Fighting Spirit*, in which, through the eyes of a doctor, I examined morale, in my experience as much a matter for treatment as a bullet wound. This book recasts my lectures at Staff College, Camberley to British and Commonwealth officers. Another book I wrote I called *Florence and Helen*. This was based on letters written by Florence Nightingale to my great-aunt Helen. Florence was loved by four men. She could have married but she didn't. She said the only person for whom she ever felt genuine passion was her female cousin Marian Nicholson. I have the letters written to my great-aunt and they form the last chapter of the book.

In those days after the war I could still play the pibroch. But eventually I found I couldn't play because the disability in my neck prevented me from tuning the bagpipe for you can't do one without the other. But I went on judging till about 1973 and I was convener of piping at the Northern Meeting in Inverness. Among other things I was responsible for selecting the judges. I was succeeded by Colonel David Murray, a very distinguished piper and he in turn was succeeded by another friend Brigadier Rory Walker. Piping gave me a lot of pleasure.

My earlier life as an army doctor was an eventful and fulfilling one.

Medical Missionary

DR JOHN WILKINSON

EARLY one morning in January, 1947 I stood on the deck of a Union Castle steamship, which had just dropped anchor off the port of Mombasa in East Africa to await the coming of the pilot. Spread out before me were sandy beaches with their mango and palm trees, and scattered amongst the trees were the huts and houses in which people were beginning to stir, while a new day dawned. For me it was to be a notable day, because in a few hours I would be landing there to begin the work I had been looking forward to for many years.

Ever since I was a boy at school I had been conscious of God's call to be a medical missionary. I had been brought up in Newcastle-upon-Tyne and there I was a member of the congregation of St Andrew's Church of Scotland. Its minister at that time was the Revd Dr Horace R.A. Philp, who had been the pioneer medical missionary at Tumutumu in what was then called British East Africa. There was no doubt that he was a great influence in my decision to train as a medical missionary.

After I left school, I was accepted for the medical course at Edinburgh University and also as a student of the Edinburgh Medical Missionary Society (EMMS). So began five happy years of student life in the company of those who like myself were intending to become medical missionaries.

We were very fortunate in our teachers at medical school. Several of them were doctors with an international reputation who belonged to the last generation of general physicians and surgeons, before the advance of medical knowledge gave rise to increasing specialisation and the fragmentation of medicine. They combined their expertise in medicine with a fine ability to teach. They trained us in a clinical medicine which depended more on the use of ears, eyes and hands and less on laboratory investigations, diagnostic imaging and endoscopic examination than is the case today. This was good training for a situation in which these facilities were not to be available, as they were not in my own case once I reached East Africa.

One of the advantages of being a student of the EMMS was the extra practical training provided by the Society in the Livingstone Dispensary in the Cowgate in Edinburgh. There students of the Society learned to dress wounds, to extract teeth and to dispense medicines. Later in their course they became resident in the dispensary as 'Coogate doctors' under the supervision of the resident physician. All this was invaluable clinical and social experience in what was then a densely populated area of old Edinburgh. During my time in the dispensary I was able to do extra work as a medical student in the Deaconess Hospital in the Pleasance, which was then a Church of Scotland hospital but in 1948 was taken over by the new National Health Service.

I had early taken an interest in theology and so after I qualified in medicine in July 1941, I went on to study theology at New College in the University of Edinburgh. After I had completed my first year there, I was called up for service with the Royal Army Medical Corps, as the Second World War had begun while I was still a medical student.

Most of my army service was spent with a casualty clearing station, which during active operations is the first point at which specialist surgical treatment of the wounded is available, and at other times cares for both medical and surgical cases, as required. This gave me invaluable experience in acute surgical and medical diagnosis and treatment which was to stand me in good stead when I arrived in East Africa. My unit took part in the invasion of North Africa as part of the First Army, and I went ashore with the initial landing at Algiers in November 1942. It then moved east with the Fifth Corps as they advanced towards Tunis. Once the campaign was over in North Africa, the unit took over the Italian Hospital in Tunis and served as a general hospital for troops in the Tunis area.

In the various quiet periods in the fighting in Tunisia and after the fighting was over, I was able to visit some of the main archaeological sites there. In fact, at one time I was on temporary detachment from my unit to provide medical care for a company of Royal Engineers who were camped beside the ruins of the important Roman city of Thurburbo Maius. I was thus able to indulge my interest in archaeology at first hand. Later when I was in Tunis I got to know the Director of the famous Bardo Museum there, and learned from him, and from the exhibits he so lovingly cared for, a great deal about the archaeology of Tunisia and North Africa in general.

After the capture of Sicily my unit crossed the Mediterranean to land at Taranto and join the Eighth Army. Then began the slow advance up the Adriatic coast through the mud and snow of an Italian winter on the eastern slopes of the Apennines. Once the Italian campaign was over I was transferred to a military hospital which had taken over an Italian army barracks at Mestre, which is the mainland town opposite Venice on the Venetian Lagoon.

One bonus during my stay at Mestre was that since we were not very busy medically, I was appointed education officer to the hospital. My main task was to arrange educational tours for the convalescent patients and staff of the hospital. For this purpose I was able to enlist the services of an Italian art historian who had been Professor of Fine Art at Yale University in the United States and who now lived in Venice. With him as guide, I toured Venice and Venetia, arranging tours for the hospital. In the course of this I was able to see many of the artistic treasures of this region, that were not normally shown to visitors. One of the most fascinating places to me was, of course, Padua, with all its historical medical associations and the Arena Chapel fresco cycle painted by Giotto. The sandbags which had protected these frescos during the war were just being removed at that time.

At Mestre we became the referral hospital for the army medical services in the Venice area, and so I was able to gain a great deal of useful experience and training, which stood me in good stead later. My interest had by now become more medical than surgical, and I was recommended for grading as an army medical specialist. However, before my new grading had been approved, I was discharged in order to continue my theological studies.

In due course I completed my studies at New College and was appointed a missionary of the Church of Scotland in July, 1946. In September I was ordained to the ministry of the Church of Scotland by the Presbytery of England in St Andrew's Church in Newcastle, and in December I set sail for Kenya.

The Church of Scotland had begun missionary work in Kenya in 1891 at Kibwezi, midway between Mombasa and Nairobi. In 1893 Mr John Paterson, an agricultural missionary, joined the staff at Kibwezi and for the first time introduced the cultivation of coffee to Kenya. Today, coffee is the main cash crop of the country and one of the mainstays of its economy. However, Kibwezi was found to be an unhealthy place and located in a sparsely populated area and so in 1898 the mission was moved to Kikuyu beyond Nairobi. Then in 1908 work was begun at Tumutumu, followed by the establishment of Chogoria in 1922. Medical work was included in the work at each of these mission stations, and in due course hospitals were built to provide more permanent medical facilities.

In January 1947 I took charge of Tumutumu Hospital, which was the hospital established by Dr Philp in 1910. The origin of the name Tumutumu is unknown, but it was given to a hill sacred to the local Kikuyu people that stood opposite Mount Kenya. It was this mountain which dominated the northern horizon of Tumutumu and was covered with eternal snow and glaciers. It had always provided a mountaineering challenge to the missionaries and they have left their names on its maps. There is even an Arthur's Seat! Tumutumu was about eighty miles north of Nairobi, along what at that time was an earth road which often became impassable due to mud and water in the rainy seasons, of which Kenya, being on the equator, had two. The nearest administrative centre to Tumutumu was Nyeri, about fifteen miles away, also along an earth road. Nyeri was where Lord Baden-Powell, the founder of the Scout movement, spent his last years and now lies buried.

The original building erected by Dr Philp still stands and is still in use. It is a corrugated iron structure with a central hall and various rooms opening off this hall. It was paid for out of a fee which Dr Philp received from caring for an injured American elephant hunter on the slopes of Mount Kenya.

When I assumed charge of the hospital, it had about a hundred beds and provided medical, surgical and obstetric services for the population around. Patients also came from far distances, such was the reputation of the hospital. It had a small leprosy hospital attached to it which was always full. At the time at which I arrived, there was no doctor there. The previous doctor had been an Italian prisoner of war who had been withdrawn for repatriation, and responsibility for the hospital and the patients had devolved on the Scottish matron. The warmth of her welcome reflected her relief at the arrival of a doctor!

It is difficult to imagine the conditions in which the mission staff lived and worked at Tumutumu then. They were housed in stone or corrugated iron houses which were constantly invaded by white ants, which devour wood and paper but do not bite, and sometimes by black ants, which do. The roof spaces of these houses were infested by bats which gave rise to the characteristic unpleasant smell associated with bat infestation. Water was piped from a stream several miles distant and as the pipe ran on the surface of the ground it was at the mercy of anyone who wanted a convenient and free supply of water for his garden. He had only to puncture the pipe with his hoe to obtain it. So there were days when there was no water for house or hospital until the leak had been found and repaired. Water was piped to the hospital and houses, but there was no hot water system in either. Bath water had to be heated in large tins over an open fire outside and then carried in to fill the bath. There was no electricity, and oil or pressure lamps had to be used in the house or in hospital even for operating in the theatre. There was no water-borne sanitation, but only 'the wee hoose' down the garden, as the deep pit latrine was called.

Over the years, of course, conditions have been improved, and it was a great pleasure to me to be able to instal hot water systems and indoor water-borne sanitation in the houses at Tumutumu and so make life a little more comfortable for my colleagues. Also, electricity eventually became available when a local waterfall, on the River Tana near Tumutumu, was harnessed for this purpose. The East African Power and Lighting Company was responsible for this, but because the electric supply was not always reliable, the Company was sometimes called 'The East African Powers of Darkness'! The provision of electricity made a great difference to life in the hospital and the houses. It meant we could have adequate lighting in the wards and especially in the operating theatre at night. Also, we could use refrigerators for the storage of drugs and vaccines, and could instal an X-ray machine and other electrical appliances we had not been able to have before, and this meant we could provide a better service to our patients and more comfort for the staff.

When I arrived at Tumutumu, many wartime restrictions were still in operation. Essential foodstuffs were rationed and drugs were not always obtainable in adequate amounts. Limited supplies of sulphonamide drugs were available but there was no penicillin. The hospital had no X-ray facilities and fractures had to be treated by manipulation without their aid. Some of the diseases I had to treat were unfamiliar and in some cases their effective treatment was unknown or the appropriate medicine was unavailable. This applied to such diseases as tuberculosis and bubonic plague.

Tumutumu was one of the early places from which the protein deficiency disease now called kwashiorkor was described. Dr Gillan, who had been a colleague of Dr Philp's, had written an article in the local *East African Medical Journal* describing the features of the disease, with the result that in East Africa the condition was often called 'Gillan's oedema'. Later the name kwashiorkor was adopted from West Africa.

Another disease which I saw at Tumutumu, and of which I made a special study, was one to which the local African name of onyalai had been given by the doctor who first described it in Angola in 1904. This condition is a disorder of the blood platelets and for some unknown reason is now much less common than it used to be. In a Zambian hospital in 1968 I saw a whole ward full of patients with onyalai, but now it seems to be much less common there, too.

It was my research on onyalai which led me to examine the incidence of disease and the causes of death in the Tumutumu area, which was known administratively as South Nyeri District.

I was able to consult the in-patient and out-patient records of the three hospitals that served the District and so collected a great deal of clinical medical information. This information I then embodied in a thesis which I successfully presented for the degree of Doctor of Medicine of Edinburgh University in 1956.

Another result of my papers on onyalai was that they stimulated my literary interest, for they became the first of many articles that I wrote for a number of medical and theological journals. Eventually, this resulted in the publication of two substantial books, one a study of healing in the New Testament and the other on Christian medical ethics.

I had met missionaries of the North Africa Mission in Tunis and elsewhere, but until I arrived at Tumutumu I had no first-hand experience of life on a mission station as a member of staff. I need not have had any anxiety, for from the first I was accepted as a colleague and given all the support that I required. I was very impressed with the devotion and dedication of my colleagues. The work of missionaries has been much criticised and maligned in recent years, especially by those wishing to find subjects on which they might write books in the current debunking and psychological tradition. Much of this criticism is ill-informed and unbalanced. It is often alleged, for instance, that the early missionaries made no attempt to understand the culture of the people among whom they worked, and in any case were more interested in destroying it than in preserving it. This was certainly not true of the early Scottish missionaries who worked among the Kikuyu people. They systematically studied the religion and culture of the Kikuyu people and sought to show how these were in fact a preparation for the gospel, much as had been the case in New Testament times. They showed how Kikuyu ideas of God resembled those of the Old Testament, especially in the requirement of sacrifice, such as used to be offered on Tumutumu Hill.

Among those who accuse the missionaries of destroying indigenous cultures are students of anthropology, who in the interest of their science wish to see continued all the old practices of the people which were prevalent before the missionaries came. But this is to ignore what is probably the most potent factor in the changes in indigenous cultures, namely, the influence of secular western civilisation. The missionaries may sometimes .

have been responsible for introducing the concepts and practices of such a civilisation because they themselves have come from it and cannot escape its influence. But they did not see the transmission of such an influence as part of their essential task, which was to preach the gospel and to serve the people. In fact, they were often called upon to mediate between the people they served and those who embodied the ideas of secular western civilisation. This was particularly true in those areas of Kenya where European settlers came into contact with the Kikuyu people. This sometimes led to opposition by the settlers to the work of missionaries.

The early missionaries studied the Kikuyu language, which is a Bantu language based on quite different principles from those of the Indo-European family of languages. It was a Scottish missionary who prepared the standard grammar of the Kikuyu language and began to translate the Bible into that language. More recently he did important work in the compilation of an Oxford Kikuyu-English Dictionary. During this work he was very conscious of how the Kikuyu language had been influenced by English words and usage since he had first published his grammar. This is a good example of how outside influences may affect Kikuyu thought and culture.

Most of my patients spoke Kikuyu and not English and so I had to learn Kikuyu in order to be effective in my work, especially as medical misunderstandings can often have humorous, and even disastrous consequences. Because of my double qualification, I had to learn not only how to speak to patients in hospital, but also how to preach to a congregation in church on Sundays.

The policy of the Church of Scotland Mission from the beginning was to concentrate on establishing centres or mission stations where educational, medical and Church facilities were provided for the population. The concentration of facilities in this way meant that all the missionaries were familiar with the work of all the departments of the Mission. One result of this arrangement was that all the Scottish missionaries came to know about the unfortunate results of the Kikuyu custom of female circumcision which produced difficulties for women in childbirth and which were being seen in the Mission hospitals. This meant that the Mission sought to persuade Christian parents not

to accept circumcision for their daughters. This issue was made
a political one by people opposed to the work of the Mission
and led to a secession from the Church, with the formation of
an independent Church movement. Much of my surgical and
obstetric work at Tumutumu was due to the anatomical and
obstetric results of female circumcision, which in some cases
were fatal. This action on the part of the Mission is sometimes
seen as an example of a missionary attack on an indigenous
culture. If this is to be admitted, then it must be in light of the
fact that female circumcision is a custom which may result in the
death of a mother, or more commonly of her child, who cannot
be delivered naturally because of the anatomical result of female
circumcision. It is encouraging to know that this custom is now
officially discouraged in Kenya,and this is a vindication of the
attitude taken up by the missionaries.

The majority of the staff of Tumutumu Hospital were
African, for only the matron and myself were expatriates. I was
very impressed with the work of African nurses and the support
they gave me. Several of the senior staff had been trained by Dr
Philp and still had a high regard for him. One of them was an
excellent anaesthetist and very skilled in the use of chloroform.
When I was operating it was always a comfort to know that he
was giving the anaesthetic. When he was not available, I often
had to anaesthetise the patient myself before scrubbing up to
perform the operation.

Part of my responsibility as medical superintendent was the
maintenance of hospital buildings and equipment. In this I had
the support of the African staff who had been trained in building
and carpentry by missionaries sent out from Scotland to provide
practical training for young Africans. However, practical training of this kind was not popular, for the young people wanted
'real education' from books, and so these 'industrial missionaries',
as they were called, were withdrawn or given other duties. It is
interesting to see how a new emphasis on practical training in
education has now arisen in Kenya because of the need of the
country for artisans and craftsmen.

Although the medical service at Tumutumu was mainly
provided in the hospital, the needs of the community around the
hospital were not forgotten. Six dispensaries or health centres
had been established in the district, staffed by enrolled nurse

grade staff. These were visited regularly by the doctor. These visits were often difficult to achieve in the rainy seasons on muddy roads with no Land Rover to negotiate the mud. They represented the nucleus of a community health service which could be expanded when more staff became available.

After a year at Tumutumu I was transferred to the main station at Kikuyu to make way for a a more senior doctor who was now available for Tumutumu. Kikuyu Hospital had been opened in 1908 and had good stone buildings and X-ray facilities. It was also near Nairobi with access to a referral hospital and good laboratory services, as well as regular medical meetings and conferences. The result was that I could offer a better standard of service to the patients and keep up to date with local medical opinion and practice.

One of my colleagues at Tumutumu was Jean Ewan who had come out from Scotland several months before I had, to take charge of a special teacher training course there. She had received a great welcome as the first post-war missionary to arrive from Scotland. Because of the war there had been no new missionary appointments for eight years and none of the missionaries had been on leave to Scotland for the same period, although some had taken leave in South Africa. After the course was finished Jean was appointed the first headmistress of the Alliance Girls' High School at Kikuyu. This school was the first secondary school for African girls in Kenya and many of the leading women of modern Kenya society were educated there.

In January 1949 Jean and I were married in the Watson-Scott Memorial Church at Kikuyu, and then set off in a borrowed Ford coupé for Moshi in Tanganyika (now Tanzania). We spent part of our honeymoon climbing Mount Kilimanjaro, the highest mountain in Africa, and we reached the highest point of the mountain, which is 19,340 feet high.

After our honeymoon we packed up our things at Kikuyu and set off for Chogoria, about 180 miles to the north of Nairobi on the eastern slopes of Mount Kenya. This is the most isolated of the three hospitals established by the Church of Scotland Mission, and the road in those days became quite impassable in the rainy seasons. However, we moved in the dry season and met dust and not mud. Chogoria, then, became our first home together and there our elder daughter was born. Chogoria has an attraction all of its own, and we came back there in later years with our family of two daughters and a son, and they all look back on their time at Chogoria with great affection. Also, we were able to have our family with us until they went to secondary boarding-school for Jean was able to teach them at home, and this was a great joy to us.

As I gained more experience of the country and its development, I was involved in wider responsibilities in mission and church-related medical work. I took part in consultations and negotiations with Kenya government medical and health officers and national trade union officials, and represented church interests on the Nursing Council of Kenya and numerous other bodies. I was foundation chairman of the organisation which co-ordinates the medical work of the Protestant Churches and Missions in Kenya and continued in that capacity for thirteen years. This gave me the opportunity of visiting church and mission medical facilities in other parts of the country. I was invited to visit other countries in Africa for conferences and surveys, and this allowed me to see the medical services which were being provided by churches and missions in Nigeria, South Africa, Tanzania and Zambia. I was also involved in international conferences on church-related medical and health care work held in Germany, Switzerland, Italy and the United States.

Meantime Kenya was progressing towards independence. In this matter of independence, the church preceded the State so far as the Church of Scotland was concerned. In 1943 the Presbyterian Church of East Africa came into being as an independent body. It arose out of the work of the Church of Scotland and was autonomous, although at first it depended a great deal on the advice and support of the Scottish missionaries. However, it gradually took over responsibility from them and for many years has had complete control of all the work which was originally established by Church of Scotland missionaries. Missionaries do still go out from Scotland to Kenya, but they work under the direction of the Presbyterian Church there now and not under the Church of Scotland. Missionaries are still welcomed as the church is still anxious to preserve its links with the Church of Scotland.

The advance towards political independence in Kenya was

not going so smoothly and we still had to go through the Mau Mau period before independence would come. We were at Tumutumu when the Government declared a state of emergency in order to contain the Mau Mau. This was in October, 1952. When this declaration was made, a company of the King's African Rifles turned up to camp on the school football field and stayed there for most of the acute stage of the emergency. We had a number of incidents during this period. I was performing an emergency Caesarean section one night, when a patient was murdered in the male ward about fifty yards from the operating theatre and almost under the noses of the Home Guard. Then one night one of my expatriate colleagues was attacked in his house and his hand slashed by a gang in search of money.

Independence finally came to Kenya in 1963, a year which found us half-way through a tour of service at Chogoria. The change of government made little difference to us for life continued much as before. Law and order was maintained and the normal processes and services of both central and local government went on. The new government had a sound foundation on which to build, and on which it did build to form a stable modern state.

After home leave in 1966, we returned to Kikuyu where I once again took over charge of the hospital and remained there until we finally left Kenya in 1975. Since our initial arrival at Kikuyu in 1947, the mission station had developed in various ways. The Alliance Boys' High School there had expanded and had been able to put up some fine new buildings to cope with this expansion. The Alliance Girls' High School had expanded, too. The church had established a training centre for church members and elders, and a small primary boarding-school. A little further away but still on church land, there was a teacher training college. All these institutions looked to the hospital for medical services. For most of this time I had a medical colleague, which was a great relief because during much of my earlier service in the church hospitals, I had been the only doctor on the staff of the hospital I was in.

In March 1975 we left Kenya and arrived back in Scotland with our future unknown. A few months later I was appointed a community medicine specialist in the National Health Service in Edinburgh.

This was not our last contact with Kenya, however, for in 1980 I was invited to conduct a survey of church medical work in Malawi and on our return journey from Malawi, my wife and I spent two weeks in Kenya. During this time we visited all three of the hospitals where I had worked. It was a great pleasure to meet my former African colleagues, and to see many former patients who remembered me as the doctor who had treated them or members of their family in the past.

My wife and I look back with great pleasure and happy memories on our time as missionaries in Kenya. It was indeed a great privilege to serve the people of Kikuyuland and to find such real and lasting satisfaction in our service and the opportunity of sharing with them the good news of Jesus Christ.

Hospital Chaplain

THE REVEREND MURDOCH MACBETH MACKAY

THE GREATEST influence for good in my early years was that of my mother, Mary Anne Brown of Aberdeen, who trained as a nurse in fever, general and maternity in Aberdeen, Dundee and London. She was deeply religious and a devout Christian. I can still hear her singing Sankey & Moodie-type hymns as she did her housework. When she was dying of cancer at the early age of fifty-three, I heard her singing very faintly 'Jesu, lover of my soul, let me to Thy bosom fly'.

I was born in Dundee in 1912, where my father had a college to prepare students for what were then compulsory and competitive examinations for the Civil Service. He also pioneered correspondence courses for young people in the Highlands, many of whom won high places in government service.

My father spoke fluent Gaelic and was a good communicator. He understood the Highland peoples' difficulties and needs, having himself been brought up on a Sutherland croft. Life there was, in many of its circumstances, primitive but education and religion had a high priority. In 1913 my father decided to establish a similar college in Canada – the new education act supported and encouraged this. He wasn't there long before the war broke out and nobody was interested in further education or in his college project.

My mother, to keep the home fires burning and feed four growing boys and a husband, went out night nursing. My recollections of Montreal where we stayed, are few. I remember the snow and keen frost and my father going up to a complete stranger and rubbing his face with snow to bring back the circulation and prevent frost bite, and also the windows of homes where stars represented the deaths in France of sons, and of one home with four stars.

We returned to Scotland on the *Empress of France* when the war ended, and settled in the north of Scotland where there was room in our grandfather's house. My grandparents were both dead but the house had been kept for any of the family who needed it. I am glad that my early life was spent in Castletown. It had everything for growing boys, yet nobody was well off. It was a place where you had to do most things for yourself and I believe it developed character and independence. It was a village near the sea and, unlike most of Caithness, it had trees.

There was a three-mile stretch of sand washed by the Gulf Stream where we taught ourselves to swim in the bay. We fished from the rocks and, when hungry, jumped over the dyke behind us to grab a turnip from the field to satisfy our need. Farmers never objected to us taking one and employed us to 'howk' turnips, rewarding us with a pail of milk. It was a barter economy in those days. There were rabbits in the quarries for the pot and white fish from the salmon fishers who did white fishing, too. These fishermen came from Johnshaven with their families for the season, year by year, and they were all MacBays by name. Some married and remained.

The village school was thorough. We could take our Higher Certificate there and go on to university and many, like myself, did so. What enabled Caithness pupils to get to university were the bursaries given by the Carnegie Trust, which paid our fees. I had an additional bursary that almost paid my digs, which were 22s.6d. per week for full board.

The village street was a mile long, of houses built by the villagers from reject stones from the quarries. The sawmills cut flagstones and exported them to London from the harbour, for paving stones. Some of them are still there today. It is a very hard stone, but the arrival of cement finished the industry. You can see these flagstones in cotters houses on the floor, scrubbed smooth and clean by the housewife, and in use by farmers for dykes to shelter animals from the Caithness winds.

We had little pocket money and couldn't buy tennis racquets or golf clubs so we had to depend on team games like football and netball. We got about on cycles, if we had them. I remember riding on the back step of my brother's cycle to my very first football match to play at Halkirk seven miles away, yes, and all the way back. I liked football and played wherever I went and didn't give it up until I was fifty years old.

I would not have changed life in that village for any other place and still go back to it as often as I can. As people in the village lived together, so they died, and were buried in the local cemetery side by side – tinkers and tailors, soldiers and sailors, some who made their names in the outside world in peace and in war and came back to retire, and those who never left it.

My football career began with that game at Halkirk when I was only twelve. The top game in the north was between Caithness and Sutherland and I was still at school when I represented Caithness. Later, I played for Aberdeen University, was captain and a soccer 'blue'. Aberdeen Football Club asked me to play but I preferred to keep my amateur status. Then followed a trial for Scotland. At university I was President of the Athletic Association and was able to encourage others to take part and not leave university without knowing the value of team games and the friendships that can be made.

It was through football that I met Bert Bowyer from Elgin who played in the university team, and who turned my thoughts to the ministry of the Church of Scotland. The church had been part of my life from my earliest days. I was baptised in Dundee and when we arrived in Castletown we went to the Free Church – the 'Wee Frees' where my grandparents had worshipped. My mother, brought up in the United Free Church in Aberdeen, couldn't put up with the long dreich services and we joined her church.

Sunday was a special day. Enjoyment was frowned upon and people were not supposed to cook or knit or whistle or play games. We played football on the q.t. The thought of becoming a minister never entered my head although I attended Sunday School and was in the Boys Brigade. Ministers were a breed apart and we had to salute them when we met. Ministers never played football.

My mother died when I was at university. I have always

regretted that she didn't know that I would be a minister. I think she would have been pleased. I will never know what she sacrificed to send me and my brother to college.

My father had been a baillie in Dundee. Now he was a county councillor and a very dedicated one. He helped to get a district nurse appointed for the village and water laid on to the houses, when previously we went to the well and had dry lavatories. But we saw very little of him and got very little financial help from his endeavours.

Now my thoughts were turning towards the ministry. My football friend was an assistant in a church in Aberdeen and invited me to take a Sunday school class – later it was a Bible class. I had graduated MA and wanted to be a missionary, but what kind of missionary I wasn't sure. I thought a medical one could do most to help native people so I applied and was accepted. I had second thoughts just three weeks before the medical term started. I applied to Christ College, Aberdeen and had just these three weeks to pass the entrance exam in elementary Greek and Hebrew. My friend, Bert, helped me and I got through. Three years later I was licenced to preach. As the war had just started I could not get a passage to India, where I wanted to go, so I spent the year of waiting at the Teachers' Training College. This proved a worthwhile exercise as I later had jungle schools to look after in India.

While still a student in Aberdeen, I was called into the office of the University Principal and offered a commission with the rank of Major if I joined the Army. He said "You won't be going to India now that the war is on." I thanked him but declined his offer. I believed I had a higher commission and that took precedence. Little did I realise then how involved I would become with British troops as a missionary.

I was home in Caithness when the call came to join my ship at Hull. My youngest brother, Alistair, had contracted tuberculosis and I was the only one there to look after him. How could I leave him on his own? I remembered how Mary Slessor had left in similar circumstances and things worked out for her family. Believing God would help me as He had helped her I left, and so it was. Help was at hand, from the girl friend he later married and from his sister-in-law.

I sailed on a Dutch ship to India, via the Cape and the

Persian Gulf and on to Bombay. The journey lasted fifteen weeks. During the journey in convoy a submarine appeared, turned away from our ship and sank a row of ships on our other side. One with munitions blew up. It was during this time that we were busy helping a Canadian doctor who had come aboard to operate on a passenger to save his life. He asked me to give the anaesthetic while he amputated a leg, which I did. When we reached Bombay I collected my salary at Wilson College, which was our Church of Scotland Mission College there, and left by train for Bihar and the Mission Station at Bamdah, where Dr MacPhail had his hospital. I remained with him for a few weeks before going to Pokhuria, where I was to be for the next seven and a half years.

The Santal Mission of the Church of Scotland was situated well into the jungle. The Santals as a tribe were experts at turning jungle lands into paddy fields where they grew their rice. We had a church and school buildings and a bungalow. This latter was built a few feet above ground by a missionary who didn't like snakes. I went one better as I had a dog the snakes didn't like. Pokhuria is 200 miles north west of Calcutta. Twenty miles south were the Dhanbad-Jharia coalfields, run mostly by Scottish and Welsh mining managers. Some of our Santals worked in the mines, coming home to their villages with baskets of coal on their heads each weekend, to cultivate their paddy fields. The Santals are the largest tribe of aborigines, of whom there are nine million in India. Their language had been put down in Roman script by missionaries. They are a small race, very dark in colour, almost negroid. Round the mission some could speak a little English. In the coalfields the European community had clubs where they met socially and I had a service in English for them once a month.

My only break in seven years was to go home in 1945 to get married to Nancy Jenkins, to whom I'd been engaged since 1939. Nancy was a secretary, and Welsh born. Her father had died when she was nine years old. I met her when I was a junior assistant at Holburn Central Church where she was soprano leader in the choir. Her Welsh gift was to take her singing on the BBC and for the Arts Council. She won the Golden Voice Competition of 1937 for the whole of Scotland, singing opera, and was in the last eight for Britain, in London. On one occasion

I heard her singing on the BBC's overseas programme while sitting on the verandah of my bungalow in India, after the announcer had asked "Are you listening, Mac?" Nancy and I were married in King's College Chapel in Aberdeen on February 28th, 1945. I returned to India shortly afterwards and Nancy followed later when she got a passage.

It was during this interval that I saw the need to set up a Church of Scotland canteen for our troops awaiting transport home. They were in tents near the railway station at Dhanbad. They had just come out after three years in Burma and were longing to get home. They had no social facilities and were getting into trouble with the Anglo-Indian railway community. I got the go-ahead from the committee of the Church Huts and Canteens and established a hut with a large sitting-room, writing-room and kitchen. I supervised it from the mission, travelling to and fro on my motor bike.

The canteen was a great success, but I realised what a help Nancy and her music could be with the canteen troops. She had been singing to troops all over the Grampian area and in concert with the Poles and their great choir. For her voluntary service she received an award from Scottish Command. The church recommended that she go out to India as an officer in the service of the Huts and Canteens and this she did with the rank of Captain.

Let me return to the mission. Ruel Soren, a young Santal christian who had been in the Air Force and could speak English, used to visit me, and over a cup of tea we would discuss his taking further education. The end result of this was that he graduated in divinity and after a very quick rise, became the Bishop of Patna. Years later he came to Scotland to see us and was invited to preach before the Queen Mother. He is back in India, now retired and doing translation work for the church in Santali. "Encourage, encourage, encourage. Nothing matters so much," said the Rev. Dr Leonard Small, Moderator of the General Assembly at the time. A colleague wrote in the Centenary Souvenir of the Mission 1871–1971 "If bringing that man into the church of Christ had been Mr MacKay's only contribution in India, it would have been enough to justify his seven and a half years in missionary service." There were so many opportunities to raise the status of these lovable people and give them a chance to use their undoubted skills and talents.

Another time I found a little child who had fallen into the open fire in the courtyard of his home and been very badly burned down one side. His mother said "Moti is going to die. We have tried all our jungle medicines and nothing helps." I asked permission to try our *sahibs'* medicines and got the child taken to the mission. He recovered, stayed with us until he was well and then was handed over to one of the church elders to be brought up. Moti is now a pastor in charge of a village church.

At our railway station there was an Anglo-Indian community. The local baker told me of the plight of two children whose widowed mother had just died and who had no one but an Indian servant with them. I got the local magistrate to allow me to take little Heather (seven) and Maureen (four) to stay with me at the mission, and later I fought for and won in the High Court at Patna the right to keep them. They were educated at Dr Graham's Homes in Kalimpong and later came to Scotland to be with us. Now Heather is a fully qualified nurse, married, with two sons and living in Denmark. Maureen is married and lives near Elgin.

In 1947 Nancy caught an infection in a kidney and we returned to Scotland where a surgeon removed it. He advised us not to risk going back to the heat of India. He had been working in the Middle East and knew the dangers of further infection. There was a Home Mission post vacant at Middlefield, Aberdeen, and we spent the next thirteen and a half years there from 1948 to '61.

Middlefield, Aberdeen, was very different from the mission in India. It was a town charge and they were fine people on the whole, with large families. The first minister had been there from 1938 and when the war came only half the building programme had been completed. All he had was a hut for a church. I inherited this wooden building but later a granite church was built.

I had been there a short time when my youngest brother Alistair, who had tuberculosis, died. When he had to undergo an appendix operation he did not recover. He was only thirty-two. Alistair had owned a motor business in the village, which my brother George came home to take over.

The hospital where Alistair died denied us the visiting time to stay with him until the end, and I will never forget his face as we left for the last time. My experience with him has made me realise how important it is for relatives to have access to their loved ones at all times of crisis.

At Middlefield we furnished the new church from various sources. Out of its congregation came three missionaries, three who married ministers, two who became organists in other churches, and twenty-five girls who took nursing training and are now scattered all over the world. Yes, and hosts of young folk from that fellowship joined other churches when they moved away to homes of their own. Two names stand out from my time there; Miss Helen Whyte, the deaconess; and Miss Mary King, at the Royal Cornhill Hospital.

While I was at Middlefield, the Presbytery Clerk, the Rev. Dr A.R. Taylor offered me the part-time chaplaincy at the Royal Mental Hospital, as it was then called. I had never been in a mental hospital in my life and I hadn't the time but he assured me there was little I was expected to do. I had to take a service on Sunday afternoon and make an occasional visit. He said I would be paid expenses for my car.

Professor Millar of the department of mental health encouraged me to go to America in 1953, where there was a new course for ministers being arranged at Boston State Hospital. It turned out that I was the first student from Britain to take the course and the hospital had to be given permission by the state to admit me. I was there for four months in residence along with a selected group of young American ministers. I had the advantage of having had at least some experience in a mental hospital, which was more than any of them had had.

The Boston State Hospital was a 'poor law' hospital with 3,000 patients and the conditions were primitive compared to anything I had seen over here. The USA have private psychiatric clinics that are first class and we visited a few of them. One feature that did alarm me at the BSH was the number of very psychotic patients. I had never seen anything like it in Aberdeen. When I joined my ward, there was a piano there. When I left it was in bits, broken up by a patient expressing her anger. This was considered therapeutic.

I put a lot into this course of study and profited greatly from it. There were seminars and group meetings with all staffs represented, at which we could share in the discussions on an equal footing. At the end, I received the Certificate of the Institute of Pastoral Training, which enabled me to get the whole-time chaplaincy appointment when it came up at the Royal Cornhill Hospital – a new name – some years later. This appointment was the first in Scotland for a mental hospital. It led also to my participating in the teaching programme at Christ College and the status of Honorary Lecturer in Mental Health at the University of Aberdeen.

The Royal Cornhill Psychiatric Hospital had 700 patients in residence, plus a group who came as out-patients for treatment or to attend therapy sessions. The majority of the in-patient population were aged. Very few were bedridden because the policy was to get patients up and keep them active, although it meant more work for the nursing staff. Nancy and I had ward services for them and it was quite common to see the old folk, who had not spoken for years, mouth the words of a familiar hymn. What we preached in our Sunday services in the chapel was the love of God. The sermons lasted about ten minutes. In a mental hospital the chaplain has a better chance of building up a relationship with patients because, unlike general hospitals, we have them longer and there are fewer of them. On the other hand, working among the mentally ill demands a degree of concentration that is demanded in no other sphere of the ministry. After a few interviews one can really feel drained. There is, however, the feeling of how worthwhile it all is. The knowledge one gains about a patient's condition one shares with other members of staff in the conferences composed of psychiatrists, other doctors, senior nurses and ancillary staff and also the chaplain's assistant.

For the long-stay patients the chaplain is, in most cases, the only minister. Mental hospitals are the most neglected by the clergy. This, I am glad to say, is improving as divinity students are now being introduced to courses in our hospitals. The visit of a patient's own minister does much to reduce the sting of the stigma that attaches itself to this illness. Patients dread going home as much as going in. I remember suggesting to a patient who looked 'browned off', that I would take her out to visit her relatives, to which she replied "My sister came to see me and said she would be back in two weeks' time. That was twenty years ago and she hasn't been back since."

When a patient dies, the chaplain or his assistant makes all the arrangements for the funeral if there is no close relative or if the relatives don't want to know, and this is not uncommon. A patient came to us from Peterhead Prison, who was very ill and died. I arranged his funeral and took the service. I was alone except for the undertaker. There was a wreath with a card which said "From his mother". There was also a crest of a noble family on the card. Poor mother – no doubt he had broken her heart but he was still her son.

Suicide is not common in our hospital, but sometimes it happens. A woman, who knew what she was doing, cut an artery and didn't summon a member of staff until she knew it was too late for anyone to save her. I think the staff were glad that I was in the clinic at the time so that they could express their shock and guilt feelings. If somebody makes up his or her mind to commit suicide, there is very little anyone can do to prevent it. It is important, however, to watch for signs of this when anyone is depressed. When a patient does not succeed in killing herself or himself, but makes a bold attempt, the reaction is a sense of acute guilt. If the chaplain is around, he can help. The job of the hospital, someone has said, is "to cure sometimes, to alleviate often, to comfort always." We can all do the last.

Included in the chaplaincy is a hospital and school, Woodlands, for the mentally handicapped at Cults, five miles from the RCH. This came into my chaplaincy when I was appointed whole-time in 1961. The children are from babies to sixteen year olds and come from the Grampian area and from Orkney and Shetland.

Woodlands is an amazing place of staff devotion and children's happiness. The tragic side of it is felt by the parents who have to accept a handicapped child when they expected one who would be normal, then to hand the child over to the care of the hospital because they cannot keep it at home although they have tried, and then to face the feelings of failure and guilt. For the most part they are lovable children and they are loved and cared for twenty-four hours each day by a devoted staff. "Do nurses have favourites?" I once asked a senior nurse. "Yes," she replied. "Every nurse has a child who is special to her." "Which is your favourite?" I asked. She pointed to the least attractive. "Why that one?" "Because I thought nobody else loved it." What could I say? I was deeply moved by her reply. It is easy to love the attractive – it takes Christian love to love the unattractive.

Miss MacDonald, who was my assistant, is a graduate teacher with added pastoral training at St Andrews University. She has built up a wonderful relationship with these children since she started. Good work had already been done but there was no literature on the subject. Now she has a weekly club for the children and has the assistance of a band of willing helpers from the community as well as Sunday schools for both the young and older groups. One thing we realised very early working there was the children's love of music and their joy in singing. With Nancy's musical gifts we soon had a group of songs that were firm favourites. Before we left, we had a pile of fifty or so songs printed on large cards of varying colours, so that they were recognised immediately they were put up, even though the children could not all read words. Through the vehicle of song we were able to get the right atmosphere and put across the message of God's love in Jesus. Joy and happiness were always the key note and we were all uplifted by the pleasure we got from them.

There was a request by parents for a church service in which parents and children could join. Dr Drummond spoke to me about this request and we arranged with Mr Anderson, the minister of Mannofield Church, to hold a service there twice a year – Christmas and summer – and so it has gone on with wonderful co-operation from parents and staffs. Other centres for the handicapped were contacted and joined in with us.

In all three centres where I have worked, I have had to build. In India it was to reconstruct the church building which the white ants had made dangerous by eating away at the wooden beams. At Middlefield, it was moving from a hut to a more permanent place of worship. At the Royal Cornhill Hospital it was planning and supervising the work on the new chapel. There we had inherited a chapel that was also a thoroughfare between two sets of ward buildings, the old and the not so old. During a service it was not unusual to be interrupted by people passing through, for a purpose sometimes necessary, sometimes frivolous. Before we left, a chapel had been created out of a former patients' lounge and canteen. It is now a thing of beauty and a joy to worship in. For years I had tried to get the Hospital Board to erect a new chapel in the grounds, but money could never be provided. Then a new administrator was appointed – Mr Bain – and he got things moving in the interests of the patients. He offered me the patients' meeting place which had chapel-like rafters, and that really made the reconstruction worthwhile. The patients had the old chapel converted for them into a far more suitable place for socialising.

I was glad that the chapel was completed and dedicated by the Aberdeen Presbytery before I retired. Now the patients have a chapel worthy of the worship of Almighty God. Now they have a quiet place where they can go during the week for reflection and prayer.

"The problem of the elderly," says one of our consultants, "and what to do to solve it, is one of the most crucial problems facing medicine today." This problem is worse where patients are living in the community with little or no support from families and friends. We can admit elderly people only as patients die, with the result there is a long waiting list of people in the community becoming older, feebler and more demented. This puts an added strain on the services. it would be even worse except for the loving care so many elderly people receive from their own families at home.

In a mental hospital we deal mainly with feelings and emotions. A young woman suffering from anorexia nervosa came to us from a general hospital where she had been a patient for two weeks. After a few days with us she said, "There they had no time to talk, here a nurse will drop in from time to time and have a chat to find out how I feel. It gives me the feeling that I am being treated as a human being."

To know how a person feels one has to make contact and the whole point is to gain an understanding of the patient, to listen to his problems, to find out how he feels about them and to lay the foundation of a helpful relationship. Patients expect to meet doctors and nurses when they go to hospital, but they do not always expect to meet a chaplain on the staff. I have come across patients who have never, before meeting me, spoken to a minister anywhere. This can create a certain embarrassment and make the first contact more difficult.

I think it was Dr Ken Morrice who said, "To be sick is to be afraid." To be ill in a mental hospital adds to that fear. That makes it imperative that, with a patient on admission, our first task is to work through these fears and anxieties with him.

People visiting patients have anxieties too, and even divinity students coming to us for practical training express these fears and some have been known to opt out of coming.

Interviewing is one way of getting information, and the interview between a chaplain and a patient has a special quality about it; a spiritual quality – or ought to have. Strong feelings are aroused in all of us by the thought of treatment and operations and it helps if someone on the staff spends some time with us to talk about these feelings. Doctors have difficulties doing this in some places and often shy clear of dealing with a patient's religious problems when they arise, hoping that the minister or chaplain will take them up.

I was called to a general hospital by a young surgeon because his patient was refusing to agree to a blood transfusion, should it be necessary during her operation. She told him that she was a Jehovah's Witness and could not take somebody else's blood. When I called to see her, it took some time before the truth came out. She was not a Jehovah's Witness; she was afraid. When undergoing a previous operation the anaesthetic hadn't acted properly so that she could hear everything that went on in the theatre, but couldn't speak and tell the surgeon. She felt it could happen again and was afraid. I asked the sister on the ward to inform the anaesthetist and ask him to reassure her, which he did. She had her operation and did require a blood transfusion.

In a mental hospital the treatment that sometimes causes anxiety is ECT, which, put simply, is electric shock treatment. There are many other treatments but about this one the public shows a great ignorance and patients come to us with strange ideas of what happens. ECT is never given without the permission of the patient or relatives and is fully explained beforehand. It does not relieve everyone, but those it helps, it helps quickly and takes them out of the state of utter misery we call depression. Depression can affect any of us at any time but when it becomes acute it needs hospital treatment.

The patient who is depressed can look physically well and yet feel so down in spirit that his normal interest in other people is totally obscured, nor has he any interest in his work nor even in his home and family and he has lost his faith. Even God seems to have deserted him. For such a patient ECT can be a life-saver.

Personality disorders have among them those with drink and drug problems. To change their personality is difficult if not well nigh impossible. In every one of us there is an anti-social element; for most of us this does not get out of hand, but for people with weaker personalities there is always the possibility that they come in conflict with the law and find themselves referred by the courts and put into our forensic wards.

The alcoholic is a most difficult person to treat successfully and there is an increase in referrals; sadly the increase includes females. The secretly-drinking bored housewife is no longer a stranger in the consulting room nor in the hospital. This produces problems in the home and in the children. Children in such homes reveal behaviour disorders, poor progress at school and petty thieving. One observation by a leading psychiatrist, Dr James G. Henderson, dealing with the problem of the alcoholic, is worthy of note: "It is unrealistic to consider that everyone with a drink problem can be salvaged and returned to a useful place in society. Many alcoholics do not wish to stop drinking and nothing short of death will end the condition," and he goes on to say this: "Society should give a clear message that being drunk is unacceptable behaviour and is not amusing or smart."

The most common complaint that brings people into hospital is depression, and people suffering from this symptom can be helped. We cannot change their circumstances nor can we deal with the people with whom they live and who are usually part of the problem, but we can help them to get back to their communities in a happier state of mind. Most depressed people suffer from a sense of loss, especially the loss of love. This is how one patient put it to me. "They," (meaning the family,) "they gave me a Mini but they gave me no love."

A feature of our work in the hospital that is engaging us more and more is the number of calls for help among the staff at all levels. I hope that this is an indication that the services of the chaplain and his assistant are recognised as including staff and that what we do for patients and relatives is an indication of our caring and concern for all.

Behind all my service has been a strong faith in God through Jesus Christ. This has sustained me at all times. Life has had its difficulties but somehow whenever I have followed what I believed was God's will for me, these have turned out not to be difficulties but opportunities. Looking back along the road I have come, I feel a deep sense of gratitude to God for the way He has led me and for the tasks He has given me to do.

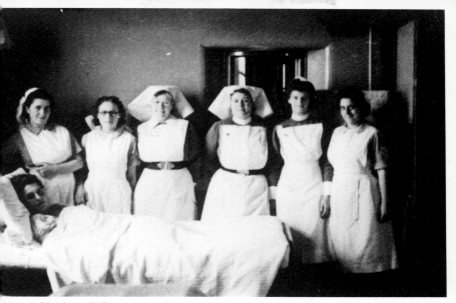

isbeth Hockey (left)
ing at Watford in 1939.

Major-General Frank Richardson,
CB, DSO, OBE

Arnhem railway bridge blown up
he enemy during the Allied advance,
n the RAMC dealt with many casualties.

Dr John Wilkinson and his wife visiting a dispensary near Chogonia, 1949.

The Royal Cornhill Hospital where Murdoch Mackay was Chaplain for 35 yea

he Rev. Murdoch Mackay

Peggy Fulton with staff

and (standing in middle) supervising patients.

Jimmy Savile after his investiture with OBE, with his mother and Joe Tyrer.

Joe Tyrer on duty.

Tom Chambers in retirement.

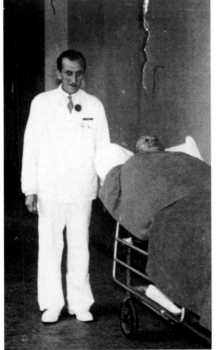

Pioneer in Occupational Therapy

PEGGY FULTON
MBE

LOOKING back over my eighty-nine years, I can say that I have had a most eventful life. I was one of a family of five and my father was a Victorian and Edwardian doctor. This I suppose is an account of how I became involved in occupational therapy and of some of the strange occurrences that seemed to keep happening to me.

My father was a medical graduate of Glasgow University and the first three members of our family were born in Muirkirk – Rosina, Moll and Bess. But my brother and I were born in Manchester, where father had his practice. He was not only the local GP, but was also responsible for the well-being of the employees of the large Eglinton iron works. I can remember as a child the terrifying thrill of watching the almost blinding red of the molten iron rushing into the pig beds. He also added to his busy practice several orphanages and a home for crippled children.

My mother was a lovely woman and I discovered from an aunt that from her queue of suitors a short list consisted of a well-known painter, a bacteriologist and luckily for us, a doctor. We became known locally as the 'fascinating Fultons'.

Ours was a busy lively family but in the early nineteen-hundreds domestic help was available. As babies my brother and I had a devoted Scots nanny. We had a cook, a housemaid, a lad hired from an orphanage who dealt with cleaning shoes, coal fires, and delivering medicines; and a dear old washer-woman Mrs Hall, who always smelt of soap. She did gigantic washes, using a three-legged dolly, a scrubbing board and a boiler. William Blount our coachman was part of our family. We also had a beautiful chestnut mare. Nellie was the fastest horse in Manchester apart from those used in a fleet of small traps that rushed round the town dumping bundles of newspapers for distribution.

The cobbled streets of Manchester did nothing for my father's writing up of his notes. There is a story about my mother being phoned up by someone who said they thought they had a letter from Dr Fulton but weren't sure. To which my mother said "If the writing looks like Charles something, that is my husband. His name is Andrew!" How did the poor chemists deal with such things?

After a time my sisters and I were sent to the Manchester School for Girls and my brother to Manchester Grammar School. I wasn't academically inclined and apparently my vocabulary was unusual at times; my brother had read to me everything and anything. I remember once when my brother and I went back on holiday to Muirkirk and the housemaid mentioned she'd lost something, my comforting remark was "Isn't that damnable!"

The time came when the family began to go their separate ways. Rosina went to the Royal College of Music in Manchester. Moll went to a famous school in Denmark for gymnastics. Bess, who adored children, went to the Princess Christian College in Manchester, which trained nannies. My brother went into medicine. That left me. What was I to do?

Fate took a hand in this. My father had gone to northern Italy for treatment for what was thought to be sciatica. He planned to return there the following year but the First World War made that impossible. Eventually he came up to Chalmers Hospital in Edinburgh where he was operated on by Sir Charles Stiles. He was given only months to live but he lived for five more years. While he had the operation we stayed in the house of Father's cousin Dr John Boyd, in Dunoon on the river Clyde. He was in France at this time with the RAMC.

It was here that an odd thing happened to me that pointed the way to my future life work, although I had no idea of it at the time. Dunoon was holding a fête and I was encouraged by my sister to have my fortune told. I went into a gypsy's tent. I don't remember what she looked like and she never looked at me. She had a bowl of blue liquid in her lap which she kept turning round and round. She told me of my nephew's birth, of my father's death and said there was a letter coming from a fair man across water. I didn't believe her then, but it all came true.

After my father's death, his colleagues helped themselves to his practice, the estate agent sold our house to a friend and our furniture was put in store. The fair man across water whom the gypsy had foretold proved to be my youngest uncle, George, who lived with an older sister and her daughter near Philadelphia, in the USA. It was he who wrote to my mother saying, as she and I had had a terrible time recently, why didn't we go out to them for a holiday?

We meant to stay for a few months but with relatives in Colorado and Wyoming and with other friends to visit, it was fourteen months before we returned home to Britain. But we were there only some months before we went back to America on the insistent invitations of the family, and this time I was to find my true vocation.

When we were in the USA a friend suggested that I should go into occupational therapy. My cousin rang up the head of the School of Occupational Therapy, and to my amazement it turned out that the father of the Principal of the Philadelphia school had been a bursar of Aberdeen University. In no time the Principal arranged to see me and contacted Mr Kinnear, who was President of the American Association of Occupational Therapy. I am more than grateful to those who helped me to get started in my course at the school. Here I was introduced to the practical work that was always related to its therapeutic use. The lecturer in charge of crafts had actually lived with the Navajo Indians and she passed on to her pupils her vast knowledge of their crafts, for instance the basket work in which they excelled.

I went out for clinical work to various hospitals. I vividly remember one patient who was weaving who said to me "It's lots of fun to be crazy when you can do work like this." I became aware of the value of humour when patients could be induced to laugh at themselves and most importantly at us, although I was slightly shocked when a head therapist at one hospital quoted to me a rhyme which went:

> Mary, Mary, quite contrary
> How does your psychic grow,
> With naughty neuroses
> And silly psychosis
> And complexes all in a row.

Many years later in Aberdeen one of my patients delighted me when she wrote an epitaph on our superintendent:

> Here lies the body of Dr Dods-Brown
> Physician, surgeon of great renown,
> Dig deep down and by his side
> You'll find a bottle of formaldehyde.

Occupational therapy was the prevailing treatment for psychiatric patients in the early days before things like ECT treatment came along. Gradually, over the years, a wider range of treatments built up; chemotherapies, brain surgery and so on. In a children's hospital I found a little scrap of humanity whose brother had set her alight. She was clothed in bandages and took a dim view of the world in general and the staff in particular. I had been warned that she was more than difficult. One day she came up behind me and as I stooped for something, small arms as if made of steel came round my neck, as she did her best to choke me. I gasped out "Do you know, I've never had such a lovely hug." That seemed to do the trick and all was reasonably well. But I found it hard if I was within hearing distance when the poor mite was having her dressings changed.

I was sent to a general hospital where there was a young man who had been gassed in the First World War. To my amazement I discovered he was, like me, from Manchester and knew our coachman William Blunt and his family. Then the head occupational therapist at the Pennsylvania psychiatric hospital, Mary Fulton Boyd, took me on. In her I found a friend, and a true occupational therapist. She allowed me six weeks with her instead of a month. She was amazing in controlling supposedly uncontrollable patients. Her quiet serenity influenced all of us.

Once, her second-in-command and I were in a side room when we heard Miss Boyd quietly calling. When we rushed through to see what was wrong, we found a very manic patient had pinned her by the wrist to the wall but the near-panic was on our side not on hers.

Some patients I have never forgotten. One was a huge fireman from the railway who proceeded to kick out the mosquito netting door, then snapped apart pipes that were about an inch thick. Memories of some of the patients come back to me. There was a man who introduced me to his nurse saying "This is Miss Fulton. I don't know if it was her father or her grandfather that put the first boat in the Hudson." He had a lively imagination.

There was one lad who was an alcoholic partly due to his having cooked all his food in alcohol. Years later at a banquet of the military section of occupational therapists in New York, I learned that the lad had made an excellent recovery and had written a book on it which was selling extremely well. While I was a student at Philadelphia I was told there was a patient, an Englishwoman, who wanted to see me. When I arrived at her ward, she was in hydro-therapy, lying in her bath washing her wigs. I'm afraid I didn't score very much because I did not know all her titled friends. I could only run off one titled relation, Lady Elizabeth Seton, far back, who had eloped with the estate agent. However, she didn't hold it against me for as I hurried across the courtyard below, there she was at the window stark naked, singing "Will ye no' come back again?"

I returned to England in 1923 after doing six months at a hospital in New York. I thought I'd start off in a psychiatric hospital, so I went to Cheadle Royal, but the superintendent at Cheadle Royal was only interested in his patients growing vegetables. I applied to Papworth Hospital, which in those days was primarily interested in TB, not heart. They weren't interested in patients until they were ambulatory. Then I applied to the Heritage Craft School, run by Jesse Boots. They were willing to have me but couldn't give me a salary, which wasn't much use. Then my cousin with whom I was staying at the time said he could get me an introduction to Percy Smith. I gathered he was one of the big men in psychiatry. I wrote to say I'd like to do occupational therapy. He, thinking I was an American, wrote back and said that if I hadn't found employment in

America he wasn't sanguine about me finding it in this country. I replied, explaining that I was a Scot and perfectly willing to work in England.

I went for an interview. Dr Smith, a consultant in psychiatry, was a dapper little man, in morning coat and striped trousers. He said "My dear young woman, we've had occupational therapy in our hospitals for years." No luck there. I went to see the Superintendent at Crumpsall just out of Manchester. I found later the man was a drug addict. When he told me that the patients washed the dishes and scrubbed the floors, I told him that if I was melancholic and he made me do that, I would go manic. He was so shocked to be treated like this by someone who looked about seventeen that he burst out laughing. But he gave me a number of useful introductions.

One of these introductions was to Porter-Phillips who was head of Bethlehem Royal in London. He was the most handsome man I've ever seen. He asked me what I would need. I said, "Give me one room, half a dozen patients, let me work with them, let me see what they can do. If it's no good, I'll go quietly away." He explained that he would have to put it up to the Board. Alas, he wrote to me saying they were moving the hospital into the country and the Board would not have anything to do with the idea of starting occupational therapy.

After more attempts and months of frustration a miracle happened. I went up to Glasgow to be bridesmaid to a cousin. My sister in Glasgow told me there was something going on at Gartnavel, a hospital originally for mentally disturbed patients. So I got an introduction to Professor Henderson, who ran Gartnavel. He had a young art student who was doing painting with the patients. Professor Henderson said, "Miss Fulton, it is extraordinary that you should come today. I have a superintendent coming from the North of Scotland from a hospital that wants to put in occupational therapy. Could you go north?" I agreed that I could.

Dr Dods-Brown, the Superintendent of the Royal Mental Hospital, now Cornhill Mental Hospital, in Aberdeen, wrote to me to tell me not to take any other post. With my mother I went north. So began my great adventure and my life work.

Dr Robert Dods-Brown, whose father had been a Provost of Edinburgh, had great influence with the Board. When they wanted to put me into a place where there were a lot of work-men, he said no, and I was put into a sixty-foot army hut to start with. It was so cold that overnight a tumblerful of water froze. I asked one of the old ladies "What do you think of this?" She said, "Thank God, my teeth weren't in it!"

They had private patients in the old mansion house and after a bit I started there, with half a dozen women. I had got them going when the chief arrived to tell me, with a charming smile, that there were half a dozen men waiting for me. I worked very hard from July up to Christmas and then occurred another minor miracle. I'd asked for more staff for the patients because I couldn't watch them all, and if a patient had suicidal tendencies, I really needed someone else there. There was a famous wood-carver called Wills who had a school for wood-carving in Aberdeen, whose son was also a wood-carver. He had been through the war in the Gordons and had been wounded in Italy. So Dr Dods-Brown suggested that the lad came to me. He could design as easily as most people could write. He was a godsend. He didn't know anything about the medical side but we told him all we could and he designed projects for me and helped the patients to work together. He was with me until he retired.

Things were beginning to happen in the world of occupational therapy and I got to hear about them. We used to meet at different hospitals to find out what was going on, and eventually during the Second World War we managed to get together a Scottish Association for Occupational Therapists. Because of the war we had to take three hundred patients from a hospital at Kingseat outside Aberdeen when they turned it into a naval hospital. My hut went for sleeping accommodation for the staff. I had to clear everything out in one day and my own staff of three was scattered through the hospital.

Then I got students sent up from the Astley Ainslie Hospital in Edinburgh. Colonel Cunningham who was running Astley Ainslie had sent for two Canadians to help start occupational therapy. So I got students helping with the clinical work for three months, which was splendid.

We were progressing all the time and in 1954 we had the First International Congress of the World Federation of Occupational Therapists in Edinburgh. I was elected President. It was a great occasion that made all the previous pioneering efforts worth while. Professor Norman Dott, President of the Scottish Association of Occupational Therapists, was also Chairman of the Congress and gave the message of welcome to the delegates from Australia, Canada, Denmark, India, Israel, New Zealand, South Africa, Sweden and the USA. Dr Dott, who was appointed in 1947 to the Chair of Neurological Surgery in Edinburgh University, was always very supportive of occupational therapy. He was a marvellous man and a very good friend.

Once I had a letter from an American, saying he gathered I took people from abroad and he'd love to come and work with us in Aberdeen. Would it be possible? By this time the Board had let me have a Swedish student and two from Africa. I wrote back to say, "If you require teeth or a wig, you'd better come and get them free here." The writer decided he must come to see who wrote letters like that. A great pair came from America and spent six months with me. I enjoyed them very much.

I was appalled at the ignorance of people about psychiatry, so after we had been running a certain length of time, and when we wanted to get rid of the saleable work our patients had done, we hired the ballroom of the Music Hall, and our first sale was opened by Sir Arthur Rose, who was Commissioner for Lunacy in Scotland. It seemed a good opportunity to educate the rest of the medical world in what we were up to. I sent a cutting of the event to Porter- Phillips in London. He replied that they now had occupational therapy in Bethlehem Royal. Princess Maud Carnegie came and opened a sale for us. The need was for publicity, so I talked to Women's Guilds, Rotaries, Churches, Business and Professional Men's Clubs: all sorts of organisations. I was asked to talk to the university people about our work. A colleague told me to make it light and not to forget the humour. Later a superintendent came rushing down to me and told me I had raised in Parliament the fact that we had no after-care at the Royal Mental Hospital. I said, "Dear me, how did I manage that?" Then I remembered. "Ah, I was giving a talk to Rotary. Our MP must have been present."

At first we didn't have occupational therapy at Aberdeen Infirmary. I was rung up from there once by a physiotherapist who told me they had a patient who had fallen off a hay-wagon and damaged his spine. He was becoming very depressed because he lived in a tied cottage and would lose it if he could not keep his job. So I went up to the Royal and saw this very nice chap. His grasp was very bad, so I went down to the docks and got cord and built up a shuttle that he could hold and manipulate. But I think the thing that helped him most was the personal contact and the reassurance that he wasn't going to be incapacitated for ever. Strangely enough, years later when I was in the Infirmary with pneumonia, the sister brought a doctor to see me. I had never seen the man before, but he told the Sister he knew about Miss Fulton, who had put one of his patients back on his feet. It turned out to be the man who had fallen off the wagon and broken his spine.

The physiotherapist at the Royal had earlier said to me that he wished they had occupational therapy at the Royal, because the exercises we did with them continued to hold their interest. Happily they got occupational therapy, in the course of time.

I remember one rather funny incident about then. Dr Casson, the sister of the famous actor, Lewis Casson, had a nursing home. At one point she wrote to offer me the headship of the school. I didn't want to teach; I wanted to work with patients. I happened to read the letter in the department and the chief's son also happened to be there at the time. I said to Mr Wills "Listen to this." Robert the son got such a shock he told his father. My salary went up at once. It was rather funny. My assistants' salaries went up as well. So that was all right.

My successor at Aberdeen was an old student of mine, Agnes Cook, who did much that I should have done. She is also retired now and sometimes comes to see me in Edinburgh. On one visit she said, "Do you realise it is sixty years since you started work as the first qualified occupational therapist in Great Britain?" How time passes! I got my diploma in occupational therapy after my work in this field in New York. But today that would not be enough. Today the medical authorities in the NHS encourage university or Open University diploma studies in occupational therapy. I have loved occupational therapy work all my life. It is good to remember we have had Scots on the World Federation and that the President at the time of its first Congress was a Scot, because although I was born in Manchester and my parents moved down there, we returned to have all our holidays in Scotland and I have always regarded myself as a Scot.

There have been so many good things to remember – recognition by the Council in London. Then one of my joys – the Grampian School for Occupational Therapy was started in Aberdeen at Woolmanhill; it's in the centre of the city, where you can get a bus to any hospital. It has a wonderful head, Miss Paterson. The school has a splendid staff and is absolutely first class. They asked me to give the diplomas to the first class of graduates. I was thrilled to bits. Our patron is the Princess Royal.

All in all, my life has been one extraordinary thing after another. I may have got the MBE but the people deserving credit are those that worked with me – bless them.

Hospital Porter

JOSEPH TYRER

I WAS born in Leeds over seventy years ago. My father and mother were born and bred in the Dales. As a matter of fact, they called my mother the Queen of the Dales. There were ten in her family and everybody knew her as the Queen. My dad worked on the railway as an engine-driver and was often away from home. There were five of us in our family and I was the youngest.

I went to Roland Road School. I didn't like school, but I was a good attender and when I left at fourteen I had a fancy to be a farmer, so I went back to the Dales and I had two or three years up there in farming. But the time came when I thought I'd like to be at home. I had a good mother and I missed the family. Also if I started working there, I'd help her a bit.

Back in Leeds I started learning how to drive, and I got a job as a lorry driver on haulage. I was just old enough to get a licence to drive for H.H. Woodward who made packing cases and things like that, which I took to Liverpool and other places.

I did that for a few years; then I got a job driving a traveller about. I drove the firm's van for the next few years, but I had to stop because of illness; a duodenal ulcer which perforated twice. When I recovered, I went back to the job of driving the traveller, which meant I was on the move quite a bit. By this time I was married and my wife wasn't keen on my stopping away, perhaps two or three days at a time.

Then came the war and I went into the Fire Service, and was stationed at Bootle. I was transferred from there to Hull, and went into the Army Fire Service. While I was there I had a nasty accident. We were going out to a fire and in those days you didn't sit on the vehicle as you do now. I was standing fastening up my coat as we went round a corner and I was thrown off onto the street. I was in hospital for over a month. The matron told me it was touch and go whether I was killed or whether my brain was permanently damaged.

I was discharged and went up to work in Avro, where I did general maintenance work on aeroplanes.

After the war I saw a job advertised for a porter in Leeds General Infirmary. My own doctor said to me "You are just the chap for a job like that." I went for an interview with Mr Hulligan who was to be my boss. He told me he would give me the job and I was put in the best department in the hospital, the X-ray department. For twenty odd years that was where I worked, as a porter in Leeds General Infirmary, and in time I became Porter-in-charge.

I may say I worked hard at the job. You had to fill in sheets about all the jobs you did. With your name on them, the sheets went down to the office next morning where Mr Hulligan read them. One morning a telephone call came to say I had to go down to his office. He told me he was going to sack me. I said "What have I done?" He said "You're working too hard. From your sheets I see you're doing more than all the others put together." He looked at me and said "Now, I want you to be down here on Monday morning. Bring your white coat. You're going to work with one patient for a month."

So on Monday morning down I went with my white coat over my arm to meet the gentleman with whom I was to work for a month. When the gentleman came in, who did it turn out to be but Jimmy Savile. That was the first time I met Jimmy, and our friendship has lasted to this day. There was a campaign going on in those days to help Britain and Jimmy had come in to do his bit. He came in for one month and years later he's still going strong.

At that time he'd come in three or four days a week and I can tell you he worked very hard, with the trolleys and chairs and all the jobs I did with the patients, getting them to and from the wards for X-rays.

As time went on, Jimmy Savile got a lot of money for the Infirmary, which provided equipment for treating people, by doing runs and taking part in marathons. Jimmy was keen on fitness. He got money for kidney machines and things like that and we thought the world of him there. He thoroughly deserved his OBE, and Leeds University made him an LLD.

Jimmy wrote a book in which he said of me, "Joseph is a millionaire, not in money but in his attitude to people." I've been lucky in my job because I've always got on well with everybody. On the day I retired I got a telegram which said "All the best, my brother, from your old pal, Jimmy Savile."

I shan't forget the time Jimmy got his OBE. We had a party at the Queen's Hotel in Leeds. Then we caught the sleeper from Leeds to London, the three of us, Jimmy, his mother and me. He always used to call his mother the Duchess. We booked in to a hotel and then we went to the Palace. There is a photograph which shows the three of us. Jimmy, through his hard work, had come a long way from the days when he was a collier in Yorkshire. I was glad Jimmy's mother lived to see him get the OBE for he thought the world of her and got her a lovely flat in Scarborough. I went to her funeral in Leeds. Jimmy Savile still keeps in touch; once, for instance, to say he was going off for eight days on the QE2. It has been a lovely friendship.

I would start my job each day at eight o'clock. First I'd see that all the trolleys were ready for working that day, all clean with white sheets on. We had about ten to twelve trolleys in X-ray. I had to see that the oxygen supplies were all right. I've actually got one here in my home as my breathing is now affected. I picked up an infection. I was in hospital for five weeks and Jimmy used to come in and visit me.

But regarding the job. We serviced all the wards when I developed the knack of how to lift the patients. There's an art in it, and you've got to learn it. One important thing is to do that job right, you must be kind and understanding, so that the patients get more confidence. Sometimes when they come out of theatre they are confused, even for a few days, and if you're bringing them down for X-ray, you've got to be very careful and know how to talk to them. Sometimes a patient had to be anaesthetised when X-rayed; perhaps the brain had to be X-rayed. When the patient came round, you took him back to the ward. If he hadn't come round, you had to take him to the recovery room.

Dr Lamb, who was consultant radiologist when I was there, still keeps in touch with me. He comes and sees me and brings me flowers and plants, for he has never forgotten me. It's good to know I can go any time to the Leeds General Infirmary where I had so many friends. Over all the years I worked there I never had a wrong word with a Sister or anybody else. For me they were happy times. I don't know what the secret is, but I've always tried to treat all people with kindness.

Changes go on all the time in hospitals. For instance, Sisters used to be very strict. I think the atmosphere is easier now. Discipline was extra strict. I remember a Professor Johnston in the X-ray department. When you went on duty in X-ray, you had to have your white shoes on, your white trousers, white coat, collar and tie. At that time there were five of us. If you went in without a tie, he'd say to the Porter-in-charge "Tell that man to get a tie on or get him off." Today things are diferent.

Looking back, I can see how important a job like a porter's really is. The task of taking sick people to and from the wards is a job worth doing well, as sick people need a lot of encourage-ment and a lot of kindness. Nearly all the patients in the differ-ent wards need to come down for X-rays so you are on the go each day and you are in and out of the wards all the time. I must have done hundreds of miles of walking and pushing. It helps you to realise that hospitals can't do without their porters. As well as his good health, a porter's attitude is all-important. That's my motto. When I started, you didn't go in for the job for the money, for there was little money in it. You went into it because you wanted to and you felt you had the right attitude. When I was promoted to Porter-in-charge all I had was two to three shillings a week extra but to me it was like an honour, almost like being a Sister of a ward.

I've got memories of many patients. There was Jim Windsor who was one of the biggest and richest bookies in the city and he was in a private ward. I had to bring him down for an X-ray. So in bringing him down and taking him back I made friends with him. He owned a big club in Leeds. We got talking and I told him I was glad to see him looking better. I said to him "Would it be all right if I visited your club sometime?" He asked for my address and about three or four days later an honorary membership card arrived for me. I've had letters and cards sent me from many patients saying they hadn't forgotten me.

There was one young lady who was a cancer patient, Ray Popplewell. Her people were big merchants. I used to go up and see her every day. She was a lovely pianist and told me she'd love to play a tune on the piano. I said "I'll see my boss and if it's all right with him, I'll bring you down to Littlewood's Hall where the piano is and you can play it." I wheeled her down two or three times and she played and do you know, the place was full to hear her play. I've got a plant outside in the garden that she gave me the money for. She died at twenty-one years of age. When she was dying, only her husband, her mother and me were allowed in to see her. She was a lovely young woman.

There was a lot of happiness and good humour too. I used to love flashy ties, ties of all colours and whenever I appeared I always got a cheery greeting and a reference to my tie.

When the time came to retire, to speak the truth, I didn't want to. But in fact I went on after I had retired officially. After a couple of years when I thought of stopping, Jimmy suggested I did what he did: go in for a few days a week. So I worked sometimes with Jimmy and sometimes with the other lads voluntarily till I finally gave up. I remember when I was pushing the trolley with a patient on it I thought it should be me on the trolley, being pushed along at my age. But it was all worth it.

I always used to go to the Christmas party. It was good meeting all my old friends. I've been a fortunate man, working in a fine department of a great hospital.

Ambulanceman

TOM CHAMBERS

I WAS born in Kendal, Cumbria, in 1910. My father was an iron-moulder with a local firm and he had fought in the South African War and the 1914–18 War. My mother died of cancer when I was only six years old and there were five of us. My grandmother took care of the three youngest including me, until she was too old to do it, then my older brother went into lodgings and I went to live with an aunt.

I worked at different things from when I was ten years of age, just to keep myself. I helped in a garage and worked in a bakehouse. When the Irish navvies were digging their way through to Manchester to lay the water-pipes from the Lake District, they lived in a lodging-house and I'd take bread there for them every day.

Then when I left school at fourteen I went to work at Netherfield with K-Shoes. I was the boy who fed the heeling machine with nails. In 1928 I joined the St John Ambulance and that was to affect my whole life. I was to be twenty-nine years in the St John's.

In 1938, before war broke out I helped with the evacuees from Newcastle to Kendal, taking them to the different homes where they were going. Then on Saturday, September 2nd, I was told to go to the St John Ambulance Centre for a medical and to report to York Military Hospital on Monday morning, September 4th. It was then 1939. War broke out on September 3rd and I was off on the 7.15 a.m. train to York. So my training in ambulance work began in earnest in the Army, No. 8

Company of the RAMC at York. I had actually been there for a fortnight's training in 1937 as a member of the St John's.

We were sent to Strensil to look after the King's Own Yorkshire Light Infantry. This was at the Queen Elizabeth Barracks, seven miles from York. We were at the medical reception centre as men were coming in from all over. We did thousands of innoculations and vaccinations and worked with two MOs on medical examinations. We did all the sterilising of the instruments as there were no throw-away instruments in those days. Before the war in the St John's I had watched operations and had done duties in wards, as part of my training. After Strensil I was called back to York and promoted to corporal. I was ordered to Burn Hall, a Red Cross convalescent home, again not far from York and was there for disciplinary purposes and to see that the arrangements for pay were carried out. We had men from all the services. I think my time there was probably the hardest I ever had in the forces, even with the work in the Advance Dressing Stations in the desert and in Italy. I was up at 6 a.m. to make sure they all got up and washed and shaved and it was midnight before I finished. I arranged concerts and sports and had a cricket pitch made for them.

I was keen to get back to the RAMC. One day the Princess Royal visited us and I took her round. Suddenly she said "Don't you ever feel you want to join a RAMC unit again?" I said "Very much so." They had tried to get me back many times but the Commandant, a Red Cross lady, had blocked it because I suppose she felt I was too useful at Burn Hall. I still have a letter from her thanking me for all I did.

Soon after I was posted to Leeds; then in 1942 to Glasgow to join a convoy. I sailed as part of a general hospital on the *Strathnaver*. The convoy of fifty-three ships refuelled at Freetown in West Africa and then reached the Cape. We had four days in Cape Town before embarking again for Suez and then we entrained to somewhere near Cairo. That was before Alamein. Unfortunately I broke an arm in Alexandria and I was posted to the 13th Light Field Ambulance. We would go into the desert and bring back casualties.

After that I was sent to the Lebanon where there were big manoeuvres on the Turkish border, I think to prepare for landings on the European mainland. I was still corporal under a sergeant in charge of C Section, Advance Dressing Stations, part of an independent brigade. My sergeant had an accident there when he was lighting a primus stove. There were spirits around and he had put a match to it, thinking it had gone out. It blasted back and burned all his chest. They took him to hospital and I was then in sole charge and had to deal with those who were sick and any casualties from manoeuvres. I had three ambulances to transfer serious cases to hospital.

When manoeuvres in the Lebanon were finished we went to the Sudan for six months, working in the general hospital, both in general wards and in the theatre. Earlier, in Egypt, I had gained my first-class nursing certificate.

After service in Egypt and the Sudan, I joined the 13th Light Field Ambulance. We were sent with the invasion force and landed in the south of Italy – I was right through the Italian campaign from start to finish, from Sicily right up to the River Po in the north of Italy, attending to our men and also to hundreds of enemy prisoners. I was promoted to sergeant while in action in Italy.

When the war ended, after further service in Austria and again in Italy, I came back to my wife and daughter and to work in Netherfield in Kendal where they guaranteed us ninety shillings a week for twelve weeks. I left after ten months when my wage was fifty-three shillings a week, the same as it had been before the war.

I saw an advertisement in the local paper for two driver-attendants for the Ambulance Service in Kendal. This was run by the Kendal Town Council. Another chap, William Stewart, who became a mayor of Kendal, and I, applied for the jobs. My MO had written a glowing testimonial. William and I got the jobs and I started in the Kendal Ambulance service on April 14th, 1947.

The Burgh had three ambulances at that time. One had been given by a gentleman from Windermere. Another was given by a gentleman from Kirby Lonsdale. These two were green Ford ambulances. The third was an old Austin model which had been used for ambulance work as well as isolation cases. We were notified about cases by the police. People 'phoned them and they passed the message on to us. Then the Council made the

Fire Chief the Ambulance Officer. Not that he knew anything about ambulance work. It was just that William Stewart and I were attached to the Fire Station. It meant that the Fire Chief was the boss. There had been one chap working the ambulances before William and I started but he had had no training like us. So really we were the first two ambulance men who had had proper training.

We were immediately thrown into all kinds of situations. We had road accidents, removals for operations, sudden illnesses. We went all over the county with what were called transfers. A place like ours in the Lake District had a great many tourists and when they had accidents they went into the local hospital, Westmorland County Hospital. It wasn't large enough to keep people for long periods and when they were a bit better they wanted to get nearer home so we transferred them to other places. A great little hospital was ours in Kendal and I've never heard a bad word about it, the staff were so kind to people. They have built a big new hospital now on the outskirts by the A65.

The Ambulance Service was taken over from the Burgh by the County Council. More men were recruited. Mr Stewart, who had joined with me, left to go into business on his own and the chap who was there when we started also left to go into other work, so I was now foreman driver.

We transferred with the Fire Service from our old site in Aynam Road to new quarters beside the Police headquarters, so the Police, Fire Service and Ambulance Service were together but they had their separate headquarters. The Fire Service and Ambulance Service were now quite separate. We were all under Westmorland County but with the reorganisation of the counties in the early '70s, we became Cumbria. The Chief Ambulance Officer was at Carlisle and they appointed a chap from Lancaster to be the Station Officer at Kendal. I was made his deputy.

When I retired we had five ambulances. We had Bedfords and Morrises, but now I'm told the bodies are being made in Ireland. At Ambleside at one time the work was done by voluntary drivers. If they were wanted, they were called out but now what with the greatly increased traffic on the Lake District roads, they've got four full-time men at Ambleside, and of

course about a dozen here in Kendal where they do shifts. In my
day we used to do our work through the day and finish at five
o'clock at night. After that, you were on stand-by and they'd
ring you if you were needed. Then you'd get paid for the time
you were out. After that they introduced shifts. The first was
eight in the morning till four. You had a break to eat, depending
on what jobs had to be done. Two other men came on from four
till midnight. From midnight till eight next morning two more
men came on. You might have to take people forty-two miles to
Lancaster and back during the night. I've known in the old days
when I was on stand-by duty, I've been out of my house three
times during the night, and that was three times during the
night to Lancaster and back – and the wife's never known I'd
been out of the house!

When William Stewart and I started, the A6 from Kendal to
Carlisle was one of the busiest roads in the country. We had
some very severe winters and I think I've picked up cases every
half mile of that road over the years, some of them after severe
crashes. I remember one Sunday afternoon years ago that a
coach coming down Shap went right over the edge down the
slope. Six died outright. This was the time before radio and I got
the call by 'phone through the police. It was after nine that
night before we got all the injured in for treatment and brought
back the dead. It was an old-fashioned coach with an open
sunshine roof. Some of the passengers had been thrown out and
a number, sadly, fell on stony ground. The road was choc-a-bloc
with cars and I was the first ambulance up there. The difficulty
was getting the injured up the slope and the crush of cars slowed
everything up.

When I got back the second time there was a great jam of
traffic. A chap came up to me and said "Where do you think
you're going?" I said "To load up again." He said "You'll never
get near it for the cars." I said "Let's get some of them out of the
road and get on with the job." A policeman further up said to
me "Do you know who you were speaking to?" – "No." – "That
was the Chief Constable." – "Well," I replied, "he should have
had the road cleared."

I've been involved in accidents on the lake. People have had
bad wounds when they've been caught in propellor blades. I've
been out all night when there were pot-holing accidents. We've

carried people down from the mountains, also we've been involved in a few train crashes, but not big disasters; and of course motor accidents of all descriptions. We did first-aid on the spot, attending to fractures and stopping bleeding. We had no radio then and had to get in touch from the nearest phone. When we did get radio, in the beginning it wasn't too successful. The range was limited.

I also had to deal with drowning incidents, both on the River Kent and down at the estuary where it runs into Morecambe Bay. I remember one case where there was a mill up Staveley way. It was many years ago. Someone had seen a little boy near the mill face-downwards in the dam. We got him out and worked on him with artificial respiration for quite a while. We rushed him to Kendal hospital and I worked on him in the back of the ambulance. At Kendal the doctor said "Carry on" but sadly it was to no avail. He must have fallen into the dam and how long he had been there I don't know.

There was a young girl at Arnside. I still have a newspaper cutting about her. We came back to Kendal at sixty miles an hour. She had collapsed in the water but fortunately we managed to save her.

I've a vivid memory of one winter night in the days when sometimes I was on my own. This time it was up Shap way. I was called out by the Fire Service which did the controlling in those early days. I went up Shap to go to a farm up a track road. There had been heavy snow and nobody had been up for a few days. What had happened was that a cockerel had flown off a wall and brought a heavy stone down onto a young lad's head. It was impossible for my ambulance to get up and a farmer who had a big sheep farm on the main road offered to take me in his Land Rover. By this time the police had arrived and we went up. We put hay and blankets in the Land Rover for the lad to lie on. We had a struggle to get up through the deep snow but we made it. The young boy, who had a depressed fracture, was semi-conscious. We lowered him into the ambulance, and took him to the Pendlebury Children's Hospital and his father went with him.

There was a happy ending to that story. Many years later I was walking through a street in Kendal when there was a tap on my shoulder. This chap said "You know me?" "Sorry, I'm afraid I don't." He pointed to the lad beside him who was wearing a grammar school cap. "You remember you came up to our farm and took him to Manchester?" I must say, looking at that lad made me realise that was where you got the real reward for your work as an ambulance- man. Those are the things that make the job worthwhile.

I was off the road for the last four years of service and worked in the office. When Cumbria took over the running of the ambulance service, there had been two men who did what they called 'sitting car' duty. They organised volunteers to collect patients to take them to hospital. They were paid per mile. When Cumbria took over, all the administration for the south part of Cumbria was done from Barrow. The ambulance cases and sitting cases were on telex and the two chaps who had been on sitting cars in Kendal were transferred to other jobs. I got the job of organising both the ambulances and sitting cars. When I finished we had five ambulances in Kendal to cover the area.

Looking back over the years I can say I enjoyed my life in the Ambulance Service. I think when I say I enjoyed it, it was because I felt it was doing someone some good. I was doing my best to relieve suffering and pain. I think it's a feeling that all the men and women have who work in the health service of our country.

Working in General Practice

DR SHEILA COCHRANE
GP

MY FATHER started his medical career in the Edwardian era. He was born in Darvel in Ayrshire, the town where the inventor of penicillin lived, but the family moved to Glasgow when he was two years old. He went to Glasgow University, qualified as a doctor in 1909, worked in hospitals in Glasgow and then did locums in general practice and also a voyage as a ship's surgeon on a Blue Funnel liner to China and Japan. This was followed by an assistantship in a London practice where the doctor sat with a cash box on his desk to collect the fees. My father didn't think this was the kind of medicine that he would like to do and left. He came to Kendal in 1912 as a locum for Dr Riddell, a GP, who was also a Glaswegian and whose family were great friends of the families of both my parents. He liked Kendal and the type of practice so much that in 1913 he purchased a practice in Maude Street from a very unusual doctor called Dr Parker. Dr Parker still lived in the house and I remember my father describing how there had to be two of everything on the table, for example, salt and pepper, so that conversation was not interrupted by passing them to each other.

When the First World War broke out there was a doctor on the opposite corner of Maude Street, Dr Jack, who was married with three young children. My father, being then unmarried, said that he was the one who should go off to the war, which he did. Sadly, Dr Jack went out to France in 1918, not long before the war ended,and he was the one who was killed. My father and Dr Jack had been great friends and had had the idea that they would like to buy all the practices in Kendal as they became vacant, put their own men into them and all work together. The First World War ended their plans.

My father came back after the war with a Military Cross, but the Kendal practice had to be built up because nobody had looked after it. He married my mother in 1919. My uncle, who was eight years younger, joined the practice a few years later. They had independent surgeries; my father still at the corner of Maude Street and my uncle in a house in Stricklandgate opposite the Kendal Post Office.

In 1927, when I was four, my father built a suite of rooms in the garden behind the house. Previously the consulting room was in the house and there was just a wee waiting-room. He built what was really advanced for that time: a very pleasant surgery with two consulting rooms, a dispensary, a waiting-room and a violet-ray room. They all had lovely parquet floors and I remember my mother looking after them with beeswax and turpentine. The small waiting-room in the house was still used as a private waiting-room.

My uncle moved from his surgery in Stricklandgate to the new building in Maude Street. The big house on the corner of Maude Street and Stricklandgate – now occupied by the solicitors Thomson and Wilson – was our home. The surgery, now extended and modernised, is still in Maude Street. My mother looked after all the books for the practice. In those days it was mainly private practice with lots of bills sent out twice a year. There was also a dispensary scheme – a kind of insurance which allowed a consultation and a bottle of medicine for a shilling. There was a lady dispenser who also acted as a receptionist. She answered the telephone and dispensed medicines, often weighing out the ingredients and mixing them with water and other liquids. The bottles were then wrapped up neatly in white paper and sealed with red sealing wax softened by a small gas burner. In those days there were not nearly so many pills, and ointments came in big jars, not in tubes, and were put into small round boxes or little glass jars by the use of a palette knife. The dispenser had to make a note of everything that a patient had and the doctor noted every call. These would be translated into bills by my mother. For years she worked with kalamazoo folders, a well-known accounting system, until the NHS came into being. She loved her involvement with the practice and supported my father in all that he did.

I was born in 1923 and although my background was, so to speak, medical, it was not assumed that I would inevitably go into medicine. I went to the Kendal High School from the age of five until I was eighteen. Maths was my best subject and when I was told that I had got 100% in the three maths papers in my school certificate, I thought I would like to try to get into Cambridge to do a maths degree. If I didn't get into Cambridge I thought I might try to read medicine at St Andrews. I had a very keen young maths teacher who was longing to introduce applied maths into the school and I was the first person to take it. So in 1942 I went to Newnham College, Cambridge and got a degree in maths.

Because it was war-time, if you were studying maths or science, at the end of your course you had to register with the Central Register and you were directed into one of the services, usually as a civilian. I opted for the Admiralty and was sent to Fairlie on the River Clyde in Scotland in the same county of Ayrshire in which my father was born. I was billeted in the Mackerston Hotel in Largs with three other girls and eighteen men, all scientists. I spent fifteen months doing anti-submarine research which involved me going out to a test ship anchored off Fairlie pier. This ship was originally the *Pioneer*, a paddle steamer which used to sail on the run from West Loch Tarbert to Islay and whose saloons had been turned into laboratories. (Little did I think that in later years I would visit Islay twice yearly and that I would find a picture of the *Pioneer* in the local museum). The research was asdic, the sonic field, and was really the precursor of the modern scanners in medicine, although at that time the oscillators were being used to scan the seas for submarines. I was in the test section, testing the oscillators in deep sea conditions.

When the war finished in 1945 and women could be released from the Admiralty to go to a university for full time study, my father said that I should decide if I wished to take up medicine and I thought that I would like to do so. If I went back to Cambridge I would have to go elsewhere for the clinical training so we thought that Liverpool or Manchester would be preferable, especially as my father had close ties with some of the consultants who came up to the Westmorland County Hospital where he was an honorary surgeon. He enjoyed this part of his medical practice very much and performed it without any monetary reward. So in 1945 I started my medical training at Liverpool University. Because I already had a degree, I didn't count as an ex-service person for a grant and my father paid for all my education. I found it comical when the Vice-Chancellor was welcoming the students and said "Now you are about to go out into the world" – I was sitting next to a bald RAF officer and quite a few of us had been away during the war.

I didn't plan to do general practice because my father thought it would be quite a hard life for a girl. I spent four years in the Liverpool hospitals – a year doing surgery with the Professor of Surgery in the Liverpool Royal Infirmary, six months doing medicine, five months gynaecology, a year at the Liverpool Maternity Hospital and eleven months at Alderhey Children's Hospital doing ENT, orthopaedics and paediatric medicine. The Professor of Child Health suggested that I might do a year of research but, as I was older starting medicine, I didn't want to do this.

I went on holiday to Cornwall for a week, thinking that when I went back I must decide what to do. I rather tended towards midwifery, but when I came back I found my father was ill with heart failure. He said if I was going to come into the practice now was the time to decide. This was June 1955. I decided that if I said no, the chance would have gone, so I started in the practice at Maude Street on September 1st, 1955. My father was very pleased. He was going to make me an immediate partner, sharing his share so that the two young doctors Oddy and Bradshaw who had joined the partnership would not suffer financially. My uncle had died two years previously. My father died eighteen days after I got home. You might have thought that it was just meant to happen.

Frankly, I didn't want to leave Liverpool. I remember going round, lamenting the fact that I had to go home. People asked me where that was. I said "The Lake District" and of course they thought I was silly because they would have loved to work here.

Starting in the practice wasn't as hard as starting my first day as a junior hospital doctor. When I went to the Liverpool Royal after qualifying, I felt the weight of the whole hospital on my shoulders and when I went to bed and heard an ambulance coming into casualty, it was an awful feeling. But when I started in the practice my father was at home for those eighteen days and that was a help. And of course there were the other two doctors. One evening when I went into the surgery, I found my partner had been called out. I opened the door of a packed waiting-room and offered to see anyone – only *one* person came. So much for the new doctor!

When I came back to Kendal we had three surgeries a day, Monday to Saturday. Originally my father also had two on Sunday but latterly they were by appointment and were discontinued when the NHS came into being. We often found that the people who came to the Saturday evening surgery had been to the first house of the cinema, so we cut that out. A few years later we stopped the Saturday afternoon surgery leaving only a morning one. In my father's day, he and my uncle didn't have a half day but after the young partners came he did have one.

It is interesting how group practices build up. Our practice in Kendal is a good example. After my father died there were three of us. Across Maude Street was the other practice which had been run by Dr Jack until 1918. He was followed by Dr Craig who took a partner, Dr Holmes. When the NHS came in they took another partner, Dr Birkett, because if you hadn't taken in a partner before July 1st, 1948 the Government would have installed someone of its own choice. So now there were three of us, and three across the road. When Dr Craig retired Dr Gill came, so it was still three and three. In 1958 when Dr Holmes was retiring, leaving two in that practice, we united with the two remaining doctors who moved over to join us. We extended the surgery so that we got better premises. Now there were four men and me. We each had a consulting room and we had a receptionist and a dispenser.

In 1973 we got permission to take a sixth partner, a very nice girl, and that was great for me. Dr Caird was with us for six years before marrying a Canadian and going to Canada. The old originals were all born within the same decade. So first one

retired, then another and another and another. I retired as a
doctor eight years ago.

There are of course differences in atmosphere and environment between practices in a very nice area like Kendal and
those in inner cities. You have the whole mix of people in a place
like this – country people and local townspeople. You know your
patients not just as a doctor. I remember seeing one of my
patients with a bad heart struggling up Beast Banks so I could
warn her about hills, etc. You were in close everyday contact
with people. Kendal is a good size and my father said that if he
had his life to live over again, he would like to do just the same.
At first people would say "You are not like your father," but
that was perfectly understandable because he was much loved.
They were very nice to me. When I retired I knew that I did not
want to leave Kendal. I like it very much. I know a lot of people
and am busy with some charitable work.

In cities now it must be hard to be a GP. A friend in Liverpool
who has a surgery in the centre of the city has had to move into
the waiting-room to continue his surgery because lads were
shying bricks at his consulting room window. There is also the
worry of having to go out in the night. When I was in the
Liverpool Maternity Hospital forty years ago and was called out
on the flying squad, there was always someone waiting to carry
my bag up the patient's stairs but today I would be worried
that someone would wallop me for my bag. In Kendal I never
felt threatened through the night at all. Kendal is very well
doctored with three big practices. Another thing about the
service here is that the Helme Chase Maternity Hospital is very
good. The doctors attend their own patients ante-natally and
during the confinement, which is nice for the patient. They have
the back-up of a consultant but the GP is often there when
the baby is delivered and also post-natally. Luckily I'm still
associated with the local branch of the College of Midwives as
their president. Kendal has been ideal. In my father's day, he
was, as I have said, an honorary consultant to the local hospital
as were three other GPs in the days before there were housemen.
They did all the emergency operations. When the NHS came in
the number of the local doctors was reduced and my father gave
up this side of his work. Two of my partners carried on with
anaesthetics for some years.

When the NHS came in there were gradual changes in attitudes and practice generally. Some people probably became more demanding with an emphasis on rights – just some. But in Kendal the relationship was and is very good between doctor and patient. Nowadays I think relationships may be changing again. You get an alteration, for one thing, because of American attitudes and litigation. There are greater external pressures on midwifery and orthopaedics for example. These give the impression of it being rather more of a business. When I think of the number of bills which my father tore up because he thought the patient couldn't afford to pay it, I realise how different things are. One family I know didn't pay for their babies, but when the NHS came in it became lucrative to have almost yearly babies! I would hate to go back to the days when you had to charge for a consultation or a visit because it meant you couldn't do extra, maybe rather unnecessary, visits without adding to the expense.

I remember a story about a farmer's wife who was not getting on in labour so my father put her into his little Morris Cowley car to drive her to the Westmorland County Hospital in Kendal. The bumpy road did the trick and the baby was born in the car. They called the baby Morris and when my father was selling the car he asked the farmer if he would like to buy his son's birthplace! Another old tale was about when my father had a quinsy – you rarely see that now – it was before he was married and he stayed up poulticing and poulticing his throat. Finally at two o'clock in the morning he opened his mouth and stuck a knife into the abscess. At that moment my grandmother in Glasgow woke suddenly, awoke my grandfather and said "There's something wrong with Jim. I can see blood." Good old Celtic sixth sense.

Looking back, I see there's been a steady development in medicine over the years, both during my father's time and mine. Consider the development of antibiotics: the speed of change has increased and now it is quite hard to keep up. There certainly has been a massive change in the drugs available, in the treatment and in the diagnosis with all the scans that you can use, with lots of hopeful changes in the treatment of leukaemia and cancers and illnesses like that. Look at the changes in midwifery. They're not just concentrating on the live or stillborn baby but on the best possible life so they may be veering towards doing caesarians sooner than they used to.

I find I am fully occupied in my retirement. Firstly there's the Save the Children Fund. Our branch was founded in 1957. It was formed to raise ten guineas to sponsor one child and one year recently we sent off £55,000 to Headquarters. Because of my practice commitments, which would limit my help at events, I offered to become the treasurer and I still am. We had a wonderful friend, Miss Cooke, who was a Moral Welfare Officer who, when she retired, was a bit down in the dumps. She offered to store our goods – pens, dusters and tea-towels – and to sell them. She built up a shop in the front room of her house selling new Save the Children Trading goods and the year she died she had sold £12,000 worth. We were distressed, not knowing what to do about our shop, but three of us bought the house, turned the upstairs into a flat and gave our branch the downstairs rent free, to continue the shop. I spend a lot of time there for I'm still the treasurer. Looking back, one of the people I admired most was Miss Cooke. I was thrilled when she got the MBE. She was employed by the Church of England and looked after a hostel for girls and women. She went the extra mile all the time. For example, once when the police found a girl on the Castle Hill in the night they wakened Miss Cooke who immediately took her in. If a pregnant youngster came to see me, I only had to phone Miss Cooke and I knew that everything would be arranged. She was a saint with her feet on the ground. She used to give so much to other people that she was almost embarrassed going up to the altar for communion because the soles of her shoes needed mending. She certainly deserved her honour.

I'm also Chairman of the Westmorland branch of the Multiple Sclerosis Society. At first I was told that it would be only three meetings per year but now it's monthly meetings and lots of involvement, which I like. I've made many friends.

I'm President of the Kendal YWCA. When you come as a doctor to a town you are often asked to do other things. My mother was on the YW committee and my father was a JP, an Alderman of the County Council and Chairman of the Kendal High School Governors. I was brought up to feel that I should give something back to the community. I am President of the College of Midwives Westmorland branch.

One of the nicest things about general practice is that you see your babies growing up and going on to have their own babies. You learn about human nature. I suppose part of me wonders, now that they say patients should be told everything, what the effect will be on some people. I remember my father cautioning me to be wary of this and he was very wise. I think you must be careful not to destroy a person's hope for their future too soon.

New doctors are now being trained not to do so much social visiting of older people. The theory is that they are less likely to miss medical symptoms on a requested visit. I know I over visited. I felt that even if you weren't giving anything medically, at least your older patients knew that you were there. We used to have an excellent team of district nurses but their numbers have been greatly reduced. Health visitors and Social Service staff are also pressed for time so old folks are visited less often.

I am so glad that people still remember my father and my uncle. There's a story that tickled me. About a year before I retired I was sitting in a patient's house and she was telling me about one of her children who had been born prematurely and had been put into a large shoe box by my father. She was saying how marvellous my father was and suddenly asked "How long have you been here, doctor?" I said "Twenty-nine years." They were quite pro-me but it was my father they revered. Another person, referring to him, said "You could *talk* to him." To me as a doctor that says a lot.

Doctor's Receptionist

EILEEN DAWS

MY FATHER'S family came from the village of Bowston in South Lakeland, and I was born in Kendal, in Windermere Road where my parents were living. I went to St Thomas's School at the bottom of the hill, then to what was known as the Senior Girls, and I left school at fourteen.

I went to Staveley to work at the box factory. We made cardboard boxes for the K-shoes factory at Netherfield. After nine years I came back to Kendal to work in the *Westmorland Gazette* in advertising.

Then I saw a position advertised for the surgery, for a receptionist. I thought 'I'll never get this job' as I was thirty by this time. 'They're sure to appoint somebody younger.' I had already applied for a job up at the hospital, typing and taking notes for the specialists, but I didn't get it. I didn't feel I could do nursing but I wanted to be involved in the medical world in some way.

However, I thought there was no harm in trying for the receptionist's job. The doctor could only say no if he wanted somebody younger. I went for the interview and the doctor said "Why do you want the job?" I said I always wanted a job where I could be associated one way or another with the medical services. I told him I hadn't got the hospital job. The general manager whom I worked for at the Gazette had some connection with the hospital and he didn't want me to leave. When I came back he offered me a rise in wages to stay on.

When I went for my interview for the receptionist's job there

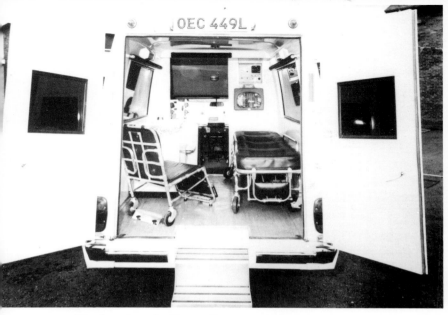

The interior of a Range Rover ambulance, 1973.

Dr Sheila Cochrane's father's house and surgery with the later addition, where she practised.

Sheila Cochrane making a presentation to Eileen Daws on her retirement as Receptionist, 1985.

Maryport, where Constance Gate was District Nurse.

Painless 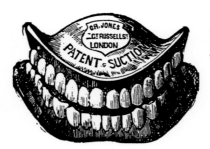 Dentistry.

ARTIFICIAL TEETH.

Mr. G. H. JONES, Surgeon Dentist,
57 GREAT RUSSELL STREET, LONDON, W.C.,
(Immediately opposite the British Museum),

Has obtained

HER MAJESTY'S ROYAL LETTERS PATENT
For his improved method of adapting

Artificial Teeth by Atmospheric Pressure.

Note.—Improved Prize Medal Teeth (London and Paris) are adapted in the most difficult and delicate cases, on a perfectly painless system, extraction of loose teeth or stumps being unnecessary, and by recent scientific discoveries and improvements in mechanical dentistry detection is rendered utterly impossible, both by close adjustment of the artificial teeth to the gums and their life-like appearance. By this patented invention complete mastication, extreme lightness, combined with strength and durability, are insured; useless bulk being obviated, articulation is rendered clear and distinct. In the administration of Nitrous Oxide Gas, Mr. G. H. JONES has introduced an entirely new process.

TESTIMONIAL.

MY DEAR SIR,—Allow me to express my sincere thanks for the skill and attention displayed in the construction of my Artificial Teeth, which renders my mastication and articulation excellent. I am glad to hear that you have obtained Her Majesty's Royal Letters Patent, to protect what I consider the perfection of Painless Dentistry. In recognition of your valuable services you are at liberty to use my name.

S. G. HUTCHINS,
By appointment Surgeon Dentist to the Queen.

To G. H. JONES, ESQ.

PAMPHLET GRATIS AND POST-FREE.

An advertisement for artificial teeth in the 1880s.

Kelvin Rees, Kendal Dentist.

Constance Gate in retirement.

Ethel Woods, Matron at Battersea Hospital 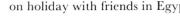 on holiday with friends in Egypt

were four male doctors in the practice and Dr Sheila Cochrane, who was on holiday when I was interviewed.

When I was told I had the job I could hardly believe it. But I was very pleased. At last I was associated with the work I had always wanted to do. I think an interest my father had had rubbed off on me. He went into the RAMC in the First World War because he wanted to do something medically, but had never had the opportunity. He was a gardener at Whitefoot, then went to work in the paper mill, Croppers of Burneside. When we were at Windermere Road if anybody had anything wrong with them, they would immediately go for Albert Daws. He would do first aid and if need be, send them on to hospital. I remember him saying when he had done a job on someone who had a fracture, the doctor later said how well he had done. Perhaps that's why I enjoyed my job as a doctor's receptionist and I never thought of moving on anywhere.

When I started, the wages were of course much lower than today's. They were paid by the National Health but again we hadn't the inflation we have now and things were cheaper then. When I started in the box factory I got 10s. a week, out of which I had half a crown a week to pay for my bus fare to Staveley. Out of the 7s.6d. that was left I paid board to my mother so there wasn't much over.

There was never a dull moment in the surgery. You never knew what would happen next. For example, one day one of Dr Oddy's patients who wasn't very well asked me if I'd sit with him. After a little the man said he felt all right. But as he walked out of the surgery he fell down the surgery steps. Someone came rushing in and said "There's a man outside lying on the pavement." Dr Oddy helped to bring him back in. The man had broken his teeth and bruised his lip. Dr Oddy saw to him and we got a car to take him home.

I remember Dr Cochrane once calling me. She had a little boy with his mother. He had cut his hand very badly and needed some stitching. He was screaming and every time he screamed the blood pumped out. They couldn't hold him and Dr Cochrane asked me to help. She said to me "You don't mind blood, do you?" I assured her it didn't bother me. So I helped to hold his hand while his mother held and comforted him and Dr Cochrane put a few stitches in.

We had to summon ambulances for anybody we thought might have had a heart attack, if they told us they had chest pains. The doctor would leave them with a nurse in the examination room while an ambulance was called. We used to have contact with the police, perhaps involving drug addicts. I remember we had a burglary. They were after drugs. As far as I remember, they couldn't get into the dispensary because the door was locked and they took some petty cash. We had a burglar alarm put in.

We had to be ready for anything. If we had to send a patient up as an emergency, even before the doctor had time to ring for his card, my colleague Eva or I would have taken it out and gone along with it. So the doctor didn't have to bother ringing. He got the card and report without any delay. Unfortunately nowadays younger people perhaps don't realise the same need for urgent action and I've seen the doctor having to come down himself for the card or report.

There was always a good spirit in the practice and we got to look on the doctors as our friends as well as our employers.

Many things have changed in the practice over the years. Take the filing of cards. We got the cards out for the doctors. We used to cut strips of cardboard to number the cards for identification. We used to get offcuts from the *Westmorland Gazette* office to make the strips or Eva my colleague and I would get them from Bateman and Hewitson. I recently went to the office and they told me that nowadays they pay a great deal of money for what I got for nothing!

I believe a Practice Manager was appointed last year. But that was after I retired. It is a lady and she does the wages, delegates the girls' jobs in the practice, does the rotas for the doctors, and all the organisational jobs. I suppose in the NHS more and more non-medical jobs are being created because the service is growing all the time.

You saw things changing as time went on. There was an increase in the paperwork we had to do, in connection with the filing and the reports. We of course had typing but there weren't nearly as many letters to do, going back twenty odd years. The change was in the amount of work I had to cope with. Eva and I did the letters between us but in those days we never seemed to have too many to do. Many more people are being referred to the hospital than used to be.

Another change was that nurses were now doing a lot of the work the doctors previously did: taking blood tests, doing dressings, ear syringing, innoculations. Then if a doctor wanted to examine a patient he would do it in his own examination room or send him or her to the nurse's room and with the nurse there have the patient examined. Then the nurse had to fill in forms, e.g. for a blood test. Everything seemed to need a form.

When I started there wasn't a nurse attached to the practice. There had been district nurses. We got three district nurses specifically attached to the surgery who would go to see the doctors' patients. That number rose to five or six who would look after our patients. But we didn't get an actual surgery nurse till about twenty years ago. That was Hazel Proctor. There are now about four nurses attached to the surgery.

The forms the nurses had to fill in went up to the Path. labs at the hospital. I'd get them from the nurse or the doctor and perhaps fill them in myself if they weren't filled in. I'd put them in a box and take them up to the hospital at ll.30 or ll.45 so that, if they had to go to Lancaster, they could go by van from the hospital. What they could do in the laboratory at Kendal they did. If not, they went on to Lancaster in the afternoon.

I retired in 1985 and have had quite a busy time since then. I am President of the local WI and have another year to go. I enjoy that. I worked in the tea-bar of the local hospital and also do hospital radio. On Wednesday nights they have a quiz in the wards. I go through it on the radio and then go round and give people forms to give the answers. It's quite an easy quiz to give everybody a chance. All in all, I've had an enjoyable life as a receptionist doing what I wanted to do and that has carried over into my retirement.

District Nurse in Cumbria

CONSTANCE GATE

I WAS born in 1909 and I was to spend most of my nursing career on the west coast of Cumbria. There were seven of us in the family including Mum and Dad and we had a very happy life. My parents were lovely people. My father was a Weights-and-Measures Inspector. I used to have great fun with my brother who was the eldest boy; I was the youngest girl. I would aggravate him, out of mischief. He had a girl friend whom he eventually married and her maiden name was Herring. When her letters came for him I used to get them and say to him "Miss Fish has written to you." He would be furious with me and would beg Mother to hide the letters when the postman came and not to let me see them. I was only about nine or ten at the time and it was all good fun.

I got married in 1940 and my husband was a Cumbrian born and bred. I've lived here in Maryport ever since. My husband had a gents' outfitters business in the main street that his father had had before him. But his heart was never really in the business. He was a historian and a model engineer, a real perfectionist who always wanted to be working with his hands. When he left secondary school his father wanted him to go into the business but he became an apprentice at Mr Wharton's foundry down by the docks. Later when the slump came he got a job in electrical engineering, for he was a gifted man who had been good at science at school.

In the early days before I was married, when there were no vacuum cleaners and washing machines and Mother had her hands full, it was decided I should stay at home and help. I didn't like it. Then a friend of mine who was in the St John Ambulance Brigade invited me to come along and Father and Mother allowed me to go. I loved it from the minute I went. The nurses were called VADs in those days. I worked hard at home so that I could go and do voluntary work at the infirmary in the afternoons. As a result I realised I wanted to be a nurse and nothing else. My father warned me it was hard work and I wouldn't get much pay, but my mind was made up. A nurse I'd be. I'd even stop in the infirmary till nine or ten at night and I wouldn't have minded stopping all night.

Father and Mother were getting worried. What was I doing out till that time of night? One day Father said "You know, they won't give you a gold chain for what you are doing. Do you really want to be a nurse?" Later Mother asked me if I really wanted to leave home. I told her that I did want to be a nurse. She said that Father and she had talked it over, and if I really wanted to, I could. After that I couldn't get going fast enough in case they changed their minds. I wrote to the hospital and they sent me an application form. It had to be signed by my parents. My father had been very doubtful about my enthusiasm, and had reminded me that it would be hard work. Now he took his fountain-pen – and I've never forgotten the words he said then, which have helped me many and many a time when I might have thrown it all up. He turned to me and said, "Remember, my dear, if they don't want you, we do."

I got experience in many places: in Huddersfield, then as a night staff nurse in Worcester. I did my midwifery and fever training. One of the girls I trained with went to Hammersmith and we kept in touch. She suggested I joined her so we could have good times together, so I went to Hammersmith and did my district nurses' training for about two and a half years. Then I went to Devon as a district nurse and then to Gillingham in Kent.

I met my husband Dick through my other brother who was a great sportsman. He brought his girl friend Eleanor to supper. Eleanor was Dick's sister, and though I didn't know him then, I had heard a lot about him. I was seventeen.

Years later he wrote to me when I was an assistant matron in Huddersfield. When I opened the letter it had a lot of postcards in it, all views of Maryport and the district. He had described them all on the back and he wrote·"I'd like to show you these myself." That was how it started and how I came to be in Maryport. We were married on November 30th, 1940. By that time Dick had taken the shop over. His father had died and his mother pleaded with him as she didn't want the business to go out of the family. He also volunteered for the Fire Brigade and was kept very busy.

One night a lady came and introduced herself as Miss Illingworth, Superintendent of the District Nurses from Carlisle. She said she'd heard I'd done a lot of district nursing and one of her nurses had had a major operation and she'd be off months and could I help her? Miss Illingworth suggested I might do part-time, even that would help her. Well, I started by doing three days a week, then it got to a week, then doing holiday duties. The Superintendent came down from Carlisle and told me she'd been looking at my worksheet. Apparently I was putting in more hours part-time than the full staff nurses. I told her I'd been happy and that it suited me. She said "Well, I think you're being very foolish. I realise there's room for another nurse in Maryport. You're not getting holidays with pay and you're not getting a pension. So you think about it." By then I had two girls growing and I asked my husband what he thought. "It's your job and you understand it," he said. I thought, well, I could give it up if it didn't work out. So I became a full-time district nurse in Maryport.

When I first started I walked everywhere. Then the authorities decided they would buy me a bicycle. After that Dick bought me an autocycle. I had that for years and they made me an allowance of a penny halfpenny a mile for the petrol. But as I was out in all weathers on the autocycle and often got soaked, I asked if there was a chance of getting a car, and at last I got one.

My permanent area was Maryport although sometimes I went beyond it. Maryport used to be a mining port. It was much poorer in those days. There was a fishing fleet when the docks were open. Boats from Spain and other countries came in for coal from the pits. There was a shipbuilding yard down at the dock, Ritsons Yard. So it was the families of miners and fishermen and townspeople I worked among. There wasn't the poverty I had seen in London and other places. You never saw children without shoes, but difficulties were often due to bad management in the home. There were some parents then, just as now, who didn't care.

The object of district nursing was to train families as one went round, to educate them as much as possible in hygiene and make sure children were taken to have their injections against polio. The health visitors used to back us up and we used to back them up.

We hear today of children being put into care. I had a case where two children were involved. A doctor rang me up to ask if I'd be good enough to visit a house and see an old man in it, give general attention and give the children a bath and put them in clean clothes. I went about five o'clock and it was winter time. I knocked and knocked on the door but nobody came. I knew I had got the right address. I looked upstairs and there were two little faces at the window: a dirty filthy council-house window. I motioned them to come down and open the door, which they did. I asked where their mother was. They didn't know. I said "I've come to see a man," and they said "That's Grandad. He's upstairs." I went upstairs, expecting to see a poorly old man in bed, and there was a man as dead as dead could be. I looked at the children and asked them if they had had anything to eat. They really were like pathetic little orphans of the storm. There was some old mouldy bread in the pantry. I looked in the cupboards. There was nothing.

I went to the lady next door and asked if she knew what was going on. She was a kindly woman who said the mother had gone off the previous day and she'd take the children in. The grandfather probably hadn't been dead when she left. I told her I'd be back, and rang the NSPCC. The doctor was a fine man, the loveliest doctor, and one who really cared. When I told him he said "Oh, Nurse Gate, what have I let you in for?" I said my chief worry was for the two children who had been left all night. I told him I had rung the NSPCC. I went back to the house and when the NSPCC Officer came he was disgusted. But that was the only time I had children taken into care.

There was another one that was a borderline case. A

colleague was going away on holiday the week before Christmas and asked me if I would go to a certain lady in Loweswater Road. She couldn't remember the number but it was only a short little road and I'd recognise the house because the gate was broken off. The woman was pregnant and due any time and her blood pressure had to be taken twice a day. I was on my way to this house when I met one of the doctors. He asked if I had been to Violet's yet. I told him I was on my way. "Oh, good," he said, "for she has a Christmas present for you."

I found the house with the broken gate, with crusts of bread all over the drive. When I got in and looked at the kitchen floor, do you know what there were for carpets? Old army coats that the Home Guard used to wear. I just stood and looked and asked Violet to explain. She said they hadn't a carpet so she'd had to put them down. It was a council house living-room. The furniture was quite all right. The wallpaper on the wall was beautiful, and looked very professional. But on the sideboard was a big goose with its neck hanging down, dripping blood on the floor. I knew then what the doctor had been laughing at when he joked about a Christmas present.

The middle leaf of the dining-table had been taken out and in it were empty baked bean tins and cellophane wrappers that had held bread. The ashes from the grate were right out into the room, which had chip papers all over it. You never saw such a mess. She herself was in an awful filthy state.

I took her blood pressure, which was all right. She was twenty-eight years old. I asked her if she couldn't have made some effort to make the place nicer for the children.The two youngsters who were sitting on the settee were really filthy. "What's wrong with the children?" she asked. I said "Don't you think they could do with a good bath?" She said they'd had a bath earlier but I knew they hadn't. I had two girls myself and knew when children had had a bath. I said "Wouldn't it be nice, as your room is beautifully decorated, to keep the rest of it clean. Who decorated it?" "My husband," she replied. "He's a painter and decorator. It's all right for people like you to talk." I had quite a job trying to help her to see things right.

When my colleague came back from holiday and attended the woman again, she rang me up and told me that an inspector from the NSPCC had called, went upstairs and found filth and excreta on the mattresses. He gave the parents two days to clean it up. The woman did clean it up, for she was frightened the children would be taken into care.

I had many, many friends in the town and such a lot of them knew my husband. During the depression before the war, when it was dark, Dick's father would sometimes give Dick a sealed envelope with money in it. He'd say "Now, Dick, I want you to go down street." That's what they called the harbour. He told him a house number and sent him off with instructions to put the envelope through the letter box and try not to let anybody see him. After his father died, people would come into the shop and tell him that when things were hard, his Dad saved their dignity when he gave them money.

I remember one humble house: two up, one down, with an outside toilet and water from a tap in the yard. An old man lived in it. He had been in a pit explosion and his eyes and face were scarred. Nowadays he would have had skin grafting. He had also lost one hand. I used to go and put drops in his eyes. Gangrene started in his other hand but you never heard that man grumble. When I visited him he used to tell me things about the docks and pits. He finally had to go into hospital to have his other hand off. I was upset about that. He wasn't particularly clean for he hadn't a bathroom but I always got such a welcome when I went there. I'd slip him a packet of cigarettes. He couldn't light a cigarette and he used to say. "I've been longing for you to come, lass." I'd put the cigarette in his mouth and he'd go to the mantelpiece and rest it on the edge where he could pick it up again. I'd give him his eyedrops and we'd have a good chat.

What are the qualities needed for a district nurse? I can only repeat what I was told in my training. A nurse must remember she is a guest in someone else's house and she must behave as a guest. If you make the right approach at the first visit, you've won, but if you go in like a bull in a china shop, you've lost. You become sensitive to people and the way they live. I found that often I met kindness, sympathy and understanding in working class homes that were absent in some middle class homes.

I retired in 1969 after a happy life in nursing. I attended people who are now parents and grandparents. When I go out walking I might meet someone with a child who will ask

"Remember him, Nurse Gate? You were the first to see him."
There is a fine continuity in district nursing. The day I retired
one of my daughters took my place as district nurse. Wasn't that
lovely?

Dentist at Kendal

KELVIN REES

I WAS born in Oswestry in Shropshire in 1915 and went to London in 1922, where I went to University College School. I got my Higher School Certificate and then went on to the Royal Dental Hospital in Leicester Square when I was about eighteen.

I think two things influenced me. My family were patients of a very enthusiastic dentist and he was always talking about it. Also, I left school in 1932 and at that time there was the depression; the burden of advice then was that if you possessed qualifications you should be all right, which of course holds good to this very day. I did a little market research and found that dentistry was short-handed. Subjects I had taken at school including chemistry and physics helped me to get started in this direction.

I started making enquiries about dentistry. The chap I mentioned came from the Royal Dental Hospital and I went there till 1937, when I qualified. It was associated with Charing Cross Hospital just across the road and also with Kings College in the Strand.

As you can imagine, qualifying in 1937, that year and the next was a traumatic time generally with the run-up to the outbreak of war. The population was being issued with gas masks and lectures in Leicester Square were adjusted to take in the treatment of mustard-gas, ARP and so on. Medical subjects were held in the Charing Cross Hospital, in the dental school and others in the College in the Strand.

In 1938 I spent some time in Kings College doing a bit of post-graduate work. But the atmosphere was now deteriorating. I felt that to get started in general practice I would need quite a bit of money to buy a partnership. But what was the use if a war was going to break out? So I decided to go into the Navy. I joined in 1938 and did a year in peace-time. I was stationed in Haslar Hospital near Portsmouth and Gosport, the main naval hospital in that area. I worked at the barracks in Portsmouth till war broke out, when I was sent to Skegness, to Butlins Camp which the Navy took over, and after that to Chatham. I joined the Admiralty Medical Board as the dental member. We were vetting applicants for commissions for the regular navy.

After this I went to sea for two years on HMS *Hecla*, a destroyer depot ship. I picked her up at John Brown's yard on the Clyde, a brand new ship. We were in the Atlantic quite a bit, based on the Clyde or in Iceland. In December 1941, Pearl Harbour was bombed by the Japanese and we were sent out to the Far East. On the way out we were mined and put into Simonstown in South Africa for extensive repairs, on completion of which Operation Torch for the North African landings was starting so we went north for that, but we got torpedoed and the ship sank. After two years at a naval air station near Edinburgh I went out to the Far East via America, the Pacific Islands and Australia where I spent eighteen months as a staff officer.

The war finished and they were getting temporary personnel home. But being a regular, I was sent to Ceylon to help with that operation. So all in all before I came home myself, I was lucky to have seen and been involved in dentistry in different countries, building up experience of methods and techniques. Wherever I went I used to visit the local practitioners and I contacted the medical or dental ones in each location. This was in case ships were in difficulties and they needed these addresses. I got to know most of the practitioners in Melbourne, Australia. The Australian Dentists Association learned a BDA member had arrived there, so I was made an honorary member of the ADA while I was in Australia. I was the first BDA member to arrive since the war started, so I got involved in the dental scene quite a bit and saw what was going on.

Before Australia I had been to Cape Town in South Africa and met a surgeon- and-agent who practised in the Shell-Mex building like the one in London. At that time he introduced me to the acrylic plastics which we knew about before they arrived in England. Similarly colour photography was widely used in South Africa but restrictions prevented it coming to England. Orthodontrics is the straightening of children's irregular teeth. Orthodontic consultant practices dealing with children's crooked teeth existed in Melbourne usually without the parents present! Accompanying parents stayed in the waiting-room. Informal visits by colleagues were therefore quite welcome. I brushed up quite a bit on orthodontrics, for of course there was none of it in the Navy. I saw what they were doing with plastics in denture-making. Australians went in for a lot of porcelain and gold filling; the demand for high quality dentistry may have resulted from a marked tendency toward dental caries. Despite their excellent diet, New Zealand had the same curious problem, now thought to be linked with fluoride deficiency. I also saw a certain amount of high quality dentistry in Ceylon. It was expensive! I had gone there from Australia because they were closing down a lot of naval establishments and as a regular officer I was involved in this as many chaps had to go back home to civilian jobs. We had an establishment in the jungle, about six miles out from Colombo. With the fleet coming in we had had up to about a dozen dentists there, waiting passage home now that the war was over.

I left the Navy just as the Korean War was breaking out. By this time, having been married in 1947, I had a daughter aged two and a boy a few weeks old. I first took a job in Worthing but we had no intention of staying there. My wife was born in Kendal in the Lake District so we thought we'd come a bit further north. The family arrived in Buxton and we were there for quite a few months in a very nice practice where I picked up more ideas about other people's practices. Incidentally, at Buxton I found that the altitude made a marked difference to anaesthetics. They worked fast; patients dropped off to sleep quickly. While I was there I used to make weekend trips to the Lake District and met lots of people there. I came across a practice that was for sale in Kendal. I got friendly with the chap who was wanting to retire and we bought the goodwill and the house in this very beautiful part of the country, where I was to practise until I retired.

I came here realising one should meet the needs of the local community.

After 1921 the practice of dentistry had been made more professional; for example, a register was compiled and dentists had to go through the process of qualifying. When I came here there were still a few who had been practising before 1921, mostly making dentures.

A lot of my work came in from the K-Shoes factory just down the road, where some of the people at that time did not greatly appreciate the value of the conservation of teeth and the same might be said of a lot of the Westmorland country folk.

This began to change over the years. I expect my attitude to conservation contributed to that change, and all the time all over the country new graduates coming into the profession increased the emphasis on the preservation of teeth. The development of school dentistry helped to build this up. Mothers and fathers of young children had been offered treatment in their day but a high proportion had rejected it. But when they realised what they had missed, they became much more interested in dental preservation for their children. Ten million people called up in the war had experience of dentistry and surgeries. All this changed attitudes to the worth of dentistry.

When I came there was only one bus a week from some villages and I worked all day on a Saturday. As the years went by, the increase in car ownership brought some welcome relief. The people who lived out in the country required domiciliary visits. The doctors who came with me would co-operate in that and give anaesthetics all over the area, up to Staveley and the Kentmere Valley and Orton and Tebay particularly, at remote farms where the patients couldn't get back from Kendal very easily.

But that came to an end when pressure was brought to bear by the consultant anaesthetists because it was not in keeping with modern thought to give chloroform and ether without hospital resuscitation resources on the spot. That would have been in the fifties. I used to get 7s.6d. a time for taking the car out and the doctor got paid £2 for the anaesthetic. He took his car, also. We actually made a loss on those visits. As time went on there was a move away from domiciliary anaesthetics because of the inadequacy of facilities at home to meet higher standards of care and modern safety standards. In those days country doctors would tackle almost anything. Some of the old doctors told me they'd plaster up broken arms themselves. Then they began to send people to hospital. So it was inevitable that anaesthetics would be gradually phased out from use in the home.

Another change was that a hospital consultant dental surgeon was appointed, based on Lancaster and Kendal. Before that we did practically everything ourselves. The new consultant would tackle surgeon's jobs not appropriate for the local surgery and with beds and nursing staff available the more serious cases (impacted wisdom teeth, etc.) could be treated as in-patients.

An old fever hospital in Lancaster was converted for ear, nose and throat and dental surgery. At the hospital in Kendal the consultant would give his advice on cases referred to him at the out-patient department. An orthodontric consultant was appointed. Orthodontrics was another thing they were not very familiar with in those days. Now we can all see the advantages of having children's teeth straightened out. Some of these cases were difficult. Previously you had to do them yourself but now you could get the consultant's opinion and report. This could be very helpful. Orthodontrics is in demand today; perhaps the perfect teeth seen on TV may have boosted it. But treatment may take a couple of years or more and demands co-operation by children and parents, so results are not always up to expectations. The consultant's report is also useful in persuading the National Health Service to accept the cost.

One advance in the early 1960s was the introduction of the high-speed air motor. That came from America. There were manufacturers' trade shows to which I used to go. They were mainly in London at Alexandra Palace with the occasional one in Manchester and elsewhere. I got one of these machines, a Bordern air turbine, and it was fixed to my existing dental unit. It was a remarkable machine for those days using diamond bits; you had to spray water on it to keep it cool while it was going. That led to the development of the aspirator, which has to be used with it, to suck the water out of the mouth. Then we found we needed a nurse to work the aspirator, so the idea of four-handed dentistry came in.

When I went to the exhibition in 1964 at Alexandra Palace I

found that, apart from these two items, many things including dentists' chairs were the same as they used to be. But at the next exhibition I went to in 1968 everything was changed completely. One thing that had happened was that an American naval dentist, working during the Korean war, had done dentistry under conditions without much equipment. He had people lying on a couch and found this worked very well. So by 1968 we were getting chairs which lay right back with the nurse and aspirator on the left-hand side and the dentist's things on the right-hand side. The patient was supine and the nurse and dentist were seated on stools. At this point I completely refitted my surgery to the new standards. The change was quite exciting; it made the work much more interesting and the patients, too, got very interested in it. It gave us all a new lease of life.

This way we took on more staff and, more importantly, it speeded up the work. In 1951 there had been a gross overload of work. A free service had been promised to the public ever since the end of the war. In 1948 it really started but the backlog was not cleared by 1951, not by any manner of means. The backlog had been created by people with dentures coming in for a free set. But after three years the same government put an end to it by imposing charges.

The autoclave arrived and the dry-heat sterilizer. Ultrasonic cleaning came in. Cross-infection cases had cropped up throughout the country through the much greater use of needles. That of course was mainly on the medical side, not ours. Doctors had been in the habit of boiling syringes in water, but it was found that the hepatitis organism could survive that, so the era of sterilized packaged needles came in; and if you wanted to sterilize, the autoclave was much more effective than boiling water. The medical people produced tracts on the subject and we all took note.

Acrylics came in. We used to make all our dentures on the premises at the back of the house. My old senior mechanic was a great family friend, a Scotsman from Wick. He had an assistant and an occasional apprentice. There had been no vulcanite in my student days and in my first few years in the navy. Going over to acrylics was much better. Incidentally, the ancient Egyptians were rather good at making ǎrtificial teeth. They did quite a lot of gold work.

A problem was how to make substitutes for teeth that were missing. Teeth used to be allowed to get fairly loose before they were taken out, so extractions may not have been too bad. Hypnotism was quite common in the nineteenth century and is still used. There is an active society of dental hypnotists. There was a famous Indian surgeon in the early days of the Indian medical service, who relied upon the chewing of Indian hemp to get the patients into a drowsy state. That was at the beginning of the nineteenth century. Then anaesthetics came in, in the 1830s. False teeth were usually carved from ivory blocks carefully sculpted to fit the gums. They used a spring from the bottom denture to the top to hold it up. The Duke of Wellington had some such appliance.

Then came a man called Stent, one of the fathers of modern dentistry. He's famous for having invented a mixture of something like beeswax and shellac. He heated that in hot water to get an impression of the mouth. Then vulcanite arrived, made from latex from the rubber trees mixed with sulphur. This formed flat strips of vulcanising rubber. From impressions you could make moulds out of plaster for the dentures. You warmed up the vulcanising rubber, cut it up into little bits and packed it in the mould, squeezed it up in a press and put it in the vulcaniser, a high pressure steam boiler. You heated it up for an hour or so and took it down again, and the teeth made of porcelain would be embedded in the vulcanite. This was how dentures came to be made with any degree of fitting. Porcelain teeth were set up in wax which was first of all made to fit the plaster models and the two models were moulded in their proper relationship to the upper and lower jaw in a device called the articulator. You could try them in the mouth while still made of wax and adjust them at that stage, for bite and appearance, and then finish them off in vulcanite. That was up to the arrival of acrylics.

It was interesting how that happened. We ran out of rubber during the war, when Malaya fell to the Japanese. Fortunately ICI developed acrylic resin. Acrylic resin had resulted in the manufacture, for example, of perspex, used in aeroplanes and windows. So acrylics came into the industry about the third year of the war. Also you could now make teeth from acrylics in whatever colours were required: quite nice colours.

Acrylic wasn't strong enough for some jaws. Thus you had metal dentures and metal plates for people with special problems. Chrome alloys, which are cast, are used today. Gold isn't used all that much in teeth in this country but it's still very fine material to use. Amalgam is used to a large extent in the back teeth, a mixture of mercury, silver and tin. But if you have a gold filling, it's there for life. Amalgam fillings have to be replaced every now and again. In my student days and later you used amalgams for the back teeth and synthetic fillings, mixtures of powder and liquid, for front fillings.

Coming more up to date, they now have composite fillings which can be used for the back teeth as well. The National Health Service is prepared to let you have those if you wish. If a really good case could be made out, the NHS would permit a gold filling. You had to acquire approval from the Dental Estimates Board to do anything outside the activities specified in the schedule.

The NHS started dentistry for everybody. It was entirely free for the first two years. Children and other categories are still exempt from charges. Under the NHS, the demands for dentistry were very much increased. We had to fill up a form in great detail for every patient. We specified what we had done under the appropriate Schedule for each item. Of course we had had to keep records in any case. I thought the paperwork wasn't too bad.

In those years, there was a change in attitude towards the use of X-rays in dentistry. Exposure times were reduced and screening improved, keeping the rays above chest level. Precautions were increasingly taken for staff as well as for patients. Of course, being in Cumbria with the nuclear power station at Sellafield, we were always cautious on the subject of radiation.

I retired thirteen years ago. I have lots of interests that I can pursue now. I have been Service-minded since I was in the OTC at University College School, when I went into the signals department where I was able to pursue my hobby of making radio sets. My father had a go at it too. I got interested in short waves and amateur radio and picked it up quite quickly. That interest has lasted through the years.

I used to travel around to organ recitals. I've always been

interested in sound and music and I made recordings at the parish church here.

We have quite a big garden; I do the rough stuff and my wife does the flowers. My son is in Australia and my daughter, who married a Norwegian, lives in Norway. We have five grandchildren and of course we spend quite a bit of time in Norway. I have never regretted spending my professional life in Westmorland, which is now called Cumbria. It has been interesting seeing the changes in dentistry over the past fifty years – for me, happy years.

Hospital Matron

ETHEL WOODS

BEFORE I talk about my life in nursing perhaps it would be interesting if I said something about my mother's housekeeping, during my childhood.

I was born at Gainsborough in 1901 into a Victorian family, but it was the year when Queen Victoria died, so I grew up an Edwardian.

I think my strongest memory is that our home was run on very strict, methodical lines. The routine was like the laws of the Medes and Persians. It never altered.

We spent most of Sunday in church. My father and brothers were in the choir. My mother and I (after my Confirmation) were Sunday school teachers. The younger members of the family went to Sunday school.

Our dinner was prepared in advance. The joint was put in the oven; the vegetables were prepared and Yorkshire pudding was mixed, ready to cook between services. Whatever the joint was, most often beef, we always had Yorkshire pudding. We had sauce to go with the joint – apple or horseradish, mint or caper. This was followed by fruit and custard or fruit pie. On Sundays we had tinned fruit; a great treat this, and I still feel extravagant if I open a tin.

After evensong we hurried home to prepare for wash-day on Monday. After Mother had sorted out the things to be washed, the equipment was assembled. A mangle, or wringer, was kept in the kitchen. My father would carry the wash-tub into the yard and anyone who could filled this with water. There was a wash-stool on which the tub stood, a dolly-tub which was a corrugated barrel-shaped thing with dolly-legs. In the house the copper fire was laid and the copper filled overnight.

I was good at sewing so I did the jobs in this department. After I was about ten years old, I had to remove all buttons, press studs, hooks and eyes from the soiled things and although generally not allowed to sew on Sundays, I had to pull together any tears. Mother said otherwise these would get worse in the dolly, and the buttons would get broken or bent in the mangle. I had the job of putting all these buttons and fastenings back later, but never on a Sunday.

My father always did the fireplace and lit the fire before he left for work as a bricklayer at 6.30 a.m. He also put a light to the copper fire.

For breakfast we had porridge and 'bread and dip'. Dip is the fat that comes out of bacon when it is fried. Father had the bacon and we children had the dip. After breakfast the process of washing began. First, clothes were washed and scrubbed in the wash-tub, all in order; the white things, the coloureds, then the woollens were dollied in soapy water. They were rinsed, mangled, and put into the copper wherever applicable. Others than the whites were then hung out. The latter were rinsed, blued, starched and mangled, before being hung out. When dry they were all folded, damped down, put through the mangle, then laid aside for ironing.

Mother ironed virtually everything. I was indoctrinated by being let loose to iron the handkerchiefs, dusters and cleaning rags. However, before this, the kitchen, larder, drains and outside lavatory were given a good 'bottoming': a thorough cleaning from top to bottom.

On washday we had cold meat, beetroot, jacket potatoes and rice pudding. My father, wisely, did not come home for his meal.

Under no circumstances would my mother go to bed that night till she had done all the ironing. She had three flat-irons which she heated on a trivet hung in front of the bars of the fire. I'll draw a veil over a wet Monday, though the ironing was done just the same. Mother said if it was left it would throw all her week out.

On Tuesdays the whole house was swept and dusted, for

you'll understand nothing much was done on Sunday or Monday. My mother would go into the market on Tuesday afternoon where she could buy for one shilling and sixpence, in old money, thirteen bananas, thirteen oranges, a cucumber, and something for tea such as haddock or herrings. We always had lots of green stuff from our allotment.

The Sunday joint had been made to last Monday while on Tuesdays we had shepherds pie. If any was left Mother would make meat paste for tea. Tea was the last meal of the day for us five children, although if the boys went to choir practice or something connected with the church, we had cocoa and a biscuit when they got in.

Wednesday was a fairly light day. In the morning we cleaned everywhere, then in the afternoon Mother, and later myself, went to the ladies sewing class connected with the church.

On Thursday it was the turn of the bedrooms. The sheets were changed and all mats and carpets were taken downstairs to be shaken and beaten. The windows were cleaned. About every four weeks the stair carpet was taken up, shaken, beaten and put back the other way round to spread the treading as she said. The brass stair rods were polished, mostly by me.

On Fridays all the downstairs rooms were turned out and given a good cleaning. My father did not light the fire on Fridays. He just cleaned the flues. Mother black-leaded and polished the steel fender and the fireirons, and polished bright bits of the range. I think the hearth was made of stone and this was rubbed with hearth stone. All the windows were cleaned inside and out; the door steps and window sills were cleaned. Friday was the day for polishing the bright things, copper kettles, candlesticks, horse brasses and so on. It was quite a job, for after I was eleven this was done by me. On Friday afternoon Mother baked. She would bake a cake and make white, brown, currant and carraway seed bread; a large quantity of small tarts with jam, lemon curd, ground rice.

We had these for tea. We longed to have 'bought' cake and bread but we never got it for nothing was bought that could be made at home.

On Saturdays we had fish and chips for dinner. For the whole family this cost one shilling. On Saturday mornings any jobs that may have been overlooked were done. In the afternoon we all went to the cinema which cost one penny each and that included sweets. In the evening my parents went into town where they could buy meat more cheaply, mostly sirloin.

At Christmas we would have either pork or rabbit. I never saw turkey till after I left home. Each Saturday my parents bought one pound of boiled sweets for four pence. We did not have regular pocket money but if we were given a penny we could spend it as we liked.

We were not well off. My father was a bricklayer, properly trained and indentured for five years. He handed over his pay to my mother. I can well remember seeing him hand over three gold pieces. He was very skilled and could do carpentry, plumbing and decorating. He also repaired our footwear. Father did work for private clients in the evenings and on Saturday afternoons. He had an allotment and grew every kind of vegetable possible.

I do not remember that we ever had marmalade. Mother never made this but she made jam. I do remember being told to take a shilling from her purse, a basket and my small sister's push-cart and buy a stone of plums, or gooseberries; or another time to take half a crown and get a stone of strawberries or raspberries to make jam. When I was old enough, about eleven, I had to stone the plums, top and tail the gooseberries and pull the strawberries. At that age I didn't much like this as I was choosey about soiling my hands; as you remember I was sewing a lot from the age of ten.

When my youngest sister was born I was ten and I helped my mother to make her shortening clothes.

From the money Mother got from father she had to pay rent, insurance, put away so much each week for our shoes, and also had to try each week to put a little by in case of bad winter weather; for if no inside work could be found by the employer for men like father, they were stood off without pay. There was no social security then.

As for clothes, Mother used to buy remnants and make night-wear, undies and dresses for my two sisters and myself. Later on I helped with some of this. I don't recall having any new clothes after eight. I inherited my clothes from a young aunt, from cousins, from the children of Mother's friends. I don't remember that I minded this. Whatever Mother sacrificed for herself, we were always well turned out.

Mother enjoyed seeing her 'whites' blowing on the line. I'm sure she loved ironing and I've known her to have fifteen girls' dresses in the wash, not to mention our frilled undies and my young brother's white sailor suits; she ironed everything.

Later in life I bought her an electric iron but I know when my back was turned she stuck to her own flat-irons till my brother gave them to salvage in the war. Her great joy was to see us all nicely dressed. She once told me that the only time she enjoyed us all was when she had two in the pram and the other three holding on. Even when I was a hospital matron she still regretted we were not all at home being biddable!

These were the Edwardian days when there were no washing machines and no school dinners. I can honestly say I never knew Mother to owe a single penny. What we could not afford we could not have.

I was at home with my mother for two years after I left school. My girlhood had been a training for nursing although I didn't realise it at the time. It had taught me to respect true discipline and hard work and the worth of ordinary human beings.

I left home aged eighteen years and in 1920 began my nurse's training at The Yarrow Home, Broadstairs, a convalescent home for children. I was driven to the station in a 'White Hart' (horse drawn) bus; my mother took me to London, but as it was August Bank Holiday and crowded on Victoria Station, she was not allowed on the platform. We did not know about platform tickets! I was very shy and nervous, frightened even, as, in fact, I had rarely gone out unchaperoned.

My mother said they were sure to meet me but they did not. I had ten shillings, I think, and was advised by the station porter to take the only transport available, an open horse-drawn carriage.

The matron said that she had expected me sooner, and I was to get quickly into uniform and on duty. My mother had told me that I would not have to work until Tuesday, this being Bank Holiday. She was wrong.

I had been instructed to get three blue/grey overalls made. At home we knew blue, we knew grey, but blue/grey was a closed book to us. I had blue; very bright blue. I was wearing a nice lace-trimmed silk blouse. I put on the overall and wore the silk and lace collar outside, pinned with a pretty blue butterfly brooch. The nurse who came to fetch me was stunned. She tucked in the offending collar, removed the brooch and pinned revers up to my neck with a safety pin. If the nurse was shocked it was nothing compared with the effect I had on the matron. A look of horror came over her when she saw the bright blue overall. She had me into blue/grey in no time and when my mother visited me some months later, I was quickly fitted out with a proper uniform before she arrived.

I cannot remember what I did that first evening – just stood helplessly around I think, but I did hear the staff nurse say she had a proper fool in her ward and she felt like beating me with a brush! Next morning, on duty at 7 a.m., I had to wash fifteen girls, dress those who could get up, take them down to prayers and breakfast, attend prayers, take breakfasts up to bed patients, feed them and wipe their hands and faces. After this I had to help the staff nurse to make fifteen beds and cots. It was 9 a.m. by the time I had my own breakfast. Then I had to dust the ward, day rooms and verandahs, clean the locker tops and the sanitary annexe with four lavatories, one sink, two baths and ten basins, which were set into slate, and slab fold and hang the fifteen towels so that they all looked alike.

My off duty was 10 a.m. to noon or 2 to 4 o'clock in the afternoon. If the latter, I could finish off the things mentioned which I almost certainly did not get done in the time allowed. If I had not done them, I was not allowed to go off duty. If off in the afternoon, I had to do extra work in the morning until lunch time. This was to scrub out the lockers and a great many cupboards, wash hairbrushes, polish a great deal of brass and copper, and, in winter, do the fireplace and keep the fire going. I often let it go out!

On Sundays we had four hours off duty. My first Sunday I was off from 10 o'clock until 2 p.m. when I went to church. When I got back I removed my hat and went to lunch wearing a very pretty dress, I remember. As I went into the dining-room I had a sense of a united in-drawn breath. The matron attended this meal, so there was never much talking, but on this occasion there was none at all. I did not think I had done anything wrong – all too easy – but did feel this deadly silence had something to do with me. After the meal I was taken aside by the sister who told me that never under any circumstances whatever, or at any time, should I appear with my head uncovered. I must wear either a hat or uniform cap. I was later told that in case the matron had to get up in an emergency she wore a garden hat with her night attire, but I think this must have been a leg pull. I do not know the origin of this rule, but I do know that it was observed in all the hospitals in which I worked until about 1940, when I guess we had better things to worry about. I can only conclude that it was a foible of Florence Nightingale's backed up by the biblical instruction that women should keep their heads covered.

I was in fact slow and it was some time before I got all those jobs done, and I was for ever in trouble. I was slow, added to which my feet hurt. I had been trained to help my mother in the house and look after my four younger brothers and sisters but not, I repeat not, for fourteen hours a day. The hospital children were put to rest after their dinner. This I had to supervise, then play with them indoors or out. Then they had high tea after which I had to bath them all. There was only the staff nurse and myself and I do not recall that the staff nurse did a hand's turn except for the beds, temperatures and medicines, but perhaps I was biased!

When the children were settled in bed I had to go through the clothes they had worn that day and mend them where required, even on Sunday. To this I objected, but not out loud. I had been brought up to 'keep Holy the Sabbath'. I fervently hoped that Matron would have to pay for this, not me. At home I had not been allowed even to look at sewing on Sunday so did not see that this should go down against me in the Golden Book! I well remember getting into the bad when I found a child who did not know any prayers. I taught her to say 'Gentle Jesus' and 'God Bless . . . ' but I was in trouble because it was not my affair.

For quite a while I was always behind but slowly I improved. Eventually I was allowed to play the organ for hymns, then promoted to taking the 'little walk'. Try to be quick, dressing about ten toddlers in the outdoor garments of the period, about eight each, then to keep them from falling or straying! Next I was promoted to the 'big walk', much dreaded if boys were there.

I was then taught to do small surgical dressings. Surgical

tuberculosis and osteomyelitis were very common. As time went by I became good enough to take children to London and hand them over to their parents, taking other children back with me. This cured me of train sickness, to which I had been a martyr. I dared not leave the children and would never have lived it down had I had to hang out of the window. I was never sick again.

I was at last given the great honour of doing a few nights on night duty, in sole charge of a hundred children and all that entails. It is not possible to tell of the innumerable tasks I had to do. I was in a mad rush for about a month then, as I said, I improved. I guess that by then I had learned some good tricks from my superiors which showed me how to cut corners and get my tasks into the allotted time.

Life was not all misery! We had our own tennis court and garden, and we were only ten minutes from the sea. The matron allowed us to have ballroom dancing lessons in the Home, then to go to small dances, chaperoned by the sister. We had plays at Christmas in which I took part.

I remained in this place for three years. I was paid eighteen, twenty, then twenty-two pounds, a year. I did not have an allowance from home. Of course we lived in and had part of the uniform provided.

With hindsight, I think these were the happiest days of my life, once I got settled to the hard work, but many were the tear-stained letters to my friends, but not so to my parents. They did not really wish me to be so far away, and had my father known how unhappy I was at first, he would have taken me away.

I made many friends, the last of whom died in 1984. In spite of my early fear of Matron I kept her informed of my subsequent progress, and she wrote to me until her death in 1970. Apart from being happy I learned many things. How to live in an institution, how to manage my money and my life. I also learned a few things that I believe to have been of great value to me and to others when, later, I had young women under my care. Amongst these were, that under no circumstances would I ever allow a new nurse to report for duty at busy holiday times, nor would I ever put a young woman straight on duty without food or drink. When I arrived at The Yarrow Home I had spent the night in London, but the matron did not know this. As far as she knew, I had travelled some two hundred miles, yet she did not offer so much as a cup of tea. I also saw to it that no one was expected to rush, as I had, trying to fit too much into too short a time. I did, of course, learn much more, but the things which were done to me at the beginning I never forgot, nor inflicted on others.

It is now some sixty-eight years since I set out. Times have altered. To the matron and my parents I was just a young girl to be kept in order. Nowadays at eighteen years of age they are no longer young girls!

In late 1923 I went to Sheffield Royal Hospital for general training. I qualified as a State Registered Nurse, gaining 297 out of a possible 300 marks in my examination. On the strength of this, I managed to get a scholarship to Jessop Maternity Hospital in Sheffield to take the Certified Midwives' Board exam. It was a six months' training scheme and fees were charged. When I did so well in my exam for qualification as a SRN I was offered either a gold medal or free training at Jessop Maternity. Up till then at Sheffield Royal I had been getting paid, and while I was waiting for the course at Jessop's to start, I had in hand only one month's pay from Sheffield Royal, which had been £36 per annum. So it was the free training at Jessop that made the maternity course possible. I was desperately hard up. Mother thought I was rolling in money because at one time I had been getting £18 a year and that figure stuck in her mind. I remember her saying "If I had £18 to my own cheek and been all found I would be in clover." But twenty-eight shillings a week did not go far. I was given material but had to pay for my uniform to be made. I also had to get shoes mended and buy clothes, soap, toothpaste, paper and stamps to write home and save up the fare of three shillings and sixpence to go home on my monthly day off.

Not all my memories of the Maternity Hospital were happy ones. Saturday supper the whole time I was there consisted of only a twopenny pork pie and one tomato, with no bread and butter. If one got back from the district round, say five minutes after the meal was served, it would all be eaten. And if one was unwise enough to go to the kitchen, the woman there would say she had sent up the correct number of meals – if one got nothing, too bad!

I was housed in a flat belonging to the hospital. There was a bath but no hot water. The flats were infested by lice, bugs or fleas and the best way to get rid of them was to stand in a bath of hot water which of course we did not have.

I had very long hair and it was impossible to wash it properly during this time. I came out in red patches all over my body. Knowing how important it was to prevent infection among mothers and babies, I told the staff nurse who told Matron and I was seen by a skin specialist. He diagnosed it as seborrhoea. He got it better but I realised it had been due to the fact that I had no hot water for washing.

Apropos of having to do day duty after a night out, one night the midwife and I were out from midnight till 12 noon next day. We got no midday meal that day but had to wait till the evening meal and had to do our normal duty till the day's end. Looking back, I sometimes wonder how we put up with it.

But despite all this, there was plenty to laugh at and as a pupil midwife my experience of life was growing all the time.

Rules laid down by the midwives' examining body were that each pupil was to deliver twenty babies, five of whom were to be delivered on the district under the supervision of the district midwife in the home of the mother. All first babies were delivered in the hospital. After that, the mothers were delivered on the district, i.e. at home, and I had already had one or more uncomplicated deliveries.

We pupils had to do the five home deliveries in our own time. As these were not first babies it was by no means unusual for the baby to arrive before the midwife could get there. They were referred to as BBA or Born Before Arrival, and did not count towards our five deliveries. We did our training on the maternity wards and labour room during the day and the five home deliveries at night. I think we knew when we were on call so no time was wasted. There was only one District midwife so if more than one mother went into labour a day staff nurse was expected to go out with the pupil. The staff nurses objected to this and always made a fuss, maintaining it was not their job.

On an occasion I have in mind, when I arrived at Reception I found there were three fathers waiting. These were the very poor who certainly had no phones in the home or even money for public phones. There was an argument going on among the staff as to who should go out, the district midwife being out already. I was no more keen than the next one on going out at dead of night and did not want a BBA. The night sister told me to run along, saying she would send the midwife when she came in. This was, in fact, my last district delivery.

I collected the nearest father, who took my bag. The time was about 2.00 a.m. It was a cold winter's night with soft, wet snow falling; very dark except for the occasional band of light from a gas lamp and quiet; the only sound the hurried patter of my feet and the clomp, clomp of the heavy boots worn by the father. Cobbled paving, or setts, glistened in the odd beam of light. So anxious was I not to have a BBA that I did not notice at all where we were going. I just followed the father. After we arrived, all I could remember was that we had climbed a long flight of stairs.

Labour was well advanced. There was a good fire burning in an open grate and plenty of hot water in kettles, saucepans and pails. (These fathers were very experienced.) I noticed a pegged rag rug at the bedside and I asked the father to remove it and spread newspaper round the bed. There was no gas, electricity or water laid on. I had to work by the light of an oil lamp as best I could, though the father was a very able helper. I prepared myself and my equipment and prayed that the midwife would soon arrive. She did not.

All went well. The baby boy was safely delivered and the mother had no tear. (All mothers seem to get torn now but we were in very bad trouble if stitches were needed.) There was still no midwife so, having made the mother comfortable, I set about the baby. As I did so, I felt a very strong sense of being watched. As I have said, I had been in such a hurry to arrive in time and so concerned by the non-arrival of the midwife, that I had taken no notice of where I was. The lighting was dim but now I looked around and found that the room was a very large attic with mattresses on the floor in one corner. I saw three or four pairs of eyes watching my every movement and I had not heard a sound. No reason for that little family to ask "Where did you come from, baby dear?"

In another corner there was a coal stove and a mangle and other washday equipment. In another there was a table and kitchen things and lastly the parents' bedroom. I was shocked to know that children had been present. The room was about twenty-five feet square, dimly lit but very clean. The mother was aged forty and at first I was filled with incredulity that anyone so old was having a baby! I was twenty-four. When I had cleared up the midwife had still not arrived. I looked around again and was appalled to find there was no door – no means that I could see of getting out. I had a moment of panic until there was a loud knocking on the floor. The father then moved the rag rug and revealed a trap door. He lifted it and the midwife appeared.

The mother and baby having been vetted and all found correct, we left. It was now about 5 a.m. and I hoped to get a little sleep before I had to go on duty at 7 a.m. The midwife had a bicycle. There were no motor cars then, or at least not for nurses and other lower forms of life. As I had no idea where I was in the slum area of that great city the midwife kindly walked with me. She then told me that I had gone off with the wrong father so at the hospital they had had no idea where I was, and while I never fathomed how that had come about I think they had found me by a process of elimination. But that was why the midwife had been so long delayed.

Since then, much water has flowed under many bridges and in a long life of service I have often had life in my hands, but never again did I feel this so strongly as I did on that dark, cold, snowy night. Indeed a night to remember.

Some time later I returned to Sheffield Royal Hospital where I was appointed sister of the Bernard Male Ward. After a year I received an appointment at the Battersea General Hospital where I got certificates in hospital administration, housekeeping and cooking.

From then on I held the posts of ward sister, night sister, theatre sister, home sister, assistant sister and tutor. Then I was appointed assistant matron.

About a year after this I became matron of a small hospital in Hertfordshire, where I stayed until the outbreak of war. With the war on, I was appointed Matron of a larger emergency war hospital where I remained till the end of 1944. I was then invited to return to Battersea as matron and I stayed there until I retired.

Even then I did not retire completely, and continued to work part-time as a staff nurse in geriatric wards until 1967. In 1972 I returned to my home town of Gainsborough.

I had always wanted to be a nurse, even as a small child, and it has been a rewarding professional life.

One interesting aspect of my career was the training of student nurses. I trained a great many nurses from different countries and I have been on several trips abroad to stay with some of them, which has been one of the chief enrichments of my life. My students come from as far afield as America, Persia, Russia, Sierra Leone, Jamaica and New Zealand.

Nursing has run in the family. My sister Mary, who lives in Oxfordshire, made it her career. At the time when my promotion to assistant matron at Battersea General Hospital was recorded in *The News* over fifty years ago, it was stated that Mary had just passed her SRN examination with honours. Mary went on to carve out a distinguished career in nursing and our careers came together for a time when we were both at Battersea.